D1276385

The Making of the King

1066

Alan Lloyd

The Making of the King
1066

Dorset Press

NEW YORK

FOR DAPHNE
AND SIMON

This edition published by Dorset Press
a division of Marboro Books Corporation,
by arrangement with Henry Holt & Co.
1990 Dorset Press

ISBN 0-88029-473-6

Printed in the United States of America

M 9 8 7 6 5 4 3 2 1

Contents

Author's Note

The Making of the King: 1066 is an attempt to trace the stories of 3 outstanding men in early mediaeval history, Harold of England, Harald of Norway and William of Normandy, to that much-noted year, nine centuries ago, when their careers finally and irrevocably collided. 1066 is its destination and its climax. At the same time, a broad effort has been made to suggest something of the environments which produced the main characters and their achievements; something of the everyday realities surrounding the greater, and more familiar, events. In undertaking a reconstruction aimed at general interest, I have drawn gratefully on the expertise of a wide range of specialists without whose scholarship the production of such a book clearly would be an impossibility. In particular, I must acknowledge my use, as arbiters on the main course of events in England and Normandy, of Professor F. M. Stenton's *Anglo-Saxon England* and Professor David C. Douglas's *William the Conqueror*. For the history of Harald Hardrada I have relied, with some reservations, on the original story by Snorri Sturlason. Other sources are included in the bibliography at the back. In dealing with the problem of quotations from early material, I have inclined to the consultation of more than one interpretation, in places paraphrasing to suit the general usage of the book.

I am indebted to Messrs J. M. Dent & Sons Ltd and E. P. Dutton & Co. Inc. for permission to reproduce material from the *Anglo-Saxon Chronicle*, translated by G. N. Garmonsway (Everyman's Library Edition).

'Good against evil, youth against age, life against death, light against darkness, army against army, foe against foe, injury against injury. . . . Ever shall the wise man ponder on the conflict in this world.'

Anon. Anglo-Saxon poet

I

The Best of Islands

According to Virgil, Britain was separated from the whole world—
'*penitus toto divisos orbe Britannos*', a theory which did little to restrain
the enthusiasm of many early and militant visitors, including the
Romans themselves. Nevertheless, Roman and Greek observations
were for long accepted, even in Britain, as a prime source of geo-
graphic data on the island. This led to confusion, for while Livy and
Fabius Rusticus compared the shape of the country to an oblong
shield, or a battle-axe, Caesar, for instance, visualised a triangle
standing on the point formed by the intersection of east and west
coasts. Again, Ptolemy, believing that Scotland trended to the east,
described the island as an inverted Z.

Great store was set, in early times, on computing its circuit, which
Agrippa, decorating a very broad margin with delicate precision,
declared to be not more than 28,604 stadia, nor less than 20,526
stadia—a stadium being about 202 yards. During the subsequent
Anglo-Saxon period, those of the inhabitants who were sufficiently
erudite to record an opinion seem to have settled for a north-south
measurement of about 800 miles and a breadth, 'exclusive of promontories' as it was usually calculated, of from 200 to 300.

Thus, a little before the half-way mark of the sixth century, the
monk Gildas, one of the earliest British authors, wrote:

The island of Britain, situated on almost the utmost border of the earth
towards the south and west, and poised in the divine balance, as it is said,
which supports the whole world, stretches out from the south-west
towards the north pole, and is eight hundred miles long and two hundred
broad, except where the headlands and sundry promontories stretch
farther into the sea.

Gildas, who took a critical view of his 'stiff-necked and stubborn-minded' fellow-countrymen (all too often, for his liking, they were also unchristian), gave by contrast an appreciative description of the land:

Its plains are spacious, its hills are pleasantly situated, adapted for superior tillage, and its mountains are admirably calculated for the alternate pasturage of cattle, where flowers of various colours, trodden by the feet of man, give it the appearance of a lovely picture. It is decked, like a man's chosen bride, with divers jewels, with lucid fountains and abundant brooks wandering over the snow white sands; with transparent rivers flowing in gentle murmurs and offering a sweet pledge of slumber to those who recline upon their banks, whilst it is irrigated by abundant lakes which pour forth cool torrents of refreshing water.

This idyll was much-favoured by early writers. Indeed, six centuries later Geoffrey of Monmouth could barely improve on the same words in his *History of Britain*, 'the best of islands'. Certainly to his near-contemporaries, the oarsmen dragging their lines off-shore in the late summer of 1065, England must have presented a picture of pastoral tranquillity; a warm, luxuriant backcloth to the calm sea. Yet even among these men, some of whom had sailed far round the coast, accounts of its shape and dimensions were undoubtedly vague. The earliest detailed maps of the land surviving today were drawn a good bit later and are formidably inaccurate, one by Matthew Paris, the celebrated thirteenth-century monk and scholar of St Albans, contriving, among other discrepancies, to omit territories the size of several counties and to place the Thames estuary on the south coast.

In fact, the natural contours of the island on the eve of 1066 differed less radically from those of today. Parts of the eastern and southern shores of England which are particularly subject to erosion and deposition were either indented with bays and tidal inlets which no longer exist, or possessed headlands which have long since crumbled away. Between Dover and Pevensey, for example, a host of creeks offered moorings for small craft where there is now dry land; conversely, a small town stood at Dunwich on a site that is now largely under the waves. Thanet and Selsey, among other places, were still islands, isolated by tidal channels.

Inland, the forests, for centuries the chief source for building material, fuel and so on, were nevertheless thick and extensive. The three largest—the Weald (Old English for Forest) of Sussex and Kent, one of the last strongholds of heathenism in the south, the great Essex-Chiltern belt which survives in fragments as the forests of Epping and Hainault, and the Bruneswald, which covered much of Huntingdonshire and Northamptonshire—were prized for their timber, their game and their excellent swine pasturage: feared for the outlaws who sheltered in them, along, it was supposed, with the devils. Elsewhere, such forests as Selwood, between Winchester and Sherborne; Kinver, Arden and Morfe in the west-midlands, and Rockingham, Galtres and Sherwood further north, were similarly regarded.

Here, among wary deer and watchful owls, lurked the renegades and outcasts of society, men officially deemed to carry the 'wolf's head', who could be cut down with legal impunity by anyone, wherever they were found. Strangers erring from four great roads, where law-abiding travellers were ostensibly protected by 'the king's peace', aroused not unreasonable suspicion and were fair sport for arbitrary treatment at the hands of less wayward men. Under one Saxon law it was obligatory to shout or blow a horn when deviating from the highway through woodland, on pain of being slain or held to ransom.

The fens also provided refuge for the fugitive and the recluse. In the east, from Cambridge to York, and beyond, there was more marshland than forest. Vast watery wastes stretched for hundreds of square miles, treacherous in summer, impassable, except by boat, in winter when the unbanked rivers spread, unchecked, across the lowlands. Places bordered by marshland, such as Ely, Peterborough, Ramsey and Crowland attracted monastic communities, their subsistence guaranteed by the abundance of waterfowl, fish and eels.

Between woodland and waste, the large majority of the people, perhaps something like a million in all, depended for their existence on farming. In the hill country, the rhythm of life see-sawed from the high pastures in summer to winter feeding in the valleys and enclosures, the main concern being for cattle, sheep and bees. Honey, the only ready form of sweetening available, was an important product. In a fermented state it was used to make the potent alcoholic liquor, mead. On more workable lands, the farming was mixed. Rye and wheat, for bread, and barley and oats, for beer, porridge and animal foods, were the principal crops. Oxen were kept as the chief plough and wagon beasts, horses for lighter draught work and riding, while milk was obtained from cows, goats and sheep. Poultry and pigs were kept for eating.

Apart from London, already by far the largest town in the country, and Winchester, the second in size and seat of the treasury, a number of administrative and trading centres existed which, by the eleventh century, had become rather more than villages, though none was larger than a small market town of modern proportions. York is thought to have had a population of about 9,000, Lincoln and Norwich between 6,000 and 7,000, Thetford about 5,000, Ipswich more than 3,000, while at least thirteen others probably had upwards of a thousand inhabitants each.[1] For the most part, however, the people lived in villages and hamlets, housed, with a minimal concept of privacy, in daub and wattle dwellings where the family cooked, sheltered and slept in a single room. The heat came from a smouldering fire in an open grate, and the light from the single aperture that served as doorway and window and supplemented a hole in the thatched roof by way of ventilation. The main furnishings were rushes and straw. Here the peasantry was born without ceremony, matured rapidly, mated robustly (and, not uncommonly, incestuously) and died early, probably diseased and hungry. For the majority, a good farming year meant a hand-to-mouth existence; a bad one brought the nightmare of famine, when the poorer freemen might be reduced to selling themselves, their children, or mothers, into slavery. Bede, the greatest of Anglo-Saxon historians, dealing with a long drought in Sussex 'whereupon a dreadful famine ensued', had told three centuries before how the people were driven to their wits' end. 'Very often', he asserted, 'forty or fifty men, being spent with hunger, would go together to some precipice, or to the sea-shore, and there, hand in hand, perish by the fall, or be swallowed by the waves.'

[1] Estimates, which vary considerably from analyst to analyst, are based on Domesday statistics. These do not include London or Winchester.

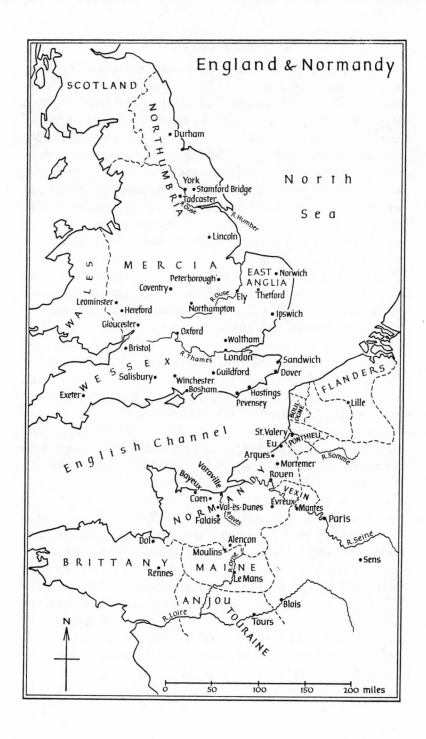

Life turned on the demands of the seasons, the landlords and the tax-collectors, all of which were both constant and heavy. Diversions tended to be riotous and all too frequently violent. Men escaped from the insecurities of life by consuming large quantities of ale, a process leading swiftly to quarrels, bloodshed and more insecurity. Cock-fighting, bull-baiting and, in some places, bear-baiting were highly-regarded amusements. Occasionally, when the barking of dogs and the blare of a horn announced that a thief had been disturbed in the act of making away with an implement or an animal, the community would set aside its work to join the 'hue and cry'. No doubt such occasions were relished. They provided the lower orders with their nearest equivalent to those ancient pleasures of the hunting field experienced by the more privileged. Furthermore, a successful chase promised the further entertainment of a public execution. Theft was a capital crime. The official attitude to homicide was more ambiguous. One way in which it could be settled was for the victim's kindred to accept from the slayer the value society placed on the victim's life (his *wergild* or 'man-price'). This might be relatively little, the equivalent in value of a few horses or oxen, or it might, in the case of a person of higher rank, be very considerable. Alternatively, the kindred were entitled to take vengeance in blood: to seek a life for a life. Since the former course made homicide an expensive pastime, and since its practitioners were commonly poor, the law effectively promoted the family vendetta. Blood feuds might persist through several generations.

It was an age in which the law, though hedged with complex formalities, left a great deal, in the final throw, to divine justice. Litigation, very much a question of one man's word against another, commonly involved 'witnesses' testifying to the trustworthiness of the word rather than giving objective evidence. Thus the defendant who could bring a required number of compurgators, or 'oath-helpers', to swear that his oath of innocence was pure, won his case and might go free. If he could not, or if the case was such that the plaintiff's oath had priority, matters were often resolved by ordeal. At least three types of ordeal are recorded: the so-called ordeals by iron and by hot and cold water. In the ordeal by iron, the accused was required to carry a glowing iron for nine feet; in the ordeal by hot water, to plunge his hand and arm into boiling water and pick up a stone. These proceedings were carried out in church, the hand then being bound and left for three days. If it had not festered in this time, the man was cleared. The third ordeal, also supervised by the clergy, was less sporting in its chances. After a three-day fast, the accused was stripped and thrown, with his thumbs and toes tied together, into cold water. At the same time, the priest adjured the water, in the name of the Father, Son and Holy Ghost, 'that thou do not in any manner receive this man if he be guilty of what he is accused, by his act, consent, or knowledge, or any other device, but make him swim upon thee to the end there may be no counterfeiting with thee, or any exploit of the enemy, that may disguise it' (*Origines Juridiciales*). If he floated he was guilty; if he sank, he was innocent.

Those found guilty of theft, house-breaking, arson, homicide by secrecy or witchcraft and treachery to their lord, among other crimes, stood a strong chance of being hanged or beheaded, though evidence survives of the Church urging greater discrimination in the use of capital punishment. 'Christian men shall not be condemned to death for all too little,' declared Archbishop Wulfstan of York, who seems to have preferred mutilation as providing more time for repentance. Sometimes a town or village was held collectively responsible for a crime committed in it, then the punishment was sweeping. Armed forces were sent in to ravage the district.

Men, weaned to cruelty and callousness, could nevertheless display fierce loyalty and truth to their pledge. On the whole, they were probably a good deal less fearful of each other than of the bizarre prodigies, dark spirits and man-eating monsters which haunted their nights, dwelling, as they imagined, in bogs, forest depths and other remote parts. Fireside tales must still have reflected the dreads and superstitions handed down in such legends as that of the heroic Beowulf, whose monstrous adversaries lurked amidst 'Windswept ridges and wolf-retreats, Dread tracts of fen where the falling torrent Downward dips into gloom and shadow'. It was a brave man who ventured far alone in the dark; a rash one who broke an oath taken on relics beneath the ever-watchful eye of a god part-Christian, part-pagan and wholly terrible in wrath. Everyday life echoed the names of heathen deities their ancestors had worshipped, not always in the very distant past. Places, events, even days of the week, were reminders of such mighty ones as Tiw, Woden, Thunor and Frig. For the masses, prayer was an appeasement, an insurance. By way of double indemnity there were special charms against witches, elves, dwarfs, swarming bees or a sudden attack of the stitch.

But, from the distance of nine centuries, it is tempting to dwell on the darker side of the past and forget the other. Pleasures come simply and exuberance swiftly among people who live close to nature. There can be little doubt that when the sun was shining and the days were kind, the countryside which embraced and bound all men and women stirred veins of wonder in their hearts. One Anglo-Saxon poem tells how, in the 'soft morning rain', plants awaken and the forest teems with branches: 'Groves begin to blossom, the courts become fair, the plains grow beautiful, the world quickens.' In another, the song thrush is made to describe the 'great bliss' its melodies bring to people. 'When I chant my carols in varying strains, Men sit in their dwellings silent and still.'

Drawings, designs in metal and textiles and carvings on stone or ivory frequently, and often enchantingly, depicted birds, animals and botanical subjects. The country scenes in surviving portrayals sometimes hint at an underlying sense of humour. Beasts slyly burlesque human foibles while a serious tract of the time is occasionally invaded by impish creatures of both sexes who frolic together naked, manifestly delighting in their passion. Ironically, it was the Church, overtly playing down the image of worldly existence in favour of the glories of heaven, that had in fact become the main depository of precisely these objects of cultural enrichment and beauty which reflected most pleasure in man's earthly surroundings.

In different parts of this now distant island men used different tongues, and the difference was more than dialect. Interpreters were frequently in demand among travellers, while men of rank were brought up to be linguistically adaptable. Few others had any real concept of nationalism, and, even among them, the importance of national unity was seldom uppermost in their minds. To most inhabitants of eleventh-century England, the shire was more important than the province, the village incomparably more important than either. Their England was the village 'street', its thatched huts and farm buildings, perhaps a couple of timber halls or manors, a small church which might be partially or entirely of stone, and the immediate tracks and enveloping land. Between village and village, and thence to the shire towns, ran a tracery of unsurfaced lanes trodden flat by generations seeking the safest and easiest way about their business. Many such tracks, following the courses of diminished streams or erstwhile river beds, still ran with water in winter.

Once in a while a great Roman road cut straight and true across this minor network. Along it moved the wagons of merchants, the retinues and ambassadors of the powerful, and, occasionally, armies. To the country folk who watched them pass, their journeys began and ended in the realms of pedlar's gossip and legend. It was between just such realms, in the autumn of 1065, that the king rode with his court to Wiltshire, for some hunting. Edward the Confessor was among the first of many prominent Englishmen to be found at sport on the eve of crisis.

*

Edward the Confessor's genealogists traced his descent through Cerdic, the ancient conqueror of Wessex, to Woden, the pagan god of the Teutonic hierarchy, and thence, ingeniously, back to Adam. The theory of royal pedigree held men in thrall, giving kings an emotional potency out of all proportion to their strictly functional powers. In consequence, genealogy became a tool of politics, and the pedigrees of the powerful were inclined to demonstrate the idealism of their age. In fact, heredity was only one of several keys to the crown of this fertile and wooded kingdom. Election played a part in king-making, and so did designation. Traditionally, the king was elected by the witan, or king's councillors, at a witenagemot, or meeting of the so-called Wise Men. Historians find it hard to say just how these sages were chosen. At times the witan might simply have comprised members of the royal household, at others it seems to have consisted of such influential lay and clerical men as were at hand when the need for consultation arose, while, again, some assemblies were more obviously representative of the lords of the country. Where a candidate was weak, a number of these might appear as the junta which brought him to office; where he was strong, their approval would be sought as little more than formality. To be designated as successor by a reigning king scored a high mark in any candidate's favour, while yet another element, the cruder argument of armed strength, could upset the most sophisticated of claims. Combinations involving all these factors were being cherished patiently by several ambitious men during the latter years of Edward's reign, for when the blood line was weak the business of king-making was at its most precarious, and Edward the Confessor was childless. His closest male relation, Edward the Atheling, a half-nephew, was dead, and the Atheling's son was too young to be a serious claimant when it mattered.

Edward had come to the throne in 1042. Slowly and painfully, the predatory Viking migration had run its course. At last, England's long preoccupation with the northern approaches was challenged by new influences from the south. Edward had spent the first half of his life across the Channel, an exile at the increasingly influential Norman court. Son of the former English king Ethelred by a queen who had later married the Danish Canute, he was accepted with remarkably little opposition by both Saxon and Scandinavian interests, bearing, at the same time, the goodwill of the vigorous duchy in France. The kingdom to which Edward succeeded was divided roughly into four main administrative areas, each under the power of an earl. To the south, most directly in the king's sphere of influence, was Wessex; to the east, East Anglia, strongly Danish in character; to the west, Mercia, whose frontier with Wales was marked by the serpentine earthwork known as Offa's Dyke; to the north, Northumbria, most remote of the earldoms, bounding uneasily and often bloodily on the land of the Scots. Partly by a diplomatic attitude to his earls, and probably by a generous share of good luck, especially in the timing of foreign events, Edward's reign proved as notable for peacefulness as for longevity. In a turbulent age, such attributes alone would have assured him distinction, and, by the later years of his life, he seems to have acquired all the trappings of saintliness which were to form his posthumous image.

Ever full of cheer was the blameless king [wrote the Saxon chronicler of his reign] though for long in the past, deprived of his land, he had trodden an exile's path across the wide world, after Canute had conquered the race of Ethelred and Danes ruled over this dear land of England for twenty-eight years all told, squandering its riches. In time he succeeded, noble in armour, a king of excellent virtues, pure and benign, Edward the noble protected his fatherland, his realm and people. . . .[1]

Edward peers from the few extant coins which carry his head with a sage-like inscrutability which certainly suggests wisdom, yet which might after all be no more than venerability. The traditional picture is of a tall, upright figure with white beard, long sensitive fingers and a somewhat introspective mien. To his contemporary and devoutly fulsome biographer, he was above all things a pious king, and twenty years of childless marriage gave rise to a legend of chastity. Some have preferred to think of him as impotent, while a further alternative, at least as likely if not as chivalrous, is that his queen, Edith, was unable to bear children. Whatever their personal relationship, it would probably be wrong to dismiss Edith as an altogether meek and submissive wife. She was born of notably assertive stock and was a woman of wealth and influence in her own right.

That Edward the Confessor, with his piety and patience, was not in the popular image of a mediaeval ruler is clear. Lack of aggression is easily mistaken for weakness and lethargy, but, given that he compromised rather than forced issue with his enemies, the fact remains that in the long run he survived them, and kept the country intact. From the sum of historical comment, he emerges at least a man of forbearance in an impatient age, a cosmopolitan creature happy entertaining the 'foreigners' among whom he grew to manhood, enjoying the company of aesthetes and ecclesiastics as well as, if not more than, the soldiers of fortune who inevitably surrounded the throne.

'Christ's deputy' among his people, a king's life was by no means lacking in earthly pleasures. He travelled about the country seeking sport and amusement, living off the fat of the land. Royal visits were looked forward to with trepidation even by wealthy subjects, for whom the honour was more than offset, very often, by the cost. In a real sense, his slightest whim was a command. 'No man can make

[1] *Anglo-Saxon Chronicle* hereafter abbreviated as *ASC*.

himself king,' the homilist Abbot Aelfric could write at the end of the tenth century, 'but after he is consecrated king, he has authority over the people, and they cannot shake his yoke off their necks.'

To careerist and sycophant, the crown of England glittered enviably, seductively. Some sought a connection with gifts and smooth words. The king of Norway had once sent a ship with a golden prow, a purple sail and an armoury of gilded shields. From the Duke of the Franks, at another time, to King Athelstan, had come 'perfumes such as had never before been seen in England, precious stones, especially emeralds, in whose greenness the reflected sun lit up the eyes of the onlookers with a pleasing light; many fleet horses . . . a certain vase of onyx, carved with such subtle art by the engraver that the cornfields seemed truly to wave . . . the sword of Constantine the Great, on which the name of the original possessor could be read in letters of gold . . . the spear of Charles the Great . . .' and so on. Like other kings before him, Edward the Confessor dressed in the finest cloths, decorated by stitch-workers and jewel-makers second to none in Europe. His tastes were expensive and his interests more temporal than some were to make out. The one pastime which delighted him the length of his life was hunting.

In this he was not exceptional. Hunting was the regular diversion of mediaeval kings, a wild, exhilarating, savage version of the sport which exists today, by comparison, as an emasculated relic. Hunting accidents were plentiful. Danger was part of the stimulant; blood lust orgiastically consummated at the kill. For the nobility, this was the nearest pursuit, in peaceful times, to the practice of war, and the hunting field fulfilled a rough and ready role as a training ground for military leaders. Such men kept their eye in, also, with the bow and arrow, shooting at game from horseback, or on foot when it was driven towards them from cover. Hawking was another popular diversion, but nothing satisfied the temper of the age quite so thoroughly as the thrill of the chase.

A complexity of local arrangements facilitated royal hunting. One manor would owe the king an annual supply of hare hounds, another would provide larger dogs for stag hunting while the rent of a third might include a good sporting bird, the most valuable of creatures, or some horses. Among the counties, for example, Worcester,

Warwick, Oxford, Northampton, Leicester and Wiltshire, each owed the price of one hawk and one pack-horse a year. Three manors in Bedfordshire contributed money for dogs. Others made payment in kind, either at a fixed date, or when the king happened to make sport in the area. Wherever this occurred it fell on the local estate to provide food, drink and lodging for his considerable personal retinue, not to mention a pack of royal guests.

Fittingly enough, the curtain-raiser to the momentous events which were to follow coincided with the last hunting party of Edward's life. He was entertaining at his lodge at Britford, near Salisbury, that autumn, when messengers rode in with the news from the north. Edward's guest of honour on this, as on many occasions, was Tostig, Earl of Northumbria, the queen's brother. Tostig, self-assured, a showy man in the prime of his life, was popular with both the king and queen. Perhaps Edward was gratified by the attentiveness of this smooth personality. Perhaps Edith got on well with her sister-in-law, Judith. Perhaps Judith flattered the ageing king. One way or another, Tostig was certainly more welcome at court than among the clannish northerners of his earldom which, since his gratuitous appointment ten years earlier, he had ruled with a heavy hand, too often from a distance. Few can have imagined much love between the tough, insular Northumbrians and their alien earl, Tostig, the overbearing son of a plutocrat from Wessex. Yet fewer expected the news which now came to the king's lodge.

While Edward and his brother-in-law were hunting deer in Wiltshire, some 200 armed and influential Northumbrians, sick of Tostig's absentee government, had been doing some hunting on their own account at York. Here, in the chief town of the earldom, it seems they had run down and slaughtered his houseguards, hanging their officers from an ash-tree by the city wall. Next, they had ransacked Tostig's property, seizing his treasury and armoury, and, in solemn council, had pronounced their missing earl an outlaw. Furthermore, the scion of a neighbouring dynasty, Morcar, a younger brother of the Earl of Mercia, was invited to take office in Tostig's place. This honour Morcar had readily accepted. Now, joined by a large force of sympathisers, and with Morcar at their head, the rebels were marching into the midlands while the Earl of

Mercia hastened to their aid with reinforcements. In short, the king was faced with a general rising of the north.

He was faced also with a personal dilemma which intensified when he sent Tostig's elder brother, Harold, Earl of Wessex, to negotiate with the insurgents. For Harold returned with the sombre news that the rebels refused to compromise. Their demands, simple and final, were that Morcar must be recognised and Tostig banished from the country. As the king's chief counsellor and military commander, Harold advised that, rather than risk civil war over his brother's future, these demands should be met. There followed a stormy council at the royal lodge in which Tostig reputedly accused his brother of complicity in the revolt, while Harold swore on oath that this was not the case. A passage in the frustratingly cryptic chronicles of the day expressed no doubt where the blame lay. Recording two great councils with the insurgents at Northampton and Oxford, on the festival of St Simon and St Jude, it concluded decisively:

... and Earl Harold was present and tried to do all he could to bring them to an agreement, but was unsuccessful. All the men of his [Tostig's] earl-dom were unanimous in repudiating him, and outlawed him and all those with him who had promoted injustice, because he robbed God first, and then despoiled of life and land all those over whom he could tyran-nise (*ASC*).

Whatever partiality Edward might have felt towards his furious guest, he had little choice of action. With Tostig's own brother, Harold, the most powerful earl in the country, for conciliation with the rebels, the king was not the man to hold out for a fight. In an atmosphere of much family bitterness, Tostig, his wife, children and retainers, left England to seek refuge in Flanders, while the rebels, having expended their high spirits on the countryside around Northampton, went triumphantly home. 'Not only did they slay men and burn houses and corn, but carried off all the livestock they could find, amounting to many thousands. They took many hundreds of captives, and carried them off north with them, so that their shire and other neighbouring shires were for many years the poorer,' wrote one Saxon chronicler. The Britford hunt ended on a very sour note.

Edward the Confessor never recovered from the shock. He had been ill before, and his health, hardly improved by this anxious and emotional period, was declining rapidly as he headed back to his palace at London. As the long caravan of oxen- and horse-drawn wagons bearing the goods and chattels of the royal entourage wound across the countryside, perhaps Edward knew he was looking upon the green acres of his kingdom for the last time. Nearby, his professional bodyguard of brawny housecarls, an élite military fraternity of Scandinavian origin, would have cast curious glances at his bleak face. Maybe, jogging loosely in the saddles of sturdy ponies which were just beginning to show their thick winter coats, the soldiers speculated on the identity of his successor. By Christmas, the king had less than a fortnight to live.

On 28 December, the new abbey of St Peter, on the isle of Thorney, a project dear to Edward's heart, was consecrated while its patron lay feebly at Westminster Palace. The word palace has since acquired lavish connotations. In Saxon times it was a place of most austere grandeur, a place where, despite the finely worked tapestries and drapes, an invalid could find little comfort. The solid wooden furniture was not upholstered, there was no draught-excluding glass in the windows and there must have been times when even the dogs in the hall preferred the wind itself to the billowing smoke from the open fire. In this spartan atmosphere, on 5 January, Edward the Confessor tossed deliriously through the last hours of his reign while, in four countries, four ambitious men waited for the trial of strength.

In Norway, Harald Hardrada, reputedly the greatest warrior king in the north, advised his Russian queen, Elizabeth, and his mistress, Thora, that England soon would be his. His claim to the island throne was based somewhat remotely on an arrangement between his predecessor, Magnus, and the former king of England and Denmark, Harthacnut. It was backed, however, by the formidable reputation of the soldiers who followed him under the Land-Waster, the notorious black raven banner of the Vikings.

Immediately across the Channel, in Normandy, Edward's cousin, Duke William, a fighter of great panache, awaited the call to Westminster. William was related to the Confessor only in the female line, moreover he was illegitimate, a stronger hereditary drawback to succession. But his hopes were pinned on a telling argument. William claimed he had been named as Edward's heir by the king himself, moreover that Harold of Wessex had sworn on oath to uphold him. Then there was Tostig, lurking at St Omer. Any chance to have returned to power in England and wipe out the humiliation of his dismissal would have appealed to the former Earl of Northumbria, especially, perhaps, a chance to do so at his brother Harold's expense.

Earl Harold was the most crucially situated of the power-seekers. Virtually Edward's deputy, he was at once a likely man to hold the country together on the king's death (almost inevitably a moment of internal crisis) and to defend it against the feared attack of Harald Hardrada's Vikings. According to Earl Harold's supporters, it was now Edward's wish that this strong son of Wessex should succeed to the throne. Legend has it that the dying king made delirious prophecies of doom for the kingdom, but there is no indication that Harold held back. If 1066 promised struggles of a kind unsung in the greatest Anglo-Saxon epics, Harold of Wessex started with at least two advantages over his strongest opponents. In the first place, his power was concentrated where it mattered at the time. In the second, the whole experience of his forty-odd years had been a preparation for the leadership of his fellow countrymen.

2

A Son of Wessex

Harold, son of Godwin and grandson of Wulfnoth, was born about
1022 into a family dedicated to the pursuit of power, and not altogether untalented in the art of abusing it. Ancient saga casts Wulfnoth as a swineherd, though he has since been identified, more
believably, with a Sussex noble of uncertain rank who once deserted
from a fleet raised by Ethelred, using the ships in his command to
plunder the south coast. Godwin, a remorselessly efficient careerist,
was adroit at switching loyalties in his own interest and appears to
have condoned the most unsavoury of political tactics. He climbed
to prominence in the first place by supporting the all-conquering
Canute, whom he accompanied on an early campaign in Denmark,
becoming a great favourite with this battling monarch. When
Canute, with his position to maintain in Scandinavia as well as in
England, was forced to delegate power, Godwin was there. Canute
divided England into the four main administrative areas, entrusting
each to an earl (the title derives from the Scandinavian 'jarl', or
under leader), and Godwin was very soon Earl of Wessex.

His position was strengthened further by his marriage to a Danish
girl, Gytha, conveniently the sister of Canute's brother-in-law,
Earl Ulf. Her family was famed for a menacing distinction. It was
said to have originated from the union between a woman and a bear,
presumably on account of the ferocious or hirsute nature of its males,
or both. Godwin and Gytha reared eight children: Sweyn, the eldest,
then Harold and Edith (though the order of these two is uncertain),
then Tostig, Gyrth, Leofwine, Wulfnoth and Gunhild. Formal
education for the boys was rudimentary. 'One shall not rebuke a
youth in his childhood until he can reveal himself,' runs an Anglo-
Saxon adage. 'He shall thrive among the people in that he is

confident.' This remarkably 'modern' concept would almost certainly
have applied to the high-spirited sons of a great earl. Godwin's boys
were nothing if not confident.

Their amusements were those of privileged country lads down the
ages: picking fights with village boys, hurling stones at birds, lying
in ambush on foxes and badgers, kicking long-suffering ponies to a
grudging gallop, teasing ancient retainers and billy-goats. Daring
and resourceful, they grew up familiar with the downs and vales of
the south, and, no doubt, with an early knowledge of the capital of
their father's earldom, Winchester. Here, sheltering in a misty cradle
of the chalk downs, the Romans had built the first city, their Venta
Belgarum, as a garrison town, and, looking down from the neighbouring heights, Harold would have seen that the main street was
still as straight as a spear shaft, while its subsidiary lanes intersected
it with military precision. From the gates issued Roman roads of
similar directness to Silchester, Cirencester, Porchester, Salisbury,
Southampton and elsewhere. Through those gates, in their time,
had passed the great figures of Wessex, a heritage at least partially
familiar to Harold through legend and literature. It was here that
Cerdic's Saxons had founded their centre after splashing ashore in the
sixth century, and here that the illustrious prince was buried. And
here Coenwalch, son of Cynegils, had built a temple to the honour
of St Peter and St Paul where, by the end of the seventh century,
resided the bishop's stool or cathedra.

When, at the beginning of the ninth century, the West Saxons
defeated the Mercians and gained tribute from the Northumbrians,
it was from Winchester that Egbert pronounced the kingdom of
Wessex supreme in all England; the city became properly the
national capital. It is difficult to imagine how Harold, with a Danish
mother and a father committed to Danish allegiance, looked back
on two centuries of Viking invasions and settlements, yet he cannot
have helped hearing of the greatness of Alfred the Dane-fighter. It
was from Winchester that Alfred, with characteristic Saxon stubbornness, had waged his lifelong fight to save the very foundations of
English culture from obliteration; and it was under Alfred that the
city first achieved widespread fame as a centre of intellectual life.
During the half-century prior to Harold's birth the city had been at

the heart of the revival of art and learning that accompanied the new monasticism of Archbishop Dunstan and his strong man, Bishop Athelwold. Indeed, descending the hill into the capital, it would have been the tower of Athelwold's new cathedral that inevitably held Harold's eye. It stood square-built in two stories, four large bells in the lower, and a single bell in the upper, roofed in red tile and surmounted with pinnacles, balls of burnished gold and a huge golden weathercock which pivoted in the sun. 'Up there he stands aloft,' wrote the cathedral precentor Wulfstan, 'over the heads of the men of Winchester, and in mid-air seems nobly to rule the western world.' In the bird's claw was the sceptre of command.

Wulfstan, who, as a monk, had watched the building of this ambitious temple, recorded his admiration in verse. So many the chapels, he declared, so intricate the passages, so numerous the columns, that one might easily be lost in it. Athelwold had done nothing by halves. By creating artificial channels from the River Itchen, his workmen had brought a water system to the cathedral and elsewhere in the city. He had taught his monks to chant in more elaborate tones, introducing new cadences and hymns. He had put writers, artists and book-makers to work on new service books and on the life-stories of local saints. And he had installed an organ of staggering size and power. Seventy men toiling at twenty-six bellows were required to fill the wind-chest, according to one description, while there were no less than 400 pipes. The keys, on twin boards, were marked with letters to indicate the notes, and operated by two monks 'ruling each his own alphabet'. The job demanded much strength. Unsophisticated machinery budged only after a struggle and the sweating organists punched the keys with both fists. 'Like thunder,' declared the poet, 'the iron voice assaults the ears and drives out all other sounds. So swells the noise that as you hear you must clap hands to your ears, unable, on drawing near, to abide the brazen bellowing. All through the city the melody can be heard, and the fame and echo of it spreads through all the land.'

The sound must have struck awe in the hearts of young Harold and his brothers. So must the stories of miracles wrought in the cathedral by its famous saint. Needing a wonder-working agency for his church, Athelwold had looked to King Alfred's long-buried tutor, Swithun, a scholar noted in his lifetime for humility and a rare practicality. His humble request that his bones might lie where the rain could fall on them was violated on his canonisation, when his remains were dug up and enshrined in the newly-completed cathedral. Tradition has it that the job was delayed by heavy cloudbursts and that thereafter rain on St Swithun's day meant rain for a further forty days. At all events, Swithun, whose foresight and constructive capacity, especially in building strong walls, had once helped to save much of value from the Danes, was henceforth vulgarised as a commonplace worker of miracles.

There was plenty more in the capital to capture boyish imagination. The names of such thoroughfares as Fleshmongers', Shoemakers' and Shieldmakers' Streets speak for themselves, as do the recorded nicknames of a number of their denizens, among them Bit-cat, Foul-beard, Penny-feather and Soft-bread. 'A creature came where many men, wise in mind, were sitting in the meeting place,' ran a well-known Anglo-Saxon riddle; 'it had one eye and two ears and two feet, twelve hundred heads, back and belly, and two hands, arms, and shoulders, one neck and two sides.' Similar guess-what quizzes were popular throughout the period and Harold could probably have identified the 'creature' as a one-eyed seller of garlic or onions. Salt pedlars, cheese makers, and many others, plied their wares in the town centres. Here, too, were the men of the town reeve, or sheriff, ready to levy the appropriate tolls on business transactions while, behind the scenes, Winchester's nine or more authorised moneyers busily struck the silver pennies and other coins which facilitated trade. Moneyers who issued base coins had the offending hand struck off and hung on the mint as a grisly warning to fellow craftsmen.

Not that Harold needed to look further than his own home for colour and excitement. The immediate household of an earl, constantly moving from estate to estate in the earldom, was bustling with stewards, secretaries, chaplains and bodyguards; a set-up similar, if on a lesser scale, to the royal court. Off duty they feasted and drank with their chief in his hall, listening to harp music and songs, perhaps watching tumblers and other entertainers. When he was old enough to be present at the revelry, Harold would have seen his mother, decked in shining armlets, necklaces and a diadem of gold, filling the mead-cups of his father and the more illustrious of his guests. As the hours and the liquor flowed on, the roistering and bragging would grow noisier until, finally, it ended in torpor or, not infrequently, in insult and injury. Godwin's associates included some very rough characters and Harold must have been well versed, as a youth, in drunkenness and violence. Their drink was highly-charged. 'He who grapples with me and struggles against my strength,' wrote a Saxon poet of the sugary mead, 'inevitably seeks the earth with his back.'

The Church had long since tried, without great success, to discourage drunkenness. An elaborate set of early Christian laws stipulated:

If a faithful layman makes another drunk through wickedness, let him do penance forty days. If any priest, deacon, monk, subdeacon, clerk or layman vomits through illness he is blameless. If anyone has been abstinent for a long time and was not used to drinking and eating much, or if through festivity at Christmas or at Easter or for the commemoration of any of the Saints he has been sick, if on such an occasion he has not taken more than was ordained by his elders, he is guiltless. If priests become drunk through ignorance they are to do penance on bread and water for seven days. If it is through negligence, fifteen days. If through wantonness, they should do penance forty days; deacons and monks four weeks; subdeacons three; clerks two; and laymen one week. If anyone compels a man to get drunk through kindness he is to do penance twenty days. If he did it for spite he is to be adjudged as a homicide.

Penalties for those who 'vomit up the eucharist' ranged from ninety days' penitence for a bishop to thirty days' for a layman. 'If he casts forth the sacrifice into the fire or into a river, he should sing a hundred psalms. If dogs devour it he should do penance for a hundred days if it is with his knowledge; otherwise forty days' (*Penitential of Archbishop Theodore*). Just how contrite eleventh-century clerics and laymen felt about their excesses is a matter for speculation, but references to carousing throughout the Anglo-Saxon period suggest that regrets were temporal rather than spiritual.

Like other lads of his time, Harold, a tall, broad-shouldered youth, necessarily matured early. By the time he reached his teens he was adept at giving orders, while an introduction to estate management would have taught him the various classes of tenant-servant and what might be demanded of them under their contract. The most favoured of these, sometimes called the *geneat*, paid rent for his land and gave services when needed as horseman, bodyguard, hunt assistant and so on. Then there was a lower order, the *gebur*, who, in return for a small holding and initial stock, might pay an annual rent of money, corn and hens, plus, in some places, a lamb, 'or twopence', at Easter. On top of this, he was required to do a regular stint of ploughing and harvesting for his lord, and probably to help care for his lord's hounds and to carry his lord's seed. On his death, an event often hastened by overwork and, among other prevalent hazards, osteo-arthritis[1] and whooping cough, his land reverted to the estate. At the bottom of the land-holding scale came the so-called *cotsetla*, or cottage dweller, a general oddbody on call for all types of heavy duties who might labour the whole of August for his lord, and perhaps a day a week for the rest of the year, in return for as little as an unproductive five acres from which to scratch his own living.

Taking a broader view, Harold was aware of an acutely class-conscious populace divided, roughly speaking, into a further three categories: an upper class of thegns, an intermediate class known most commonly as ceorls (which included the *geneat*, *gebur* and *cotsetla*), and a lower and less numerous order of slaves. The slave was a chattel, to be sold like an animal or a plough. Some slaves were prisoners of war, some were descendants of those ancient Britons the Romans and Saxons had encountered in their invasions, others the offspring of freemen forced by poverty to sell their kin into slavery. Though it was contrary to law, the export of slaves persisted in the eleventh century. An Anglo-Danish lady of high rank appears to have been notorious for selling English girls to the Danes. 'Also we know full well where that miserable deed has

---

[1] Human vertebrae from the Anglo-Saxon period have been found welded solidly together as the result of heavy labour.

occurred that a father has sold his son at a price, or a son his mother, or one brother another, into the power of foreigners,' Archbishop Wulfstan wrote at the beginning of the century. Sometimes slaves were redeemed by ransom, by the goodwill of their owners or the concern of the Church. Many tried to escape their toils simply by running away; a desperate venture. One Anglo-Saxon law ordered runaway slaves to be stoned to death.

The ceorl was a freeman, at his most successful a farmer with one or more hides of his own land.[1] For a tenant-farmer, the rent of a hide was heavy. In one part of Hampshire, for instance, it involved an annual payment in money, ale, wheat, barley, wood and fencing, plus part-time work on behalf of the landlord every week of the year except three. In his own time, such a tenant was obliged to plough three acres of his lord's land a year, sow it with his own seed, mow half an acre of the lord's meadow and wash and shear the lord's sheep. Elsewhere, in the locality of rivers, the landlord demanded his rent in rods, yarn, labour on the weirs and one out of every two fish his tenant caught. For the hell of it, he required the tenant to hand over *every* 'unusual' fish.

Just as the family of an impoverished ceorl might sink into slavery, so it was possible for a prosperous ceorl to rise to the upper class, that is become a thegn. According to one late-Saxon document, he was worthy of up-grading if he possessed, among other status symbols, five hides of his own land, a church, a kitchen, a bell-house and a gate to his estate. As a thegn, he carried altogether more prestige. He was more expensive to kill than a ceorl and his oath carried more weight. At the same time, he was liable to higher penalties for his own offences, for example, in failing to answer the call to military service or to assist with fort-building and bridge-repairing when required. The thegn was the mainstay of the wartime army, by tradition the king's man. Whether he was a magnate with a hundred estates in various counties (such thegns were not unknown), or little better off than a well-to-do ceorl, farming his own land, his class distinction was a matter of the same pride.

---

[1] The term 'hide', meaning 'household', might originally have defined the area of land thought necessary to provide for a family. In Domesday Book its size seems to have varied from forty to 120 acres depending on its situation in the kingdom.

These traditions Harold learnt as he accompanied his father about his earldom. Deeper, less tangible traditions were already in his blood. Half Saxon, half Dane, his heritage flowed from two races renowned for ferocity in battle. On the Saxon side, his forefathers came of one of the most pugnacious nations of Germany. Though these people proved as industrious with the plough as with their favourite weapon, the short sword or *seax* (hence the word Saxon), after their invasion of Britain, they never lost the tradition of heroism upon which their society was founded. Many centuries earlier, Tacitus, noting the passionate loyalty between men and leaders among the Germanic races, had observed that it was 'a lifelong infamy and reproach to survive the chief and withdraw from the battle.... The chiefs fight for victory, the followers for their chiefs.' In return, the successful chief ensured that his followers received their share of the spoils of war.

Time and again, Saxon writers honoured men who stood resolutely and fell honourably beside their leaders, sometimes long after hope of victory had gone. Admittedly there was a great deal of less stoic behaviour, while the appeal of such incidents is ambiguous in itself. Certainly the persistence with which bribes were offered to opponents is eloquent of the fact that they were less persistently scorned. Nevertheless, loyalty, even to the point of death, stands out as a shining ideal. An Anglo-Saxon poet describing a tenth-century battle at Maldon told how the followers of one Byrhtnoth, an ealdorman of Essex, fought on against the Danes after he had been slain. 'Remember the times when often we spoke at the mead-drinking, when on the bench we uttered boasting, heroes in hall, about hard strife,' a young warrior urged his comrades. 'Now he who is brave may show it in the test. I will make known my lineage to all, that I was of a mighty race among the Mercians.... Thegns shall not reproach me among the people that I wish to leave this army, to seek my home, now my prince lies low, hewn down in battle.'

A second shook his spear and echoed the sentiment: '... it is the task of all of us that each should exhort the other to fight while he can grasp and hold a weapon.'

'I promise I shall not flee a footstep,' growled a third.

'He in the host who thinks to avenge the prince cannot waver nor mourn for life,' declared another, a humble ceorl.

With Byrhtnoth's loyal band falling one by one to the victorious Danes, the poem closed on a moving note of defiance from an ageing Saxon warrior: 'Thought shall be the harder, heart the keener, courage the greater as our might lessens,' he asserted. 'May he lament for ever who thinks now to turn from this war-play. I am old in age; I will not hence, but I purpose to lie by the side of my lord. . . .'

Valour in defeat, the brave loser, greatly inspired the chroniclers and poets. There seems to have been a stubborn streak in the Saxon which made him particularly tenacious in adversity. By contrast, the Dane has come down through the ages as a master of initiative, a resourceful long-range fighter whose swift, unexpected attacks were for long the scourge of western Europe. It was not only at sea that the Danes excelled in mobility. Their forced marches across England, both in deeply penetrating raids and to extricate themselves from difficulty, often astonished their enemies. On one occasion in the reign of Ethelred, a force which had landed at Sandwich, finding itself heavily outnumbered, took to the sea again, re-landed in Southampton Water and launched a winter raid of the most sweeping nature through Hampshire and Berkshire, passing through Reading and Wallingford to a point on the Berkshire Downs known as Cuckamsley Barrow before the defenders could reorganise. There is a hint of sheer bravado in this daring strategic move, for, according to an old saying, if the Danes should ever reach such a point they would never get back to the sea again. Not only did they get back to the sea, they marched brazenly past the walls of Winchester carrying their loot. 'Then might the Winchester men see the army, daring and fearless, as it went by their gates towards the sea, fetching treasure and food for over fifty miles from the water' (*ASC*). There was a lawlessness, an unpredictability about the Dane. He was flamboyant and mobile where the Saxon, once settled in England, often seemed phlegmatic and insular. From the tales and attitudes of those around him, Harold inherited both these traditions, though, as time was to show, nurturing less of the impulsive Viking temperament than his brothers Sweyn and Tostig.

Meanwhile, there were more lessons to learn. As childhood receded, Harold moved from the romance of theory to the sterner school of practical politics. He was to find it no place for the squeamish.

★

Canute died at Shaftesbury in November 1035 and his body was carried to Winchester for burial at St Swithun's. In the solemnity and emotion of the hour, few could have made a greater impression on a youthful mind than the dead king's extraordinary widow, Emma. Desirable, formidable and incorrigible by turn, Emma, 'the gem of Normandy', had been the wife of two English kings, was to see two of her sons achieve the same eminence, and went on dabbling in politics to the last. In her sixties she was accused of trying to poison the king and of too close an intimacy with her kinsman, the Bishop of Winchester. One story has it that she cleared herself by submitting to the ordeal of hot iron. Be that as it may, the better authenticated high-lights of her life are remarkable enough. Daughter of Richard I of Normandy and his vivacious mistress Gunnor, Emma's hand was first given in a diplomatic marriage to King Ethelred of England, notorious to posterity for his unreadiness to take counsel. Ethelred's reign was popularly remembered for his disastrous policy of trying to buy off the Danes and for a particularly vicious blunder in ordering the massacre of numbers of Danish settlers in the country. The strong-willed Norman girl, despising her husband's weakness and caprice, is supposed to have been equally unimpressed by their children, Edward and Alfred. Ethelred died in 1016, and when the young and soldierly Canute became King of England a few months later, the princes were in the care of Emma's brother, Richard the Good, in Normandy. The stocky Dane turned out to be as competent a monarch as Ethelred had been an inefficient one. In the role of Viking chief he had been ruthless and cruel, pitilessly mutilating hostages when it suited him, but, once the throne was his, Canute aspired to a loftier role than that of a mere crowned pirate. Realising there was no kudos in governing a ravaged and rebellious land, he had soon set about improving public relations.

In a stroke as masterly as it was unexpected, the new king had offered his hand in marriage to the widow of his late opponent. He appears to have been no more than twenty-one at the time, while Emma was then at least ten years, maybe fifteen, his elder, but the lady had considerable charms in maturity. A contemporary portrait showing her with Canute at Winchester suggested a delicate nose, large mouth in an oval face and a lively, sensual appeal surviving even the marked stylistic conventions of the artist. But Canute had not set eyes on her when he offered marriage. There were a number of less romantic advantages to be gained from the match. By making their queen-dowager his queen-consort, he aimed to reassure the English; to soften the image of the new régime. At the same time, since Normandy had been a Viking settlement and Emma's family came from Scandinavian stock, he saw the marriage as acceptable to his Danish followers. Furthermore, and perhaps most vital of all, by creating a tie with Emma's brother Richard, he hoped to obviate the potential danger from her sons by Ethelred. It seems that Emma was not distraught at the idea of scuttling the rights of her existing children. Her sole condition to the marriage, an oddly cold-blooded one coming from a mother, though politically shrewd, was that Canute should guarantee that any son she might have by him would be his lawful successor. This forced him to make a similar sacrifice, if so she saw it, to her own, for the youthful Canute already had two sons, by Aelfgifu, the Gift of the Elves, daughter of a Northampton ealdorman. Canute raised no objection to the bargain and in July 1017, this striking and wilful couple were married. By all accounts they were admirably matched. The following year Emma bore her new husband a male child, Harthacnut, whom she adored to extravagance. Meanwhile, Canute, having assumed the role of a devoutly religious and conscientious ruler, paid off the Danish army in England, set the pace for greater integration between Saxon and Dane in the country, and with his wife ever-lovingly beside him, postured dramatically as Church benefactor and penitent. For the last time, during Canute's reign, Winchester was the true focus of regal and ecclesiastic power in the kingdom, and the royal couple endowed its churches with much land and treasure. If the legend can be believed, it was above St Josse's that Canute placed his crown after the celebrated scene on the sea-shore, swearing never to wear it again.[1]

As with the demise of so many strong rulers, the death of Canute precipitated a dangerous political crisis in the country, of which Godwin's family found themselves at the centre. Harold, now old enough to take an interest in such affairs, was to have perhaps his first chance of studying his father's adeptness in manœuvre. Canute had remained true to his bargain with Emma and, in normal circumstances, Harthacnut would probably have succeeded him without trouble. But Harthacnut was abroad at the time of his father's death, opposing the threat of a new northern power, Magnus of Norway, and England found herself divided. One party, headed by Emma and largely southern in following, wished to elect Harthacnut as king in his absence, while the other, broadly drawn from north of the Thames, proposed setting up a regency with a son of Canute by Aelfgifu of Northampton, namely Harold Harefoot, as its candidate. There seems to have been little to choose between the half-brothers save that one was present and the other was not. Both were cruel, degenerate and rapacious, and though evidence of less obnoxious qualities can be found, the couple indeed represented a sad regression from the standards of their father. At first, Godwin backed Harthacnut, the early favourite, taking Emma into his protection against the supporters of her bitter rival. In the words of the chronicler, Emma 'sat at Winchester with the housecarls of Canute and Harthacnut, her son, and held all Wessex for him, and Godwin Earl was her chief man'.

When Harefoot, egged on by his mother, sent a force to the city to dispossess Emma of Canute's best treasures, however, Godwin's loyalty did not run to anything so chivalrous as a confrontation. Neither, when Harthacnut's continued absence swung the odds in his half-brother's favour, did the fervour of the calculating earl rise in opposition. Godwin was playing it cautiously; so cautiously, as it

[1] At the summit of his power, Canute was supposed to have set his throne on the seashore as the tide was rising, addressing the mounting waters thus: 'No one has ever resisted my rule without being punished. I therefore command you not to rise on to my land, nor to dampen the robes or legs of your master.' When the water came on unheedingly, the monarch leapt up and proclaimed dramatically: 'Know all inhabitants of earth that vain and trivial is the power of kings, nor is anyone worthy of the name of king save Him whose nod heaven and earth and sea obey under laws eternal.' The story was first put on record in the first half of the twelfth century by Henry of Huntingdon.

happened, that when, in 1037, Harold Harefoot was eventually recognised, formally, as king of all England, and Emma was forced to flee the country to Flanders, her erstwhile protector stayed safely at home. It seems he had already joined Harefoot's party.

Godwin's part in an altogether unpalatable incident the previous year had pretty clearly signalled his intentions. It happened after Alfred, the younger son of Emma and Ethelred, though long since a mature man, had landed on the south coast with a heavy bodyguard of Norman mercenaries, ostensibly to visit his mother at Winchester.[1] Uncertain of their reception, Alfred and his band had travelled west from some point near Dover up the Vale of Kent, no doubt casting many apprehensive glances towards the heights of the downs on their right and the inhospitable Weald on their left. It is not hard to imagine their relief when, in due course, they were met by a seemingly hospitable Godwin and conducted down into the lovely Wey Valley where food and shelter had been arranged at Guildford. Eventually, when Alfred and his friends had been welcomed and feasted, they were billeted with some care in small groups about the town. At this point, Godwin faded out of the picture and Harefoot's officers took over. It was late at night as their men moved quietly into position and, at a given signal, seized the unsuspecting visitors where they slept. So efficiently was the operation planned that hardly a blow was struck by the Normans in their defence. Many perished in an orgy of murder and mutilation, some, it appears, being scalped, and the survivors were duly sold into slavery. Alfred's own fate was no less tragic. It moved the chroniclers to verse:

> *Threatened with every kind of injury, the prince still lived,*
> *Until the decision was taken to convey him*
> *To the city of Ely, in chains as he was.*
> *When he arrived, his eyes were put out on board ship,*
> *And sightless he was brought to the monks.*
> *There he remained as long as he lived.*

[1] Historians are at variance over Alfred's motives. Sir Frank Stenton, for instance, accepts the above at face value in *Anglo-Saxon England*, while Sir Charles Oman, in *England Before the Norman Conquest*, takes the view that Alfred was 'making a snatch at the paternal crown while the sons of Canute were at variance',

Which was not for long, for the operation had been crudely performed. 'Never,' declared one version of the *Anglo-Saxon Chronicle*,
'was a bloodier deed done in this land since first the Danes came
hither.' Harefoot died a few years after the affair and Harthacnut,
finally returning from Denmark to disinter his half-brother's body
and hurl it, disfigured, into the Thames, ordered an investigation
into Alfred's murder. Meanwhile, the Earl of Wessex had reverted
deftly to his former colours. The new king found him innocent of
complicity in the crime though not before Godwin, having mustered
a host of influential compurgators to swear to the purity of his oath,
had made his judge the timely gift of a gilded *drakkar*, or dragon
ship, manned by a crew of eighty, each bearing a specially-wrought
battle-axe and twelve ounces of gold in the form of bracelets.

Harthacnut ruled for less than two years, during which, on the
words of a Winchester writer, four banquets a day were laid in the
great hall of that city to meet his apparently insatiable appetite. Even
by royal standards, Emma's favourite, it seems, was a glutton. If
he placed any faith in the old Saxon Church laws about food, he
must have resorted pretty often to that highly recommended settler
of stomachs, a hare sodden in water; perhaps even taking its liver,
mixed with pepper, to banish his jaw-ache. The Anglo-Saxons were
highly superstitious in their attitude to the things that were proper
and improper to eat. While they would eat fish which had been
found dead, because it came from another element and was 'not of
our nature', many of them would not eat horse meat, and, at one
time, it was against religious teaching to eat birds and other creatures
found strangled in nets since the Acts of the Apostles warned people
to keep 'from things strangled and from blood'. One ancient
manifesto advised:

If a hen drink human blood, it is lawful to eat it after three months; but
on this point we have not ancient authority. If anyone eat anything with
blood in half-cooked food, if consciously he is to fast for seven days, if
unconsciously for three days or to sing the Psalter. If anyone unconsciously drinks his own blood in his saliva, there is no peril. If anyone eat
anything from that of which a dog or a mouse has eaten or which a weasel
has defiled, if consciously he is to sing a hundred psalms, if unconsciously
fifty psalms. If anyone gives to another liquor in which a mouse or a

weasel has been drowned, if he is a layman let him fast three days, if he is a monk let him sing a hundred psalms. If he knew it not at first but knew it later, let him sing the Psalter (*Confessional of Archbishop Ecgbert*).

Harthacnut's end was appropriate. At twenty-five, Emma's favourite fell dead in front of a laden table. He was the guest of honour at the wedding feast of his father's retainer, Tovi the Proud. 'As he stood at his drink,' declared a monkish scribe with certain relish, 'he fell to the earth in a horrid convulsion; and then they who were nigh lifted him, but he spake not one word, but died on the sixth day before the Ides of June.' It was 1042, the last year of the Danish royal house in England. Harold Godwinson was approaching his twenties. In the side-stepping shadow of his father, he had progressed from childhood to manhood. He had observed the tactics of the most successful politician of the time at first hand, no doubt even playing his part. He was ready to try his hand alone.

3

Edward and the House of Godwin

On the first day of Easter, 1043, Edward the Confessor, elder brother of the blinded Alfred, was crowned at St Swithun's, Winchester. Heading the great English families present was Godwin and his sons. Of these, Harold probably regarded the occasion most thoughtfully. Without doubt, he was a steadier, shrewder young man, altogether more on the pattern of his father, than Sweyn, who had the makings of a thorough-going tearaway, or Tostig, whose reputation trended to vanity and arrogance. No really trustworthy likeness exists of Harold at any time of his life, though the Bayeux Tapestry, worked within a generation or so of the events it depicted and accurate in many verifiable details, shows him as tall and of athletic build with a clean jaw and fair locks falling to the nape of his neck. He appears to have sported a wispy moustache, may have been tattooed in Saxon custom on the hand or neck, and doubtless shared the taste of his times for bracelets and rings in precious metals. Like other young noblemen of his period, he wore a knee-length tunic of fine cloth, a rich cloak or mantle caught at the shoulder with a jewelled clasp, linen stockings, and shoes or ankle-boots of moulded leather stitched up the front. Perhaps for state occasions such as this he wore some sort of perfume. The age was hardly obsessed with the finer points of personal hygiene.

Around Edward, a lonely, vulnerable figure blinking unfamiliarly at his audience from beneath the gold circlet and fleurs-de-lys of the crown, hovered the archbishops Eadsige of Canterbury and Aelfric of York. After Harefoot and Harthacnut, a return to the royal line of the Saxons was welcome to many, but Edward himself inspired few hearts to ardour. At thirty-seven, the new king had spent the best part of his life in the shelter of the Norman court. To his unfamiliarity with English affairs he could not even bring the advantage of Norman military flair. His candidature for the throne, backed by the leading magnates and upheld by the witan, had succeeded less, it seems, on the basis of positive loyalty than on the general lack of antipathy. He appears to have been regarded rather as an object of inertia: a convenience. Popular sentimental reaction to his brother's murder had lent this princely-looking, middle-aged fellow, with his air of patience and resignation, a certain sympathy. But since his personal following in the country could hardly have matched that of any one of the three leading earls, Siward of Northumbria, Leofric of Mercia or Godwin of Wessex, his survival as anything more than a puppet depended on using one against the other. No one, watching Edward enrapt in the mystery of consecration, could have seen him as a Machiavelli.

As the cathedral windows framed the spring sky, and the first swallows emerged, so it was thought, from their winter fastnesses at the bottom of fens and lakes, Harold must have looked from the misty eyes of the pious Edward to the knowing and satisfied expression of Godwin, and caught a hint of rich and expanding prospects. If Godwin had ever feared the accession of one whose brother he had betrayed to the brutalities of Harefoot, it could not have taken him long to estimate the temper of this returned exile. Here, with God's blessing, was a king he could dominate. Quietly, he had lobbied for Edward's recognition, where necessary buying-off the opposition. Not far from the cathedral, moored to the leafy banks of the Itchen, rode a magnificent barge with a crew, several score strong, of expert rowers. At the stern was a golden lion while, from the stem, fluttered the flag of Wessex, a dragon, also in gold. The ship was a gift to the new king from the house of Godwin. The earl was nothing if not thorough.

But not everyone was as anxious to invest in Edward. Emma, who who had returned to England with the reign of Harthacnut, to be reunited with her property at Winchester, openly turned her back on the son she had born to her despised first husband. Many suspected the ageing queen-mother of having invited Magnus of Norway to invade the country on the death of Harthacnut. It was said that she had offered the northern king the considerable treasure she had accumulated through Canute and Harthacnut to take the country from Edward, and at least this would not have been out of character. For twenty-five years the ambitious Emma had devoted herself to her second husband and his children, neglecting her off-spring by Ethelred. It was not hard to believe she would have pre-ferred another strong Norseman on the throne, albeit a stranger, to a reminder of Ethelred's reign. On the advice of earls Godwin, Leofric and Siward, and probably without much filial compunction, Edward's earliest recorded move, having settled into office, was to descend on his mother and seize her treasure hoard, property and lands. Taken by surprise, the old lady was powerless to do anything save, perhaps, unleash a flood of Norman-French invective on her unwanted visitors. She never forgave Edward. Shutting herself away with her resentment and her memories of a remarkable and passionate past in a house at the top of Winchester High Street, she died a few years later as uncompromisingly as she had lived.

Meanwhile, in 1045, the influence of the Earl of Wessex was demonstrated very clearly by the marriage of his daughter, Edith, to the king. 'As from the thorn springs the rose, so from Godwin comes Edith,' wrote an early epigrammatist. Yet it is hard to find romance in the contract. Edward, old enough to be her father, was, by all accounts, a confirmed bachelor at this stage of his life. In any case, he must ideally have looked elsewhere for a father-in-law than in the one man he resented, perhaps feared, above any. More likely, this odd match symbolised the discomfort of Edward's position at the time; his need to comply, however uneasily, with his sponsors, especially the high-stepping Godwin family whose control was spreading in the south. Harold's brother Sweyn had already received an earldom which included a sizeable portion of southern Mercia, and now a nephew of Godwin, Beorn Estrithson, was given an earl-dom in the eastern midlands. At the same time Harold, in his early twenties, stepped finally from apprenticeship under his father to assume his first responsibilities of direct and sweeping command.

Harold's first earldom, commemorated in such surviving names as Harold Wood near Romford, and Harold's Park, Nazeing, both in Essex, was that of East Anglia, a division which traditionally included Norfolk, Suffolk, Essex and Cambridgeshire, though the limits in Harold's time are now uncertain. In any case, the appointment was both a personal triumph and a further glory in the summer of Godwin's cause. As an earl, Harold was now answerable to none but the king, his brother-in-law. His task was a large one. With the help of his deputies, a sheriff or shire-reeve in each county, it was his duty to keep peace and do justice in his earldom, to maintain its defence and to command its forces in war. East Anglian society provided a special challenge. As part of 'Danelaw' England, its culture preserved a virile Scandinavian influence foreign to Harold's native Wessex. To start with, its laws were different. For the first time in England, Danelaw courts asserted the principle of a majority verdict. And its penalties were different: generally harsher. Furthermore, as a more or less autonomous province for some time in the past, East Anglia had enjoyed a happy immunity from the heavy taxes of the Old-English kings and the grasping habits of their churchmen. The result was a less depressed populace than elsewhere. There were fewer slaves; a more robust body of ceorls. Particularly prominent was a stratum of peasant aristocracy, the sokemen, whose economic buoyancy had survived the crunch of manorial obligations which had crippled so many of their kind in other parts of the country. While the sokeman was not free from money and labour dues to his lord, these were neither as burdensome nor as humiliating as elsewhere. The freemen of East Anglia were still proud of their tradition of independence. They were proud, too, of their fighting qualities. Such people could afford to be intolerant of bad leadership. They required a just, if stern, rule, and this can have had nothing but a good influence on their young earl.

To the north, the frontier barriers of his earldom were the wide, soggy fenlands; to the south, the woods. In between, large areas of boulder-clay, providing the basis for workable, loamy soils, supported the farming settlements, each with its shared water mill for grinding corn. In the larger communities there were more mills, seven at Norwich and eight at Thetford.[1] The fens themselves were not unproductive, and the monks and others who had settled on the higher points among the marches, as at Ely and Peterborough, had reclaimed useful areas by ditching and banking. Osiers, used in

[1] Domesday refers to more than 5,000 water mills in England.

making baskets, eel traps and so forth, grew here. So did rushes for thatching and long grasses which made hay to nourish livestock in winter. One eleventh-century visitor to Ely wrote:

The Isle is within itself plenteously endowed; it is supplied with various kinds of herbage, and in richness of soil surpasses the rest of England. Most delightful for fields and pastures, it is also remarkable for beasts of chase, and is, in no ordinary way, fertile in flocks and herds. . . . In this Isle there is an abundance of domestic cattle and a multitude of wild animals; stags, roes, goats and hares are found in its groves and by these fens. Moreover, there is a fair sufficiency of otters, weasels and polecats, which in hard winter are caught by traps, snares or any other device. . . . In the eddies at the sluices of these meres are netted innumerable eels, large water-wolves, with pickerels, perches, roaches, burbots and lampreys, which we call water-snakes. It is indeed said by many that salmon are taken there, together with the royal fish, the sturgeon. As for the birds which are taken there and thereabouts, if you are not tired of listening to me, I will tell you about them as I have told you about the rest. There you find geese, teal, coots, didappers, water-crows, herons and ducks more than man can number, especially in winter or at moulting time.

The shepherds of East Anglia seem to have been troubled less by wolves than were their counterparts in the west and the north of England, where these carnivores were all too plentiful, but parts of Harold's earldom may have been noted for bears since the responsibility for providing the king with three of these animals each year, for bear-baiting, devolved upon Norwich.

There is no reason to doubt that Harold governed East Anglia with anything but circumspection. Rugged, direct, methodical, tenacious, he seems to have had a genuine talent for inspiring the respect of ordinary people, especially his soldiers. As far as knowledge of his life goes, it lacked the vices and excesses of so many leaders of his time. He was also a family man. From the lowlands of the east, supposedly Norfolk, Harold chose his concubine, Eadgyth Swanneshals, or Swan-Neck, and at least five children, possibly six, eventually filled their hall with happiness. Harold's three sons by his white-throated mistress were named Godwin, Edmund and Magnus; their daughters, Gunhild and Gytha. A fourth son of Harold's, Ulf, was probably of the same mother. The picture is one of both official and domestic stability. Indeed, had the children's uncles, Sweyn and Tostig, been anything like their father, the house of Godwin must have held the country in its hands. Unfortunately for Godwin, such was not the case and, from now on, the two eldest of Harold's brothers were to bedevil the family and Wessex, between them, almost to the end.

It was Sweyn, with characteristic imprudence, who invoked the first curse. He was returning from a campaign in South Wales, which bordered his earldom. Having extracted promises and taken hostages from the Welsh, he was in high fettle as his force clattered into Leominster on the homeward ride and tethered their ponies while they stopped to celebrate. Fertile of soil, sheltered and convenient to water, Leominster had been the site of human dwellings since the earliest times, but its reputation and development as an Anglo-Saxon town dated from the establishment there of a religious institution in the seventh century by a Mercian king named Merewalh. In the customary fashion, this foundation was connected with miracles. A Northumbrian priest, Eadfrith, travelling to the court of Merewalh, had sat down to eat some bread from his wallet when a lion appeared before him. Eadfrith offered the lion some of his bread, and the two became friends. The parable underlined Eadfrith's supposed relationship with Merewalh who, once fiercely pagan, was thought to have been converted by Christian teaching to a benign and compassionate ruler. According to one version, the town got its name from this incident—'Leonis Monasterium'. The name 'Leofminstre' actually comes into recorded usage with the time of Godwin's rival earl, Leofric of Mercia, who was probably an important benefactor of the local church.

The scandal of Sweyn's halt at Leominster involved a woman. Her name was Edgiva, and she was abbess of the convent which by now lent repute to the township. Edgiva was not unattractive, nor should it too readily be assumed that she held herself aloof from Leominster's soldierly visitors. Early bishops were sometimes as upset by the worldly behaviour of nuns as of monks. In one instance it was deplored that they spent their time making gorgeous robes, 'in which they either adorned themselves like brides, thereby endangering their own estate of life and profession, or they gave them to men who were strangers, for the purpose of securing their friendship'. Whatever Edgiva's disposition, it was sufficiently provocative to take Sweyn's fancy. Apparently he determined to seduce her. In conquering mood, the swashbuckling earl had the abbess 'fetched to him', as a contemporary put it, 'and kept her as long as he pleased' (*ASC*). Then he let her go home. Another source maintains that he wanted to marry her. At all events, few acts could have been calculated to provoke greater public resentment. Had Sweyn tortured or murdered a few prisoners, or amused himself at the expense of some slave girl, the episode would not have been extraordinary. To invite divine retribution in so flagrant a style was another matter.

Poetically enough, by the time the scandal had had good time to circulate, the worst winter in living memory was upon the country. Men, cattle, birds and even fish, it was recorded, perished from frost and hunger. Maybe, in the superstitious minds of many people, the two events were connected. Assuredly, few men, least of all the king, his most precious sensibilities outraged, were in the mood for forgiveness, and Sweyn, inspired to momentary wisdom, put the sea between himself and England, sailing first to Bruges where he found refuge with Baldwin of Flanders, then, next summer, to Denmark to join his namesake and cousin, Sweyn Estrithson, against Magnus. It can have been no great surprise to learn that he was soon on the run from Denmark, accused of another grave (though no longer identifiable) crime.

Sweyn was settling into his stride. From Denmark he returned to Flanders where Count Baldwin, no love lost for Edward, allowed the renegade to use his harbours as bases for piratical operations against the English coast. The laugh, however, was to be on Baldwin, for while Sweyn's raids were no more than a nuisance to Edward, the fugitive never having many ships, Edward was quietly mustering a considerable fleet with a view to causing the utmost embarrassment to Baldwin. It happened that the count had overstepped himself by storming the Nijmegen palace of his lordly neighbour, the Emperor Henry III, and now Henry, having collected a great army of allies, was bent on retribution. It was said that even the Pope was present in the force. Edward's role in this combined operation was to prevent

Baldwin escaping by sea, and to this effect he sailed with his navy to Sandwich where he lay until Henry had indeed gained satisfaction. Edward was still at Sandwich Haven when Sweyn, the bad penny, reappeared on the scene.

By Edward's reign Sandwich had been written of as 'the most famous of all English ports'. Far across the eastern end of the Wantsum Channel, which then separated the Isle of Thanet from the mainland, stretched a sandy neck of the island, forming a natural weather-break behind which large numbers of vessels could harbour. For centuries the fame of Sandwich Haven as a harbour and shipping rendezvous had invited the ravages of Viking fleets. Canute had used it as a refuge in his early days, Ethelred had assembled a navy there and Harefoot had seized the port from the monks of Christ Church, Canterbury, who traditionally received its revenues and tolls. When Edward anchored there, 307 dwelling houses stood in the town, many of whose occupants must have been herring fishers, for the little community contributed 40,000 herrings a year in taxes alone.

Surveying the familiar scene after his wild and comfortless travels must have been a moving experience, even for Sweyn. Long months abroad lent a special joy to the sound of Sandwich bells and the tranquil sight of the ferry making its leisurely way between Thanet and the mainland. Perhaps the great shoal of long-boats on the calm water filled him with the urge to return to his own people. Sweyn had left his pirate squadron of seven or eight ships along the coast at Bosham, and he now ventured to seek audience with Edward and his council. There is some confusion among the chroniclers as to the details of what followed. It is recorded that Godwin, Harold and Tostig held commands in the assembled fleet and so did Godwin's young nephew, Earl Beorn. Apparently Edward, doubtless influenced by Godwin, at least agreed to discuss the possibility of Sweyn's reinstatement to office, but Harold and Beorn, both of whom had received portions of the outlaw's forfeited earldom, were prominent in opposing the return of these possessions. Thus, with Godwin's family disunited over the prodigal's return, the king was safe to follow his own inclination and order Sweyn to keep out. The outlaw was, in fact, given four days to be clear of the country again. By now, the fleet was dispersing. Sweyn had to do something quickly.

While Edward remained at Sandwich with a number of ships, others were sailing along the south coast to investigate reports that hostile craft were raiding to the west. Godwin and Beorn got no further than Pevensey before they were forced to stop and wait for more opportune weather. The flat country now known as Pevensey Levels was then indented with bays and inlets, making an excellent landing area. Indeed, it was here that some of the earliest Saxons, under a leader named Aella, had disembarked to lay siege to the Roman fortress of Anderida.

At Pevensey Godwin and his nephew were overtaken by the disreputable, and now desperate, Sweyn, a wild, fugitive figure with new schemes churning his none too subtle mind. To begin, he pleaded with Beorn to help him in a final bid to win round the unconciliatory Edward. Perhaps Godwin, enduring in loyalty to his sons if not always to others, helped to rouse the young Beorn's compassion. The outcome was that Beorn magnanimously agreed to return to Sandwich with Sweyn with a view to inducing the king to review his earlier decision. Pledges were made, horses were saddled, Beorn detailed three followers to ride with him, and the party set out on its mission. 'Then as they rode,' declared one chronicler darkly, 'Sweyn begged him [Beorn] to go with him to his ships, making out that his sailors would desert unless he went to them very quickly' (*ASC*). Since this meant a sharp detour from their route, Beorn's acquiescence seems a trifle naïve, even allowing for the considerable weight attached to a pledge of honourable behaviour. Sweyn's choice of Bosham as a refuge for his ships had been a cunning one. The tree-fringed harbour was a favourite seaside haunt of Godwin and his family. Tradition told how the bell of Bosham church was once stolen by Norse pirates who were carrying it away across the creek when St Nicholas, rather than see it in pagan hands, sank their ship at a spot afterwards known as Bell Hole. When new bells rang from the church, the old bell was said to chime in from the depths of the sea. The origin of at least part of the fable was a clear echo across the water from West Itchenor woods. But if Beorn heard it as Sweyn urged him down to the harbour, there was to be no saintly intervention in the devilish action that followed. Sweyn had reckoned, correctly, that his ships would not be challenged at a place where the family connections were strong, and his credulous fellow-traveller was virtually upon them before his suspicions were aroused. 'Then they both went to where his ships lay; and when they arrived earl Sweyn begged him to go on board, but he stubbornly refused until Sweyn's sailors seized him and threw him into the boat: they bound him and rowed to the ship and put him on board, hoisted their sails and ran west to Axmouth' (*ASC*). On the wet planks of that pitching long-boat, Beorn was murdered. They buried him 'deep' at Dartmouth.

Saxon writers offer no explanation for the crime, leaving it, to all appearances, a piece of wanton savagery. Contemporaries would have deemed it by no means unique on this score. What shocked them was its element of treachery. By perpetrating a murder under tryst, Sweyn had once more displayed his singular flair for outraging the rough-hewn ethics of his time. The majority of his own crews, hardened to brutality though they were, deserted him after this. When the king heard the news, he called a mass meeting of his followers at Sandwich and Sweyn was pronounced '*nithing*', a term utterly expressive of contempt. Harold made his own attitude abundantly clear by leading Beorn's friends to Dartmouth where he collected the body of the luckless earl and bore it, with honour, to Winchester, to be interred in St Swithun's minster beside the remains of Canute. The arrival of the travel-stained cortège in the city created much sympathy and the appearance of Harold, tall, mustachioed and solemn, at its head must have gone down strongly in his favour. By his stern refusal to take sides with his wayward brother from the start, he had contrived not only to guard his material interests but to credit his public image at the same stroke.

On the other hand, Godwin's prestige had been impaired by his refusal to harden his heart towards Sweyn. It seems almost a pity that loyalty to the oafish first-born of his brood, perhaps the most endearingly human of Godwin's recorded traits, should have done so much to undermine his position. Yet the year following the murder, Godwin was again working for Sweyn's return. This time the intermediary was Bishop Ealdred of Worcester, who happened to be passing through Flanders, where the exile was lingering, on his way to attend a church council in Italy. Perhaps Ealdred, reputed to have a special talent for administering the sacrament of penance, was stimulated by the exceptional challenge in Sweyn. 'No man in the world is so very criminal,' it had been written in the canons enacted by Edgar a century earlier, 'that he may not make atonement to God, let him undertake it fervently.' The full course of penitence laid down in the regulations, including, among other things, abstinence from flesh-eating, drunkenness and kissing, cannot have come easily to his subject. Nevertheless, with Ealdred's moral support and Godwin's practical influence, Sweyn made the grade: in an astonishing sequel to the whole affair, Edward authorised the 'inlawing' and returned much of the penitent's former earldom.

Territorially, Godwin was now at his zenith. He and his sons held the whole of the south from Kent to Cornwall and as far north as Bristol and Oxford; the Mercian shires of Oxford, Hereford and Gloucester; and also East Anglia, probably including Cambridgeshire and Huntingdonshire.

Yet, powerful as the family looked on paper by the half-way mark of the century, there were signs that Edward was increasingly asserting his independence. The Norman friends he had established in the country were gaining promotion and influence, much to the chagrin of the Earl of Wessex, especially when they opposed his own candidates for office, or actually infiltrated the family earldoms. In foreign affairs, Godwin had been blocked resolutely by the witan in his attempts to obtain military aid for his relative Sweyn Estrithson's fight against Magnus, and now even events in that direction had turned, perversely, in Edward's favour. The death of Magnus in the very year of his victory had relieved England of its one immediate threat of invasion, and Edward, by eventually disbanding his standing fleet, put himself in a position to abolish the heavy tax which had maintained it for the best part of forty years. It was a useful point in his favour. The restitution of Sweyn Godwinson was another, for no one could have done the goodwill of the Earl of Wessex more harm. Slowly and patiently, Edward was inching towards his own ends. There is no evidence that he had ever forgiven Godwin for his part in the slaying of brother Alfred. Beneath the passive exterior, the icy restraint, must have seethed a volcanic resentment of his domineering father-in-law. For eight years, in all, the king reigned in the shadow of Godwin, praying, hunting and, for the most part, answering yes, before restraint snapped and the docile royal lion turned on his trainer.

*

On 29 October 1050, the year of Sweyn's pardon, the death occured of Eadsige, the aged Archbishop of Canterbury who had crowned Edward at Winchester on that distant day of the festival named from Eostre, the heathen goddess. Godwin's choice for the vacant seat, a relative named Aelfric, was ready, and the chapter of Canterbury promptly obliged by electing the earl's candidate without waiting for consent from the king. Awkwardly, Edward had already decided to bestow the primacy on the closest of his Norman confidants, one Robert Abbot of Jumièges, a monastery on the Seine, whom the king had already elevated to the bishopric of London. Robert, a worldly and ambitious man with a taste for intrigue, is cloaked in legend with an evil reputation and was, indeed, resented in many quarters for his apparent hold over Edward. 'If he said a black crow was white, the king would rather trust his mouth than his own eyes', it came to be written of the Norman. But Edward was not to be cheated of his appointment. If anything could inflame his passion to danger point, it was to be ignored on an important matter of the Church, and, in March of the following year, he hit back. At a tense meeting of the witan in mid-Lent, Godwin's choice of primate was overruled and Robert of Jumièges was elected instead. Within a few months Edward was issuing more orders.

Soon after Robert left England to receive his pallium in Rome, a custom which had become increasingly fashionable with the growth of papal influence on the English church in the past century, a party of Frenchmen visited Edward's court headed by Eustace, Count of Boulogne, the husband of Edward's sister. The king was at Glouces-ter at the time, still flushed by the success of his newly-found asser-tiveness, and the arrival of the French knights provided a circle in which, in his somewhat fastidious way, he could relax and exercise some wit at the expense of absent Saxon and Anglo-Scandinavian magnates. Doubtless, the king would have sought to impress Eustace with his recent ecclesiastical victory. Thus, with some sort of impression that the king's English father-in-law had been put in his place, Eustace eventually set out south-east across Wessex on his way home. His point of embarkation was Dover, the normal passenger port for the Continent. As a transit town and mercantile base, Dover was a place of considerable importance in Edward's reign. Overlooked by a strong fortress on its eastern heights, the seat of a sizeable monastic foundation, St Martin-le-Grand, and already possessing a guildhall, it also enjoyed special municipal privileges. The burgesses of Dover were entitled to charge the king's messengers for pilot services when these people wished to cross the Channel. Since the approaches to the harbour were tricky, local pilots were important. 'In the entrance of the port of Dover there is a mill which shatters almost every ship by the great swell of the sea, and does great damage to the king and his men,' Domesday Book later asserted dramatically.

In short, the people of Dover, where even Julius Caesar, viewing that cleft in the white cliffs, had not ventured to land, were proud of their civic rights. They paid their taxes, part to Godwin and part to the king, and expected from their visitors a measure of respect. Count Eustace and his band of travellers appear to have approached the town apprehensively, for, on the word of one contemporary writer, 'When he was some miles this side of Dover he put on his coat of mail, and all his companions likewise . . .', a reference possibly intended to impute malice of forethought, though it seems as likely that the robust reputation of the seaport warranted caution. Rivalry between Dover and Boulogne, each with fishing interests in the narrow waters of the Channel, would not have been unnatural. There might even have been an incident of some sort when Eustace and his escort had disembarked on their arrival in England. The only close accounts of what followed are Saxon, and some allowance should probably be made for bias. On this evidence, the troop from Boulogne, having reached the outskirts of Dover on the Canterbury road, proceeded to demand the best lodgings in the town. As the king's guests, Eustace and his followers were entitled, by law, to hospitality on their English travels. The claim was that they asserted this in an overbearing manner, and it seems that trouble started in earnest when one householder refused to accommodate anyone.

Wounded in the brawl that resulted, he retaliated vigorously by killing his assailant. 'Then Eustace got on his horse and his companions on theirs, and went to the householder and slew him on his own hearth. Then they went up towards the town and slew both within and without more than twenty men; and the townsmen slew nineteen men on the other side and wounded they knew not how many.'[1]

The noise of the mêlée, mounted Frenchmen lashing out with maces and swords at their pedestrian opponents, while flying hooves sent chickens squawking to the rooftops, drew the clannish burghers of Dover in an angry crowd to the street. Faced by this danger, Eustace, and those of his retinue who remained in the saddle, had no option but to turn and flee along the road by which they had arrived. Saddle-sore and humiliated, they retraced their journey to the royal court where they blurted their story to the king. Edward was furious. Without waiting to make further enquiries, he sent orders to Godwin instructing him to take arms to Dover and ravage the town. 'Eustace had told the king that it was more the townsmen's fault than his,' declared a Saxon scribe, 'but it was not so.' One way or another, Godwin's choice was a tricky one. Either he must submit to harrying his own subjects on the word of a Frenchman, or by refusing, lay himself open to a charge of rebellion. With some comfort, he looked to the stout arm of Harold.

[1] *ASC*—a parallel version puts the French dead at seven, 'and much evil was done on either side with horse and with weapons'.

4

A Trial of Strength

The king's order to violate Dover arrived soon after the marriage of
Harold's brother Tostig to Judith, a half-sister of Baldwin of
Flanders. Marriages of this period consisted of two ceremonies. The
first was the 'wedding' or betrothal at which terms were agreed
between parties, the bridegroom's friends guaranteeing his pledge to
keep the bride in a fitting manner. The second was the gift' or
bridal, when the bride was given to the groom; an occasion for
much feasting and celebration. While Church blessing was not
essential to the legality of marriage, it had been urged strongly on
the matrimonial pattern of Anglo-Saxon England for some time.
An eighth-century manifesto had been quite positive about a couple's
first duty having lawfully married: 'that is, according to the teaching
of the books, to keep their chastity for the space of three days and
nights and on the third day to be present at Mass and both to take the
Eucharist. . . .' Many religious taboos were imposed on marital love-
making, which was considered wrong, among other times, for
forty-nine days and nights before Easter, at any time during Easter
week, on Sunday nights and on Wednesday and Friday. The same
guide, *The Penitential of Archbishop Ecgbert*, stated that 'every religious
woman should keep her chastity for three months before childbirth
and for sixty nights and days after, whether the child be male or
female', a slender form of birth control no doubt gratefully ex-
ploited by many women who would otherwise have known almost
no respite from pregnancy.

The political element in Tostig's marriage was to prove useful to
Godwin much sooner, and in very different circumstances, to any
he might reasonably have anticipated. Almost before he had ceased
congratulating himself on the match, Edward's summons exploded

in his hands. In principle, the communal punishment the king ordered was not original, nor was it extreme. Earlier kings had sent punitive forces to terrorise Thetford, Thanet and Worcester, among other places, as retribution for lesser incidents. Harthacnut, for instance, had ordered the ravaging of Worcester because two of his soldiers had been killed there. But Godwin, already angered by Edward's growing intransigence, was in no mood to be urged by precedent. Not only did he refuse to obey the order, he countered by demanding that Eustace and his men should be handed over to him by the king. For good measure he also brought charges of robbery and oppression against the garrison of a castle built by some of Edward's Norman friends in Herefordshire, part of Sweyn's earldom. At the same time, he called up his forces, not to march on Dover but to threaten the king.

Harold's attitude to what was to be known as the rebellion of 1051 is unrecorded. Perhaps he would have joined forces with his father out of loyalty in any case, though he had not placed family loyalty before prudence when Sweyn had first returned to plead his 'inlawing'. Perhaps he considered the king's sentence on Dover so unjust as to warrant rebellion, though, again, the broader evidence of his life suggests he would have preferred to move diplomatically rather than risk civil strife. Perhaps, indeed, he considered a firm show of strength and resolution was the answer, in itself, to such a risk. Here was Godwin appearing in the role of the protector of Englishmen against unwanted aliens. The slogan, in effect, was 'Frenchmen go home!' and maybe Harold, like his father, believed it would carry the country. It appealed at least to his own men, for they rallied to his call to arms and on 1 September, Godwin, Harold and Sweyn massed forces at a point, believed to be Beverstone, near Tetbury, on the Cotswolds. Below lay Gloucester, the king and Eustace.

Gloucester, in Edward's reign, shared the function of capital of the kingdom with Winchester and Westminster. It was the king's habit to 'wear the crown' in each of these cities for part of the year, and at each in turn the national assembly was annually convened. Gloucester was particularly well-suited to this purpose, being handy for both Wessex and Mercia while within easy reach of the Fosse Way and other important roads. As the key to the lower Severn

Valley, it had been a prominent military and commercial centre since Roman times, and probably earlier. The city was renowned not only for the fertile beauty of the Vale, which provided its corn, and its graceful Cotswold pastures, but for its ironworks and smiths' shops. Handy to the mines of the Forest of Dean, Gloucester rendered much of its tax to Edward in iron, including thirty-six *dacrae* (by one estimate, enough to shoe rather less than two hundred horses) and a hundred malleable rods for nails. Apart from thirty-six pounds a year, the rest of the tax was made over in honey, to the extent of something like fifty gallons.

No trace remains of the king's lodge at Gloucester, though legend sites a Mercian palace to the north of the city, and the place-name of Kingsholm might not be irrelevant. Wherever he was stationed, Edward's confidence had waned very rapidly with news of the proximity of Godwin's force, and his prayers must have been urgent for help from the North. If the dates in the chronicles are right, Edward had been caught off guard by Godwin's reaction to the Dover order, for the assembly he convened to cope with the emergency seems not to have met until around 8 September, at least a week after Harold and his father arrived on the Cotswolds. Now everything depended on earls Leofric and Siward. If they stood aloof from the issue, the king would soon be swallowing very humble pie. But this time it was Godwin who was out on his estimates. Apart from the resentment aroused in the north by his presumption, perhaps he had overestimated the antipathy there to Edward's French friends, while underestimating the repugnance for Sweyn. At all events, the earls of Mercia and Northumbria, having turned up at Gloucester with their guards, expressed their sentiments quite unmistakably. Both sent post-haste for reinforcements with which to strengthen the king's hand. These were joined by Ralph of Hereford, a nephew of Edward, with his own contingent, and the two composite forces faced each other across the autumn-tinted wolds.

It was country to catch the admiration of all men: undulating beech woods, willowy valleys between grass-covered limestone escarpments, and, in the west, the hazy, jagged outline of the Malverns. For the local shepherds, the smoke of campfires rising from the buff-green mounds was a warning to call in their sheep and shut up their daughters. In both armies, soldiers from distant counties spat on their axes, harked to the Saxon poetry of the sword—'the gem of death my master gave me'—and dreamed of the rich pickings in the city and its surrounding hamlets.

It is perhaps worth noting at this point that while the thegns and better class of ceorls gathered in the opposing forces around Gloucester had made their way hence on horseback, it was their custom to do battle on foot. Neither the Saxons nor the Anglo-Danes favoured fighting in the saddle. For one thing, their mounts were small. In fact, the original ponies of the old British tribes, though up to pulling chariots in teams, often had not been large enough to ride. Among others on the island at the beginning of the Christian era had been a robust eleven- or twelve-hand forest type, a weedier Celtic pony and a thirteen-hand variety probably owing its extra size to breeding with North African ponies brought over by the Roman legions.[1] On the whole, the British stock when the Saxons arrived had been a mixed bag of small and underbred creatures. Not that the newcomers, accustomed to travelling by water and fighting as pedestrians, were very concerned. The Norsemen were more horse-conscious, but the animals they had brought with them on settling were only little ponies, skewbalds and duns. By the eleventh century, larger, stronger ponies were certainly more numerous, but the English soldier still did not fight on horseback: he was a mounted infantryman, not a cavalryman.

If Godwin and Harold had not stinted in their show of force, the prospect of full-scale military opposition revealed their inhibitions, and, while the leaders wavered, their followers, unaccustomed to inhibited generalship, now began to have second thoughts. For plunder, these simple country levies might risk their skins. In defence of their own, they would give their lives. Love of a lord or hatred of an enemy could stir them to fighting fury. But this time their lords were hesitant about spoils, and it was difficult to generate hate for the remote and colourless Edward. Indeed, the mystique of kingship touched many with awe, and there was not a little uneasiness about disregarding royal orders. Suddenly England smelled sweet, and life

---

[1] The Crispinian legion of the Roman army of occupation was mounted on North African stallions, probably barbs.

seemed valuable. After all, Dover was pretty far removed from most of their lives; the call of their homelands all too tangible. As one patriotic contemporary rationalised: 'Then thought some that it would be great folly to join battle, for all that was most noble in England was present in one army or the other, and they weened that it would expose the land to our foes and cause great destruction among ourselves' (*ASC*). And so, to the relief of all, not least the people of Gloucester, this autumnal display of warlike postures was honourably deflated by an agreement to exchange hostages and seek a peaceful settlement at a general meeting of the Witan in London later that month. The 'revolution' was virtually at an end.

Compromise was to prove fatal to Godwin. From now on the Earl of Wessex was doomed to assume the role of defendant while Edward, saved from humiliation at the eleventh hour, suddenly found himself positioned to strike. He did so with consummate skill and dexterity. As Godwin prepared to face the witan at Southwark, backed now by an even more irresolute army, the king announced the call-up of the national militia, a move theoretically obliging many thegns and freemen, irrespective of the earldoms they lived in, to join the crown force. The move strained the loyalties of Godwin's followers still further. On top of this, Sweyn was once more declared an outlaw. Prudently, as things were going, Godwin and Harold refused to face the king and witan without a promise of safe-conduct and more hostages. Edward answered with a counter-demand that Godwin and his sons should give up the homage rights of certain thegns who paid tribute to the family though actually living outside its earldoms. This seems to have been agreed, while Godwin's own request was ignored. Instead, he and Harold were ordered to present themselves in the king's camp with no more than twelve men to support them. Again they asked for safe-conduct and more hostages, upon which the king pronounced his final ultimatum. They were given five days in which to submit without guarantee, or leave the country.

The Earl of Wessex did not wait to hear more. His disheartened army was rapidly dispersing while the king's forces were stronger than ever. Stunned and furious, Godwin realised there was nothing to be done but save the lives of his family. That same night, accompanied by his wife, Sweyn, Tostig and a younger son, Gyrth, among others, he hurried south to Bosham, where ships were hastily laden with treasure. From there the party sailed for Flanders, from which place Tostig's wife Judith had so recently come. At the same time, Harold and his compatriots, including Leofwine, the youngest of his brothers in public life, had decided to make their break west to Bristol. After an adventurous journey, eluding a force sent after them by Edward and barely surviving a storm in the Bristol Channel, Harold reached the coast of Ireland, damp and dejected, defeated without a fight, a political outcast.

Edward marked his deliverance by dividing the Godwin family earldoms among his supporters and packing Queen Edith off to a nunnery. Siward and Leofric had soon returned to their own lands. At last the king felt free to handle things his own way. The result was that the Norman element in the state very much came into its own. Archbishop Robert had the king's ear, Edward's Norman chaplain, William, was promoted at the expense of an English bishop elect of London, patronage was lavished on Frenchmen at court, posts found for them in the counties. But, if we are to believe one annalist, the most striking example of Edward's affinity for the duchy of his upbringing was yet to come. On a now unknown date, perhaps in the spring of 1052, Duke William of Normandy, a young ruler of remarkable ambition and capability, sailed to England with 'a great retinue of Frenchmen' and was received amicably by a satisfied, even too complaisant, king. It was a rare event for a ruler to leave his own land on such a peaceful mission to another: it was to have unique repercussions.[1]

★

Harold's exile in Ireland was not a long one, but bitter: bitter with the unpalatable aftertaste of an unnecessary and perhaps even stupid blunder. It gave him time to review the surprisingly unskilful diplomacy that had led to the present plight of his family. In 1052 he was eventually able to hoist sail again for England. With nine hired ships

---

[1] It has been suggested alternatively that the visit was not made by William but by a high-ranking delegate.

and an assault force of rough Irish-Scandinavian mercenaries he
made first for the Bristol Channel, scanning the coastline of Devon
and Somerset for a target on which to vent his aggression. Where the
wild tableland of Exmoor tumbled to the sea through the sylvan vale
of Porlock, lay a remote manor belonging to Edward. Leaving
guard on the ships, Harold and his commandos waded ashore across
the flats and set sword and torch to the neighbourhood. Before
eventually departing, they had defeated a combined force of Devon
and Somerset levies called out to oppose them, destroyed dwellings
and crops, taken captives, and loaded themselves with plunder. It
is the only incident in the surviving record of his life in which
Harold appears in a wantonly vengeful light.

It is interesting, too, as an early glimpse of him in action as a
military commander. According to the chronicles, he put the opposing force to flight, though it seems to have been a relatively strong
one, killing among others 'more than thirty good thegns'. He then
headed south-west for Land's End. Meanwhile, Godwin was also
busy. Sailing from Bruges with a small fleet to reconnoitre the south
coast, the outlawed Earl of Wessex made a number of armed landings to test the feelings of his former subjects. At least the southern-
most counties were loyal. According to one chronicler, 'during the
time he was here in the land he won to his side all the men of Kent
and all the sailors from the vicinity of Hastings and the adjacent
coast, together with all those in the east part of the country, the
people of Sussex and Surrey, and many other places as well'. Already
a wave of resentment had swept the country against Edward's
now unrestrained Normanising proclivities, and not only in
Wessex.

Even the forty ships Edward now ordered to sweep the prowling
Godwin out of the Channel were commanded by Normans, the
earls Ralph and Odda. Helped by a storm, the veteran eluded them
and, while the royal fleet retired via Sandwich to London, slunk back
towards the Isle of Wight whereabout he settled to wait for Harold's
flotilla. One son was missing from the reunion that followed west
of Portland. Sweyn had gone off on another adventure: to seek
salvation along the pilgrims' path to the Middle East. Like many
others who rode it, he never returned. Sweyn's death was to make

Harold the successor of Godwin, and his absence alone was a good omen for the family project. Sailing east again, Harold and his father ran along the rim of Hampshire, Sussex and Kent levying assistance and calling the people to arms. 'And they did no great harm after they had joined forces, except to seize provisions, but they won over to their side all the inhabitants along the sea coast as well as those inland. Then they sailed towards Sandwich, collecting reinforcements as they went, arriving there with an overwhelming host' (*ASC*). Ahead lay the gaping estuary of the Thames, and their objective, the metropolis of London.

The old city had seen many assaults and incursions. In the earliest recorded mention of London, Tacitus told how the British warrior queen Boudicca had massacred the community while the legions of Suetonius were away in the north-west. Already, by A.D. 61, it had been full of merchants and their wares, and the Romans had eventually built a wall to protect it. Bede, the first writer to tag London the 'metropolis', the mart of many travellers by land and sea, harked back to the stubborn paganism of its inhabitants. Early in the seventh century, Seberht, king of the East Saxons, whose chief town was London, had built a church in honour of St Paul on the highest ground in the city. But after his death, heathen worship once more held sway. Only after several subsequent missionary efforts had ended in similar frustration was Christianity finally established in London. By the beginning of the ninth century a contemporary reference could describe this resilient, marsh-bounded commune as 'the illustrious place and royal city', and, later that century, it was to become a rallying point against the depredations of the Danes. In 886 Alfred the Great 'honourably restored the city of London and made it habitable', according to his friend and biographer, Asser. Alfred initiated extensive repairs to the walls which had since held firm against all attacks. At the south-western point of the town, London bridge formed a strong barrier against water-borne invasion and Icelandic saga depicted the Vikings lashing their longboats together and using the force of the tide in an attempt to penetrate it. Canute tried different tactics. He had cut a channel through the dykes in the swampy ground to the south of the bridge to bypass this obstacle, but even his siege had proved unsuccessful, the people

of London becoming subject to him only after his treaty with Ethelred's short-reigning successor, Edmund Ironside.

Edward's London, aloof from earldoms and with a population
estimated by some modern historians at around twenty thousand,
was pre-eminent among English cities both for its size and wealth.
Harold and Godwin, pressing upstream with their armada, scanning
the city distantly over the marshes which flanked both banks of the
Thames, must have pondered anxiously on their reception. Their
objective straddled two mounds of high ground divided by the
little valley of a northern tributary, the Wall Brook. On the west
boundary was another tributary, the Fleet, or Hole Bourne; on the
north, moor land, and on the west, immediate to their approach, the
fens commemorated presently in Fenchurch. Sailing upstream from
the delta of the River Lea (then a tidal estuary swamping the Isle of
Dogs) and drawing abreast of the flats of Bermondsey, the seafarers
from Wessex saw the city against a background of wild tree-
crowned heights, now the urban districts of Highgate and Hamp-
stead. Ahead, beyond the bridge, the Thames swung left to be joined
by yet another northern tributary, the Ty Bourne, its estuary filling
what later became St James's Park, and isolating the isle of Thorney.
Now the leaders of the advancing fleet could see the masts of
Edward's heavily-manned longboats, some fifty strong, rocking
gently by the grey walls.

London wall itself, tracing its course approximately from its
south-west corner at Blackfriars, ran north along the rim of high
ground above the Fleet to Newgate, from which a road roughly
corresponding to the later line of Holborn and Oxford Street ran
across country to link with the great north-west artery of Watling
Street in the present vicinity of Marble Arch. From Newgate the
wall took a north-easterly direction to Aldersgate, inclined north
again to a point slightly west of Cripplegate, then stretched east to
Bishopsgate. Two roads forked from Bishopsgate which, with
Newgate, comprised the chief land gates of the city. One of these
ran north towards Lincoln and York; the other east across the Lea
and into Essex. From Bishopsgate the wall curved south-east in a
shallow arc through Aldgate to meet the Thames again at a spot
where the White Tower was to stand in later times. On the river side

there were port entrances at Dowgate, on the mouth of Wall Brook and, away to the east, beyond the bridge, at Billingsgate. Within the walls, the city, like others of its time, was still relatively open. Small brooks coursed over green, cattle-grazed allotments, or ran beside huddled cottages, obliging washerwomen, thirsty goats and poultry with their waters.

In the market areas, the buildings crowded closer together and, since these were mostly of wood, severe penalties fell on those who started fires. Here could be bought butter, cheese, eggs, eels and salt from the surrounding countryside; fish from river and estuary; wine, spices and trinkets from abroad. In exchange, London exported a whole range of commodities from textiles and art-worked metal to greyhounds. Traders from Rouen, Flanders, Ponthieu, and farther afield, often spent so much time in the city that they became permanent or semi-permanent citizens. The ports were bustling, cosmopolitan; the streets alive with character, avarice, wit. It was the place in which to get rich quickly. Property investment seems to have been a particularly good thing. Godwin was among the many people of substance with city holdings, possessing a stone-built hall in the south-bank 'suburb' of Southwark where the lords and ladies of many outlying estates maintained town connections. The Abbess of Barking owned twenty-eight London houses. Not surprisingly, the number of moneyers in the city far exceeded that for any other English town. More than twenty were striking coins at one period of Edward's reign.

Edward's London also had its guilds, including a 'knights' gild', with their periodic banquets, their arrangements of mutual benefit and their popular custom of distributing alms. For the purposes of official administration, the city was divided into wards each with a ward-moot or assembly presided over by an ealdorman. Civil cases were settled at a meeting called a husting, while a great folk-moot was held in the open space between West Cheap and St Paul's for proclaiming and maintaining public order.

Here, the crowds must have jostled and clamoured for news of the approaching army, and of palace reaction. At low tide, the ships of Harold and Godwin could be seen anchoring off the south bank, just downstream of the bridge, while a land force which had marched

from the south to support them was spread along the strand of
Southwark. On the other side of the river, Edward's housecarles
stood ready. The king had sent north for reinforcements, but, as the
chronicles put it, 'they were very slow in coming'. Edward's Norman friends, whose alien methods of rule and misunderstandings of
local custom had caused friction in several parts of the country, were
now proving, if unwittingly, a sore embarrassment to their patron.
To the English chroniclers it seemed that they had 'promoted
injustice and pronounced unjust judgements and counselled evil
within this realm'. Nevertheless, the king had a considerable force of
levies, as well as his household troops and his fleet, under command,
and his intimates, including Archbishop Robert, Bishop William
and other Normans, were urging him to fight. By holding the
bridge, he could have made things very hard for the invaders, but
Harold and his father were not ignorant of the history of earlier
advances on the city. Knowing how vital it was to have help from
inside, Godwin had slipped ashore while his ships were at anchor,
and had 'come to an arrangement with the citizens that they would
fall in with his wishes in almost everything' (*ASC*). Popular sentiment in London seems to have swung full arc since the rebellion of
1051. Perhaps the citizens felt Godwin and his sons had been too
harshly treated at that time. Doubtless, their amiability was strengthened by discretion. This time there was more to be called than bluff.
While the men of Wessex might be reluctant to fall upon their
neighbours, at the core of both Harold's and Godwin's command
were hired crews from abroad, unsentimental professionals who
counted slaughter, destruction and rapine among the satisfactions
of their trade. They had no neighbourly scruples. In the circumstances, London, enticingly lootworthy and inflammable, might
well have been excused for putting her own busy interests before an
unproductive political argument.

As the tide rose, the waiting armada raised anchor, slid unopposed
through the bridge and veered sharply towards the north bank to
pinion the king's ships. Behind it, on the south bank, the men of
Wessex stood impressively to arms. For a while Edward wavered
indecisively, urged one way by the anti-Godwin faction among his
counsellors and another by the moderators. Finally, he gave up all

thoughts of resistance. When an old friend of Godwin and his sons, Bishop Stigand of Winchester, was despatched in due course from the palace to arrange negotiation, the news of Godwin's moral victory passed rapidly through the streets, and, before long, the inevitable city mob was demonstrating against the Normans. Archbishop Robert, Bishop William and others were lucky to escape with their lives. Mounting horses, they led their retainers in a desperate retreat through the gates, cutting down several members of the crowd, and thereafter fled the country in such haste that, according to one commentator, they put off in an 'unseaworthy' ship. Then, reported the same writer with satisfaction:

a great council was summoned outside London, and all the earls and the most distinguished men in this land were present. There Earl Godwin set forth his case, clearing himself before King Edward, his lord, and before all the people of the country, that he was innocent of the charges brought against himself, his son Harold and all his children. And the king took the earl and his children back into favour, and gave him back the whole of his earldom, and restored to him and all his supporters everything they had previously owned. Moreover the king restored to the queen all her former possessions. Archbishop Robert was declared an outlaw, together with all the Frenchmen, for they had been mainly responsible for the discord which had arisen between earl Godwin and the king (*ASC*).

At a time when he could have demanded a lot more, Godwin's virtual acceptance of repayment without interest was judiciously moderate. He demanded no reparation from Leofric or Siward, and even Ralph of Hereford was allowed to keep his land undisturbed. Queen Edith, on release from the nunnery in which she had been confined, seems to have been content to resume her place beside her once more submissive husband. Only Stigand, the power-conscious bishop of Winchester, made any dramatic gains from the whole affair. Despite Robert's bitter protests from abroad, Stigand took over the archiepiscopal chair, proceeding blandly, and as some thought, scandalously, to occupy it in duality with his seat at Winchester.

On 12 April 1053, having given the last of his talented and unscrupulous, yet not always ungenerous, energies to rescuing his political eminence, Godwin, now sixty-five, dropped to the ground in an apoplectic fit. Within three days he was dead. Thus, at thirty-one, Harold became Earl of Wessex and the greatest single power in the land beside the king; a king who had no children and was now most unlikely to beget them. From now on, Edward was to rely increasingly on the administrative and military capacities of his brother-in-law. Yet, while Harold's prospects glowed with a brilliance unmatched in England, his stint of exile had not passed without leaving a squall of nagging questions to cloud his ambition. What, he must have asked himself in particular, had passed between Edward and William of Normandy's embassy during that short but disturbing visit following the autumn 'rebellion'? There was never likely to be a conclusive answer, but of one thing Harold can have had no doubts. The duke had not turned his eyes towards England out of idle curiosity. What kind of man was this Norman leader? And precisely how dangerous were William's resources?

5

The New Duke of Normandy

William, seventh Duke of Normandy, was the direct descendant of the first Duke of Normandy, a Scandinavian emigrant named Rollo, who died about 931. If, as seems probable, Rollo was one and the same as Hrolf the Ganger, a character famed in Norse saga for his huge size, it would appear that his southerly orientation came about after banishment from Norway for plundering his own people. (In more recent times, Danes and Swedes, as well as Norwegians, have claimed the honour of nurturing Rollo.) Dudon, the father of Norman historians, described Rollo operating against England from the Hebrides before taking his pirate ships south along the coast of France in search of somewhere to settle. Robert Wace, the twelfth-century Jersey poet-historian, and William of Jumièges who wrote a century later, developed this story and, having outlined an exotic dream in which the pagan Norseman previewed his conversion to Christianity, told how the prowling dragon boats, tempted by the wide gape of the Seine estuary, eventually came to the promised land. After the grey north sea, the vivid green of the French valley and the gracious sweeps of the river must have looked marvellous to Rollo and his Vikings. Probing cautiously upstream, they came upon the first scattered dwellings, some vines, a few orchards, perhaps a patch of bright poppies.

The Romans had named this country Lugdunensis Secunda, the second of the seventeen departments of ancient Gaul, with its principal centres at Rouen, Bayeux, Avranches, Évreux, Séez, Lisieux and Coutances. After the Frankish conquest, it had become part of the kingdom of Neustria which, under the Merovingians, had once stretched from the Scheldt to the Loire, shrinking, after the Carolingian high-tide of Charlemagne to an approximation of its modern limits—that is to say, bounded on the west by the hills of Brittany, on the east by the plains of Picardy and the Île de France, in the watershed of the south by Perche and Maine and on the north by the English Channel. The first substantial Viking invasions had begun in the middle of the ninth century and when Rollo eventually landed at Jumièges, some fifteen miles short of Rouen, he was able to supplement his force with Danes and Norwegians who had preceded him to France and with whom he now advanced on the old abbey town. The Rouennais, terrorised too often in the past by Vikings to be unaware of the grim consequences of an unsuccessful action, prudently offered to accept Rollo's forces into the capital provided he guaranteed the safety of property and persons. Nothing could have suited him better, and for the next sixteen years he held sway as virtual ruler not only of the city, but of most of the province, raiding and ravaging beyond its boundaries until his gigantic frame, reputedly too heavy to travel by horse, became synonymous with dismay and panic throughout France.

In an effort to halt the murder and violation, the French king, Charles the Simple, offered Rollo his daughter Gisèle in marriage and 'all the maritime district between the river Eure and Mont Saint Michel' if the pirate chief would renounce paganism, be baptised in the Christian faith and do homage to the crown. The move, less magnanimous in practice than in theory, for Charles was giving away territory he no longer enjoyed in any real sense, plus providing himself with a barrier against further Viking attack, proved a success. Rollo, surfeited with battle (he had suffered particularly heavy losses in an engagement at Chartres, 911), bored perhaps with the restless life of a freebooter, appears to have accepted respectability on the king's terms, and tradition holds that the 'treaty' was honoured at St Clair-sur-Epte, a village a short distance from Gisors, where the big Scandinavian and his followers gathered to give token of their homage to the king. According to a well-known legend, recorded with amusement by early writers of both nations, the ritual of lifting and kissing the king's foot was performed so clumsily by one of Rollo's tough lieutenants that Charles was toppled on to the ground.

Rollo proved as energetic a legislator as he had a warrior. Having rewarded his followers-at-arms with land (scrupulously measured, tradition has it, by rod and line, thus supposedly initiating the rectilinear pattern of much of pastoral Normandy), he set out to maintain an iron discipline in his dukedom. The predatory nature of his subjects, accustomed since they could remember to live by pillage, called for the most vigorous and ruthless suppression of crime, and Rollo was quick to provide it. He was portrayed by the early story tellers of France and Normandy as a leader of great worldliness, vigour, eloquence, thoroughness and intrepidity: attributes much prized by the Normans themselves in their heyday. Insofar as the slender traces of his achievements are true, he must also have been exceptionally voracious and callous in pursuit of his own ends. On the death of his royal wife, Gisèle, an event reputedly hastened by his ill-treatment of her, Rollo married Papia, daughter of the Count of Bayeux, whom he had taken as his mistress on capturing that place. Their son, William Longsword, became the second Duke of Normandy. Longsword, repeating his father's taste for free union as opposed to Church-blessed marriage, passed his title to Richard the Fearless, his son by a mistress named Sprota, while Richard, though marrying the daughter of King Hugh of France, continued the tradition by fathering the children of a peasant woman, Gunnor. These included Richard the Good, fourth duke; Emma, wife of Ethelred and Canute, and mother of the Confessor; and Robert, who became Archbishop of Rouen where his father had thoughtfully built the cathedral. Richard the Good left the duchy to his eldest son by Judith of Brittany, Richard III, but the fifth duke died of poisoning, along with several of his barons, after a very short reign, and was succeeded by his brother Robert.

Robert the Magnificent, so called for his flamboyant taste and ostentatious manners, was cast in the classic mediaeval mould of brutality and piety. The first public act of his reign was to build the abbey of Cerisy, near St Lo, and the last, when he was still not twenty-five, was to go on a pilgrimage to Jerusalem, riding part of the way, it was said, on a gold-shod mule. Between whiles he waged remorseless war on the rebellious elements within the duchy and profitably lent his sword to influential outsiders. Above all things, he was a formidable general, successfully attacking Constance, widow of King Robert of France, at the instigation of her eldest son Henry;

effectively supporting Baldwin of Flanders against his son Baldwin of Lille, and, at one time, even launching an invasion against Canute in an attempt to restore Ethelred's line to the English throne. This expedition, mounted at Fécamp, failed when unfavourable winds forced the duke's fleet to shelter in the bays of the isle of Jersey, though the lessons learned in its planning lived on to intrigue his successor. Robert, landing at St Michel instead of England, promptly took the chance of impressing his authority on the Bretons. His methods were dashing and sanguinary. By quick decisions and long rides at maximum speed he took his luckless opponents by surprise. In one move against his refractory vassal, William Talvas of Bellême, Robert raced the length of Normandy to surround Alençon castle, where William was ensconced, forcing the earl to solicit pardon barefoot and, it was said, with the saddle of a horse on his back. Once committed to an engagement, Robert stopped at nothing. It was his belief that the greater the carnage the shorter the conflict, a maxim that would have gone down well with Rollo.

His domestic life roughly followed the pattern of his ancestors. Although Robert later indulged in a 'political' marriage with a daughter of Canute of England, his son and successor, William, was the child of an early relationship with a young Falaise beauty, Arlette, whose father was most likely a tanner, though possibly an embalmer.[1] Some time after William's birth, Arlette was married to her lover's friend, Herluin, vicomte of Conteville, though there is disagreement as to whether or not this preceded Robert's death.[2] At all events, Arlette stands out as a remarkable woman. The strength of her character is suggested in the quality of her sons, irrespective of paternity. To Herluin she bore two boys destined to fame, Odo, bishop of Bayeux, and Robert, count of Mortain. She also had at least two daughters, both of whom did well, one, Adelaide, probably by Robert, having enough of her mother's appeal to win three husbands. By the time Arlette died, at a not very great age, her father, Fulbert, had given up his profession to become an officer of

[1] The word used to describe the family by William of Jumièges was 'polinctores'.
[2] Orderic puts the marriage after Robert's death; William of Malmesbury, before it. Modern historians are inclined to place the marriage quite shortly after the birth of William, thus demolishing the touching tradition that Robert bequeathed his mistress to Herluin in the eventuality that he should die on a pilgrimage to the Holy Land.

the ducal court, while her two brothers, Osbern and Walter, also owed advancement to their personable sister.

*

William was born in 1027 or 1028, about five years after Harold Godwinson first saw the light of day in Wessex and a month or so after Robert left Falaise to assume the ducal sceptre at Rouen. The child grew up in a fertile, temperate land where cherries, raspberries and wood strawberries grew wild for the picking and where the traditional French concern for gastronomy was reflected in many products of orchard, garden and cotil. When the yields were good, food was preserved against harder times by drying, and other means. Grapes and plums, spread in the sun, shrivelled aromatically on the terraces; sea-food (chiefly herring but also porpoise, sea-dog and whale) hung in salted strips in the markets; bread, twice-baked to form a durable biscuit-like provision, was trundled by ox-cart and pack-horse to castles and ships. Pork was the standard meat, and most Norman (or, for that matter, French) families reared and fattened a pig, or pigs: coarse, hairy creatures which hunted the woods for acorns or roamed the towns quite freely eating garbage and getting under horses' feet. William would have learned, however, that many kinds of animal and bird were considered good eating, including bear, hedgehog, squirrel, heron and crow. Goose flesh was especially favoured and flocks of geese were driven to feed on the grasslands like sheep. Unlike other types of meat, the eating of poultry was not prohibited during fasting, birds and fowls being classified among species of aquatic origin. Cheese was also a popular food. One ancient anecdote greatly enjoyed by the initiated held that Charlemagne, on first eating green cheese, had cut out the green part in the belief that it was bad. Apart from cheese and butter, the Normans evolved an individualistic liquor from butter-milk, garlic and onions, called serat.

Good living, however, was largely reserved for the nobility, and exploitation of the lower orders by their predatory lords was rife. Most peasants held their land from a master, either as serfs or as free tenants, both classes possessing their plots on a hereditary basis in return for service, money or kind. The main difference was that in the case of the serf—indeed, in theory, throughout the feudal system —land reverted to the master on the tenant's death. Theoretically the lord also had the power to stop a serf renouncing his tenure and moving elsewhere, and to prevent a serf's daughter from marrying outside his estate. Early descriptions of peasant life in Normandy enumerate obligatory burdens on the tenant farmer that would not have surprised his Anglo-Saxon counterpart.

Higher up the social scale, fiefs, or land originally granted by lord to vassal as a life interest on condition of fidelity, had generally become hereditary by William's time, much like the smaller tenures of the peasants: that is, the rights and obligations of both lord and vassal were inherited by their successors. Thus the duke held title by grace of the King of France, the barons by grace of the duke, the knights from the barons, and so on. These might involve, among other things, military duties for so many days a year within a certain radius of the suzerain's castle on the part of the vassal, and, reciprocally, protection for the vassal by his lord in time of attack. Feudalism had not stopped short at the Church. Archdeaconries and prebends had been turned into hereditary fiefs; bishops commanded their own armies of knights. Almost everyone, to use a classic description of such relationships, was the man of someone else. Above all prerogatives, the right of sporting and hunting was perhaps most dearly valued by the nobles, who frequently fought to maintain or extend their varying degrees of privilege and who were not above hanging the peasant who killed a rabbit on their sweeping domains. The ownership and right to fly falcons was held in such esteem that some noblemen seldom appeared in public without a hawk on their wrists. Bishops and abbots even took them into their churches. According to one ancient law, the stealer of a falcon was obliged to feed the bird with six ounces of flesh from his own chest, unless he could pay a heavy fine to the owner and a special bonus to the king. Regional lords held their own courts of justice and were sometimes only too willing to execute sentence with their own swords. Gibbets towered wherever commoners were accustomed to congregate.

In the words of one French historian:

Everything was a source of privilege for the nobles. . . . They had a thousand pretexts for establishing taxes on their vassals, who were generally considered 'taxable and to be worked at will'. . . . We must nevertheless remember that heavy dues fell upon the privileged class themselves to a certain degree, and that if they taxed their poor vassals without mercy, they had in their turn often to reckon with their superiors in the feudal hierarchy.

Fines, tolls and tributes were levied everywhere, and endlessly, to meet the exigencies and avarice of the ruling classes, and if a man was so impoverished or simple as to be incapable of exploitation in any other way, he was driven to some absurd task to satisfy the facetiousness or sadism of his master.

Thus, we read of vassals descending to the humiliating occupation of beating the water of the castle moat in order to quieten the frogs . . . elsewhere at times the lord required of them to hop on one leg, to kiss the latch of the castle gate, or to go through some drunken play in his presence, or sing a bawdy song before the lady.[1]

The eleventh-century English monk Orderic, who lived for years in Normandy, found the ruling society a brash and aggressive one. In his *Historia Ecclesiastica* he wrote: 'The race of Normans is unconquered and ready for any wild deed unless restrained by a strong ruler. In whatever gathering they find themselves they always seek to dominate, and in the heat of their ambition they are often led to violate their obligations.' His contemporary, Geoffrey Malaterra, described them as 'eager for gain and eager for power, quick to imitate whatever they see . . . given to hunting and hawking and delighting in horses and accoutrements and fine clothing, yet ready when occasion demands to bear labour and hunger and cold; skilful in flattery and the use of fine words, but unbridled unless held down firmly by the yoke of justice'. In these, the leaders of the race, it is tempting to see shades of Rollo and his Scandinavian lieutenants, but there was more to the eleventh-century Norman than this. By the time William was born, the Norseman was already absorbed in his new environment: his language, laws and customs were French while his philosophy had been influenced profoundly by the land

---

[1] Paul Lacroix, *France in the Middle Ages*.

and those who had lived there before him. Against the fiery race of derring-doers on horseback must be placed a scheming, hard-headed stock 'with an immense capacity for detail, and an innate liking for routine . . . but mainly concerned with small economies and gains; limited in their horizon, but quick to recognise superior powers and to use them for their own objects'.[1]

This land, then, in which William took his first infant steps, was a land above all scarred with envy and distrust, a land studded with the castles and forts of highly-armed and avaricious neighbours. Often such strongholds, most of them built of wood, formed the vital defensive feature in areas bounded by a few natural barriers. They could be thrown up relatively quickly. A tall blockhouse of heavy timber was built on a man-made mound, or *motte*, which had been prepared from earth displaced in the creation of a moat. The ground floor of the stronghold, used as a well for stores and prisoners, had no direct access with the outside. Instead, entrance was effected across a steeply-inclined drawbridge descending from the second storey of the blockhouse to the far side of the moat, this bridge being cleated to give footing to horses. In William's time, these cramped and comfortless structures, with few rooms, fewer windows and often ladders rather than stairways, served as the homes of noblemen and their families. From here the knights clattered forth to harry or ambush their rivals, or organised their defence when their own territory was attacked. Since such forts were practically invulnerable to direct assault and could be taken only after long siege (unless the wood could be fired), their construction was not only an asset to the defence of the locality but also a potential danger to the ducal authority, and it was forbidden to build them without the duke's licence. A condition of this was that he might put his own garrisons in the castles of his barons if he wished, or hold hostages as guarantee of their loyalty. In an attempt to limit baronial feuding, there was a number of laws prohibiting the provocative display of armed strength. It was illegal to challenge a rival by riding out in mail order accompanied by banners and horns, illegal to take prisoners or to confiscate arms, horses or property in a private feud and illegal to lay an ambush or make an assault in the duke's forests. Nor was it

[1] H. W. C. Davis, *England Under the Normans and Angevins.*

permissible to plunder or lay waste in an action for land. Nevertheless, private wars and blood feuds flourished, even under a strong
duke, and the labouring classes had good cause to fear the very forces
whose ostensible function was to protect them.

It was to the tender mercies of his acquisitive and warlike barons
that Robert, in an apparent seizure of political fatalism, left the boy
William at the age of about seven, to embark, himself, on the opulent
pilgrimage to the Holy Land that was to terminate in his death. First
he appointed the child his sole heir, gave him seizin of the duchy,
requested the count of Brittany, his cousin Alan, to keep an eye on
Norman affairs until the child should come to maturity, and recommended the boy to the protection of his liege lord, King Henry of
France. Having overcome the alarmed opposition of his loyalist
barons to the whole venture, and having further appointed his friend
Gilbert of Brionne as William's immediate guardian, a scholar
named Thurold as his tutor and one Osbern Crépon his seneschal,
Robert then set out with a bodyguard of knights and a large quantity
of treasure to make the ambitious journey to Jerusalem and salvation.
The rest of his life is obscured in the dust of travel. Having passed
through Rome and Constantinople, it seems he was last heard of
being carried on a litter by a team of black slaves, weak from the
quartan fever of which he was to die at the Bithynian Nicaea on or
about 1 July in the summer of 1035, shortly after attaining at least the
first of his goals.

★

Arlette's son was about eight years old when it became known that
his father would never return to Normandy. His youth was an open
invitation to lawlessness on the part of the wilder barons while the
illegitimacy of his breeding, though hardly unique in ducal pedigree,
provided a convenient pretext for insurrection. Unauthorised castles
began to spring up in defiance of the child duke; crops and villages
blazed in an unholy scramble for power. William's adherents might
have quelled the rebellion in its earlier stages had they been less concerned with squabbling among each other and quicker to rally to
his banner. His antagonists were similarly disunited. Anarchy spread

on all sides. 'Treason, perfidy and impiety were arrayed in court robes,' wrote Dumoulin, 'while justice was dressed in crêpe.' All ducal edicts ordering the subjects of the duchy to lay down their arms were ignored, and, in desperation, William's counsellors eventually called on Alan of Brittany to bring an army into Normandy and pacify the barons by force. This move, when it came about, was very easily represented as planned usurpation. Indeed, Alan's ultimate intentions were never put to the proof. He was supposedly poisoned while laying siege to a castle.

One by one, William was stripped of the protection of his father's friends. His guardian, Gilbert of Brionne, was cut down in cold blood. Thurold, his tutor, was murdered. Finally, an attempt was made on William's own life at the castle of Vaudreuil, a stronghold situated on an island in the river Eure. Here, as the boy slept and the frogs croaked in the reeds outside, assassins slew the seneschal Osbern Crépon in his chamber, and, groping in the darkness for his ward, were disturbed by guards in the nick of time. For the next few years William's life becomes something of a mystery. According to tradition, Arlette's brother, Walter, was forced to flee with him to forest hide-outs to escape his enemies, but the estate at Conteville, where Arlette lived with Herluin, would seem to have provided a relatively safe refuge. It lay between the Seine and the Risle, stretching out to Honfleur, and perhaps here, learning to handle horses, to achieve skill at arms and to sail ships on the estuary, William was first able to bury the horrors and insecurity of his early childhood in a new and compensatory mood of wilfulness, even aggression. Already the struggle to hold his own against superior experience and power must have taught him a precocious cunning, the beginnings of the smooth tongue and calculated charm he was to employ to great effect later.

The physical characteristics most commonly attributed to William have included a large frame, grey eyes under russet hair, thin lips and a deep jaw. No contemporary portrait of sufficient detail survives to corroborate what might be termed the classic image, but at least his sketchy representation on coins, on his seal and in the Bayeux Tapestry does not seriously contradict it. It seems reasonable to assume that one conditioned and elevated in childhood to William's

office would have had a certain hauteur of carriage, while it may
well be, as fable would have it, that by the time he cast the *robe
d'adolescence*, in his mid-teens, his face was somewhat hard-set, his
features prematurely defined. The Norman habit of shaving high up
the back of the neck, plus the evidence of one contemporary who
ascribed to him a harsh and guttural voice, contributes to a severe,
rather hawkish picture, though he later ran to excessive corpulence.
When his liege lord, Henry of France, condescended to knight his
young vassal, the youth was undoubtedly strong, healthy and, in his
newly-donned warrior trappings, a comely enough figure.

His first chance to express this new-found manliness in action was
provided by the governor of his own birthplace, Falaise, a knight
named Thurstan Goz. Some time after 1040, Henry of France had
inaugurated a number of interventions and incursions in the duchy
by lodging an objection against a Norman fort at Tillières, on the
River Avres. Amidst the resulting confusion, Thurstan Goz, the
ambitious son of a Dane, took the opportunity of supplementing
his own retainers with French mercenaries, and, bursting with grand
ideas, proclaimed himself to be outside the jurisdiction of the duchy.
This sting was too much for William. In the face of Henry and the
French army, the duke's counsellors had advocated a judicious
swallowing of pride; but Thurstan was another matter. He could be
tackled with a fair chance of success. Accordingly, William now
marched purposefully against Falaise castle, where the rebel was
quartered, calling on the local populace to back him. They did so to
such good effect, it seems, that the stronghold was breached in a
single day, and that night its opportunist commander fled. Thurstan
was outlawed and William, flushed with his first small military
triumph, gave the confiscated lands to his mother.

As William's personal standing grew with the years, his enemies
were drawn into a more cohesive opposition until, in 1047, the
celebrated conspiracy of Bayeux brought the revolt of the barons to
a climax. The figure-head of the rebellion was William's own
cousin, Guy of Burgundy. The son of Renaud, Count of Burgundy,
and Robert the Magnificent's sister Adelaide, Guy claimed the
duchy by right of his maternal descent. He had been brought up
with William from an early age and was indebted to the liberality

of his relative for the provinces of Vernon and Brionne, including the former castle of the murdered Gilbert on an island in the River Risle. These acquisitions had fired his ambition and, doubtless jealous of his benefactor into the bargain, he now openly contended that William's illegitimacy nullified his right to the duchy. Guy's cause particularly appealed to the restive barons of Lower Normandy whose principal leaders, Rannulf of Bayeux and Nigel of St Sauveur, joined Guy and others to plan their *coup* in Bayeux itself, the heart of rebel territory. The uprising took William by surprise. He was hunting not far away, at Valognes, when news of the danger reached him and was forced to ride pell-mell, unaccompanied, across hostile country, picking his way by devious paths, until he reached the safety of Falaise. Here, the full seriousness of the situation became apparent. The whole of the Bessin and the Cotentin was in arms against him, while the loyalty of several other places, including Rouen, was uncertain. William's position was desperate. His only hope lay in his unsentimental overlord, Henry. Apprehensively, he set out for the French court at Poissy to plead his case and claim the aid of his suzerain.

As far as the French king was concerned, the almost perpetual rivalries and conflicts between his feudatories were no great hardship. On the contrary, as long as these restless and adventurous vassals were at war among themselves he was safe from the coalitions they might otherwise form against him. It was even politic that, on occasions, he should encourage their conflicting ambitions, and, since decisive victory in their midst was potentially dangerous to him, it suited him in general to support the weaker side. With this principle in mind, and doubtless an acrid indictment of Guy by William to back it, Henry now took what has been called the most momentous decision of his reign. Early in 1047 he led an army into Normandy, advancing through Argentan, and thence north towards Caen, to assist the young duke against his enemies. Meanwhile, the rebels had come in from the west, eventually meeting the king and the duke on a stretch of open, undulating ground between Caen and Falaise known as Val-ès-Dunes. Here, between two rivers, the royal army took station, Henry flying a standard emblazoned with the imperial eagle of Charlemagne and the Caesars, William reputedly bearing on his shield the picture of a pair of lions. Before them stretched the plain with its peaceful streams, tangles of wild rose, occasional prehistoric relics and, more ominously, the banners and bristling lances of their foes. Among the gaudy insignia and surrounding groups of bustle and importance denoting his principal adversaries, William would have distinguished Guy of Burgundy, like himself barely twenty and a novice to pitched battle; the great barons Rannulf and Nigel; a toothy knight known as Haimo 'Dentatus', lord of Thorigny, and, holding back from the main force, Ralph Tesson, 'the Badger'.

Together with a strong cavalry tradition harking back to the Gauls, the French had inherited a powerful stamp of war horse, often black in colour, well capable of bearing a mail-clad and heavily-armed knight in battle. Such animals had helped Charles Martel to crush the Saracen cavalry at Poitiers, had carried Charlemagne across Europe and were the pride of the Norman barons. Now, arrayed on the open plain, several hundred on either side, they carried their riders proudly into battle. As far as can be learned from the short accounts of the affray most nearly contemporary, the battle of Val-ès-Dunes was waged almost exclusively as a cavalry action. William of Jumièges wrote of 'many engagements between groups of cavalry' and William of Poitiers, exclaiming on the death of horsemen and mounts, spoke also of men being crushed and trampled. A later, but more graphic account of the battle by Wace gave it something of the air of heroic tournament, small cliques of riders detaching themselves from the conflict to wheel in search of particular rivals, ponderous charges disintegrating into individual contest. But it is grim sport that proceeds on a pitch of blood and entrails and, when the roars of '*Dex aie!*' and '*Mont-joie!*' had stirred the keenest amongst Normans and French to fervour, there must have remained many who thought discretion the better part of valour. Ralph the Badger, among other rebels, seems to have lost his nerve at the sight of Henry's army and to have switched sides judiciously in the early stages of confrontation.

King Henry, one of the older participants in the action, enhanced his reputation by joining the thick of the fighting, twice being unseated and heaved aloft again by his followers. His second assailant,

Haimo the Toothy, was himself killed in the tussle and carried from the scene on his shield. William, it appears, proved an adept beginner. 'Hurling himself upon his enemies he terrified them with slaughter,' declared William of Poitiers. It may well have been the verve of the duke's attack that prompted Rannulf, already disheartened by the Badger's duplicity, to call it a day. According to Wace, William personally killed one of Rannulf's most redoubtable lieutenants, a certain Hardez of Bayeux, after which Rannulf himself seems to have decided to look to a more auspicious occasion and, hacking free from the mêlée, retired from the fight, the Bayeux contingent following. Nigel of the Cotentin remained the leader of the rebel resistance. For a long while he fought on vigorously, his men appealing to St Sauveur for strength, but numerically and psychologically the odds were against them and, when all was clearly lost, they broke and fled in panic. 'Great was the mass of fugitives, and fierce the pursuit,' wrote Wace in conclusion.

Horses were to be seen running loose over the plain, and the field of battle was covered with knights riding haphazard for their lives. They sought to escape to the Bessin but feared to cross the Orne. All fled in confusion, striving to cross . . . by fives and sixes and threes. But the pursuers were at their heels bent on their destruction. Many were driven into the Orne, and there killed or drowned, and the mills of Borbillon were stopped with dead bodies.

Guy himself seems to have played no conspicuous part in the struggle. His plans for Normandy were smashed at Val-ès-Dunes. William's were about to start in earnest.

*

Val-ès-Dunes enhanced William's prestige and did much to establish his authority, but the victory was far from guaranteeing his survival or securing the duchy. It had scattered the forces of rebellion, but it had not extinguished them and there were to be desperate struggles ahead. His most urgent task was to isolate Guy of Burgundy, the figure-head of the rebellion, before he could start further mischief. Guy, avoiding the disastrous flight of many of his allies towards the Orne, had escaped in relatively good order to Brionne, where he had barricaded himself in his castle on the Risle. Guarded by walls of stone, and surrounded by shallow but impeding water, the stronghold seems to have been impregnable. According to the duke's panegyrist, William of Poitiers, William was soon 'terrifying the enemy by daily attacks', though, since another account of the investment of Bionne (Orderic's) put its duration at almost three years, these would appear to have grown less terrifying and more monotonous as the months dragged on. Certainly, William treated the fort with respect. On either bank of the river he put up siege-works and wooden towers from which his men could repulse both sallies from the castle defenders and any outside attempt to raise the siege or bring in provisions. At last his purposefulness was rewarded. All hope of rescue gone, Guy surrendered Brionne, his garrison emerged from the gates to beg the duke's forgiveness and, with sound political sense, William graciously bestowed his pardon upon the vanquished.

For some time, William's military career was to be punctuated by a feverish and somewhat repetitive process of siege warfare in which the tactics of Brionne formed a fairly standard pattern. To begin, the flashpoint switched to the south. Here, for a while past, Normandy's immediate neighbour, Maine, had experienced something of the internal disorder from which the duchy was beginning finally to emerge. In 1035 its warrior ruler, Herbert Wake-Dog, had died leaving a youthful successor, Count Hugh IV, at the mercy of rebellious and independently-minded vassals. Hugh's troubles were watched closely by his own southern neighbour, Geoffrey of Anjou, whose self-chosen soubriquet, Martel, or the Hammer, was not inappropriate to the methods with which he pursued his ambitions. Powerful, unsubtle and frankly expansionist, he had already waged successful war against Aquitaine and Poitou, and had driven his frontier east as far as Tours, when he turned north to try his luck in Maine. In 1051, shortly after the premature death of Count Hugh, Geoffrey marched triumphantly into the capital of that state, Le Mans, pushing his advance guards to the very doorstep of Normandy. Neither the duke nor the King of France could afford to remain inactive in the face of such developments. With Henry's blessing, William rode south to challenge the intruder.

Two key fortresses dominated the border. Domfront, the

westerly, stood in Maine, while Alençon was on the Norman side
of the frontier. In practice, however, even Alençon was remote in
its connection with the duchy. The rough and hilly country thereabouts was held by the bold and headstrong house of Bellême which
had little time for overlords, particularly William. It was important
for him to administer a sharp lesson. Surrounding Domfront, therefore, he planned a surprise night march against Alençon, forcing part
of the defences and taking prisoners. Thirty or more of these un-
fortunate people had their hands and feet cut off, seemingly on
William's instructions, after which the rest of the defenders surrendered on terms of safe conduct. Indeed, not only Alençon was
overwhelmed by these atrocities. The news struck such fear in the
defenders of Domfront that they, in turn, decided to surrender,
leaving the duke master of his southern frontier.

From the south, William turned north to lay siege to his uncle,
Count William of Talou, who was defying his nephew's authority
from a hill-top castle at Arques in Upper Normandy. The count, a
half-brother of Robert the Magnificent and an envious spectator to
Duke William's success, had picked a crafty moment to make his
challenge. Not only was the duke busy at the opposite end of
Normandy at the time, paradoxically his triumphs there at the
expense of Geoffrey of Anjou were contributing to a dangerous
change of heart in his most powerful ally, King Henry. To Henry,
ever wary of his strong vassals, it must have seemed that the young
duke he had saved from extinction at Val-ès-Dunes was gaining
altogether too much impetus for comfort. Accordingly, in the
autumn of 1053, he entered Normandy once more at the head of a
French army to support the duke's rebellious uncle. Fortunately for
William, the king's advance upon Arques was an unwary one and
he was forced to retire after being ambushed and severely mauled
within an ace of his objective by a captain of the duke's siege force,
Walter Giffard. Before the year was out, the rebel garrison and its
lord had been starved into submission, and the stronghold of Arques,
invaluable to the domination of Upper Normandy, had passed to the
duke. Success continued to strengthen William's following. In
particular, the tough and tireless young leader was attracting the
support of the new generation of Norman nobles, up-and-coming

men such as Roger of Montgomery and William fitz Osbern, who could identify their own dreams for the future with his ambition. He was to need all the armour he could muster, for neither King Henry nor Geoffrey the Hammer had finished with him yet.

Meanwhile, he had made friends, as well as enemies, beyond his own borders. The unreliability of Henry's backing had always been evident, and with Val-ès-Dunes behind them the Norman magnates supporting William had soon turned to the pressing expedient of a sound political marriage for their duke. His husbandly potential was hawked in the best of markets. Matilda, daughter of Baldwin V, the Debonair, of Flanders, and his wife Adela, was the niece of Henry of France, the granddaughter of Robert II of France, and could trace her descent on her mother's side from Charlemagne and England's Alfred the Great. Her father was a knight of the Holy Roman Empire, a powerful and independent vassal of the emperor with increasingly close ties with the French court. Politically, Matilda was immensely desirable, and, by the time Brionne came under siege, William had already made a bid for her hand. Among her personal attributes, the Norman chroniclers told dutifully of her beauty, chastity[1] and various feminine accomplishments, but her most certain physical characteristic was her astonishingly small size. In full growth she was little more than four feet in height and, since she was at the most seventeen years old when William first 'wooed' her, she might then have been even smaller.[2]

What Matilda lacked in size, however, she made up for in spirit. According to a late tradition, her first reaction to the ambitious Norman was one of scorn. The story had it that, when she rejected his advances, the duke forced his way into her chamber at Bruges and, in his fury, beat and kicked her, so impressing her with his mastery that she declared she would marry nobody else. Though historically dubious, it remains an interesting assessment of William's reaction to personal frustration. The main opposition to the match

[1] A nineteenth-century theory, given much prominence by Freeman, that Matilda had already been married and was a mother when William sought her hand, has been discredited by later historians.

[2] In 1961 Matilda's remains were disinterred at Caen. An examination of the bones showed them to be those of a woman barely fifty inches tall. By contrast, William, estimated from a single femur which survived when the rest of his remains were destroyed, stood about 5ft 10in; a man of considerable size by the standards of his age.

was less readily overcome. At the Council of Rheims in October 1049, Pope Leo IX pronounced a ban on the projected marriage. No specific objection was recorded in the edict, but it can be assumed that 'William the Norman', as Leo summarily described him, was taken to task for planning to marry within the seventh degree of consanguinity. A more mundane motive could be found in the pope's active backing at the time of the emperor against a disputatious Baldwin, hence a desire to hinder any strengthening of the anti-imperial cause. It was to be ten years before the ban was finally lifted: ten years in which William stubbornly opposed the ruling of Rome, fought opposition within the Norman church itself, contrived the banishment of yet another of his family, Archbishop Mauger of Rouen, who had openly denounced his plans, and even contemplated the dismissal of the very man who eventually engineered his reconciliation with the papal office, the brilliant Lanfranc, then Prior of Bec, who had never compromised in his disapproval of the marriage as a breach of canonical law.

Regardless of opposition, William and Matilda were wed. Baldwin had conducted his daughter to the Norman frontier town of Eu, and here, on a date now unknown (probably in 1051, though possibly a year earlier or later) the ceremony took place. Side by side before the altar, in a welter of gold and finery, the big warrior and his tiny bride must have made a remarkable picture. Forty miles to the south, where the leisurely Seine met the first faint ripples of the tide, the people of Rouen turned out to see the bride and groom celebrate the occasion in their capital. But it was at Caen that the couple left perhaps the most striking memorial to their marriage. Here, to mark the lifting of the pope's ban in 1059, William and his wife built and endowed two religious houses, one each for the devotees of their respective sexes. These fine examples of eleventh-century Romanesque architecture, the famous abbey churches of St Stephen and Holy Trinity, were to symbolise important new harmonies in the duke's career: a new harmony between Church and temporal government, personified by a growing understanding between William and Lanfranc, which was to contribute much to Norman power, and the personal harmony between William and Matilda who, for all the early opposition to their union, were to sustain a long and most fruitful partnership. Valiantly, the miniature Matilda bore her restless lord four sons, Robert, Richard, William and Henry, and at least five (very likely six) daughters. In her spare time, she was an adroit and loyal political helpmate. William never contracted a better alliance.

6

Scotland and Wales

If it is a characteristic of those who achieve great worldly success that, in the midst of the most daunting adversity, they remain beguiled by the future, Duke William was not an exception. He had been about twenty-three when, the struggle for survival in his own domain far from finished, according to one account, he hit upon the novel and forward idea of a ceremonial visit of friendship to his cousin Edward at the royal court of England. The English rebellion of 1051 had run its abortive course and Godwin and his sons were scattered overseas. Eustace of Boulogne had been handled roughly: William's embassy, it seems, was treated with resignation. No doubt England's émigré Normans were assembled to welcome them. It is only stated that they travelled with a large following, stayed awhile enjoying the Confessor's hospitality and eventually departed loaded with gifts and honours. Seen as nothing more, the outing was a first-rate advertisement for the Duke of Normandy, and it is likely that William, if he was present himself, exerting his charm to the utmost, would have gone over in a big way with his regal kinsman. William's later claim that Edward actually promised him the crown (a claim ignored by the closest English writers, though eagerly propounded by their Norman counterparts)[1] was not linked specifically with this visit, nor does any direct evidence exist that a promise was made; nevertheless, it is conventionally held by modern historians that it was indeed now that the duke received at least some kind of intimation that he stood in such favour. The mood was conducive to rapport. With Wessex bereft of its stubbornly anti-Norman leadership, Siward and Leofric more at home ranging their earldoms than

[1] Strictly, Edward would have been beyond his rights in making any such promise, though this is not to say that he did not do so, perhaps even to more than one person. Such disposal of a kingdom was not unusual.

in the special atmosphere of court life, William's limited intelligence of England must have revealed what seemed to him a rarely amenable land. Though the long hair and moustaches, the flowing mantles and metal bangles of Saxon and Dane were not absent from Edward's circle, many of the inner conclave were frankly and familiarly Norman or French. Greeted at the heart of a foreign monarchy by this exceptional profusion of their own countrymen (prelates, earls and thegns), William's embassy could be excused if they supposed the island more sympathetic to Norman influence than, in general, was the case. It would have been strange had the sum of their impressions not combined to generate an atmosphere of strong mutual interest; an interest heightened by Edward's childlessness. Before the embassy left, presents of rich tapestries, precious ornaments, hawks and hounds had been exchanged as mementos of the entente. The travellers must have counted themselves well pleased with the enterprise.

*

Their first flush of pleasure, however, was to prove a brief one. Within months, the house of Godwin was back in the ascendant, Edward's Norman friends had scattered and the stolid figure of an Englishman loomed tall again beside the prayerful and shaken king whose long-deferred snatch at the political reins of the realm had served only to emphasise his dependence on its native earls. Harold's first concern on succeeding to his father's earldom was to consolidate the unique authority it gave him. His flair for diplomacy quickly became apparent. With characteristic understanding, he resisted the temptation to give his old earldom, East Anglia, to one of his younger brothers, passing it on to Earl Leofric's son, Aelfgar, instead. Next, he displayed his goodwill towards the other veteran earl by allowing Siward of Northumbria the support of a strong contingent of royal housecarles for a long-range attack on Macbeth of Scotland, the king notorious in legend for his murder of his predecessor, Duncan.

Contrary to the legend, Duncan had not been killed at Macbeth's castle as an old man but had died young, possibly in battle, at

Bothnagowan, near Elgin. While Duncan's young sons, Malcolm and Donald Bane were carried off and reared at the English court of their grandfather, Siward, Macbeth appears to have proved a potent and popular ruler of his craggy, loch-starred lands, even finding time during his thirteen years as Scottish king to make the fashionable pilgrimage to Rome. Presumably such success had done little to commend him in Siward's eyes for, in 1054, with his old rival Godwin dead and the more conciliatory Harold holding sway in the south, the hoary old Northumbrian warrior strapped on his armour and rode north to restore his grandson Malcolm to rightful estate. The fact that no English force had marched beyond Forth since the days of Athelstan left Siward undaunted. His offensive was mounted 'by land and by sea' (*ASC*) striking north across a hostile barrier of uplands and rivers to challenge Macbeth at his hillbound stronghold in the valley of the Tay. On 27 July, 'the Day of the Seven Sleepers', Macbeth and his wrathful clansmen swarmed to meet the invaders at Dunsinnan Hill, near Perth. The details of the battle are inextricably tangled with myth. Siward depended on the crack warriors of his household force, strengthened by the royal housecarles from the south. They had endured a hard march, probably having to skirmish for supplies on the way, but they were professional soldiers with a fighting tradition and discipline which, other things being equal, must have given them a big advantage over the more loosely organised Scots. Macbeth was said to have been supported by a northern warrior prince named Thorfin who had established himself in the Orkneys and spread his authority down the west coast as far south as Galloway. Certainly there was heavy fighting with many casualties on either side. Siward's son Osbeorn was killed, as was a son of his sister and a considerable number of the regular soldiers in his force. But losses among their opponents were even heavier (including one Dolfin, seemingly a relative of Thorfin) and, in the end, Macbeth's army was routed. A characteristic anecdote, if of poor authority, later told how Siward, on hearing of his son's death, asked the nature of the wounds. Assured they were to the front of the body, the old earl was consoled, wishing no better death for his son or himself. Though Malcolm was now able to assert his rule over at least part of Scotland,

Macbeth (again contrary to later tradition)[1] survived the battle and continued the struggle from the wild fastnesses of the north until finally killed in combat at Lumphanan, in Aberdeenshire, 1057, when the whole of Scotland came under a king of predominantly English influence.

The quantity of plunder taken in Scotland seemed marvellous to contemporary writers, and Siward's expedition must have returned to Northumbria loaded with the material rewards of its venture. There would have been a great reception waiting at York, capital of the earldom and the booming commercial centre of the north. Standing high, dry and welcoming on a natural ridge in the swampy vale of the Ouse, conveniently at the farthest inland reach of the tide,[2] the city had long been a favourite base with northern traders, particularly Danes and Anglo-Danes who shipped to and from the settlements in Scotland, Iceland, Ireland and the Isle of Man as well as Norway and Denmark. Like London, it was also a depot for Continental goods from the south. According to Domesday Book there were rather more than 1,500 dwelling houses 'in the city of York in the time of Edward the Confessor', while a portion of the city was 'wasted in castles'. At the heart of York, the most ancient of its walls and buildings, dating back to Roman times, towered in disrepair, monuments to an already impressive history. Here, on the readily defensible land between the Ouse and its tributary, the Foss, the Roman's had built the fortress of Eboracum, the military capital of their northern command. Here, 200 years after the departure of the legions, the Pope's emmisary, Paulinus, had discovered the pagan Edwin of Northumbria ensconced in the crumbling relics of praetorian grandeur; and, within the great north-pointing arrowhead formed by two remaining walls, the first Archbishop of York had baptised the Anglian king in the Christian faith.

Those same stubborn bastions had survived to see the first stone church, precursor to the mighty York Minster; to see the small sanctuary in the rushy mire give root to the ecclesiastical eminence of the northern province; to see its blossoming as an educational

---

[1] Shakespeare followed William of Malmesbury against overwhelming evidence in perpetuating the myth of Macbeth's death at Dunsinnan.

[2] The tidal head is now seven miles downstream of the city.

centre in the eighth century, its development as a port of commerce with the settlement of the Danes, its establishment as a seat of earldom under Canute and, now, to welcome home its renowned earl, Siward Digera (The Strong), after his triumphant campaign in the north. As the bells rang a greeting from church to church along the old pathway between the rivers, the women and kinsfolk of the soldiers must have rushed tremulously through Bootham gate to meet the returning army and learn the best, or the worst. The loot would have been apportioned and the local soldiers dismissed to their homes. No doubt Siward offered thanks for his success to his favourite saint, the martyred Norse King Olaf.

The earl did not live to fight another battle. The year following his victory at Dunsinnan, he lay dying in his Northumbrian capital. Henry of Huntingdon later portrayed him bemoaning his ill-luck to die in time of peace, 'the death of a cow', and gave a stirring account of how the rugged northerner commanded his followers to dress him with helmet, mail, shield and sword that he might face the end in the fashion of his Viking ancestors. The story, capturing something of the essence of England's early Scandinavian stock, was not mentioned by the earlier chroniclers who touched the event briefly and matter-of-factly: 'In this year [1055] passed away Earl Siward at York, and he was buried . . . in the church which he himself had had built and consecrated in the name of God and Olaf,' wrote one, adding equally briefly, 'and Tostig succeeded to his earldom.'

On the face of it, Tostig's appointment was a provocative one, yet it must be remembered that Siward's natural successor had fallen in the Scottish war, while his only surviving son, Waltheof, seems to have been too young to hold his father's refractory subjects in awe. To choose from among rival Northumbrian houses could have been to invite a more certain danger than that inherent in the nomination of a complete outsider. Then again, for some reason Edward and his queen had a particularly soft spot for Godwin's third son. It is notable that the king's biographer sketched Tostig in the most impressive terms. Smaller in build than Harold, more impulsive and inflexible, he was nevertheless handed to posterity as a man at least equalling his elder brother in strength and daring. If Tostig was to fail, eventually, in his relationship with the turbulent Northumbrians, there is no record of anyone having raised voice against his appointment at its time: not even Leofric, though it further strengthened Harold's hand. Indeed, for a while the experiment looked very much like succeeding. Having entered into a pact of sworn brotherliness with Malcolm of Scotland, and checked lawlessness in his new earldom with a severity not unfamiliar to the Northumbrians, Tostig touched the peaks of soldierly glory by co-operating with Harold in a brilliant military campaign against the troublesome Welsh king, Gruffyd ap Llewellyn.

At the time of Tostig's northern appointment, Gruffyd, who, as an ambitious prince of North Wales had once allied himself with the English against his South Welsh rivals, was at the height of his power and looking for new victories along the controversial English-Welsh border. Nothing could have pleased him more than to be offered eighteen shiploads of well-armed mercenaries to assist in a large-scale plundering expedition on Herefordshire. The offer came, surprisingly enough, from Earl Aelfgar: the same Aelfgar to whom Harold had so recently given East Anglia. One disruptive element in an unusually settled political scene, Aelfgar had been outlawed during the Lent witenagemot in London[1] for reasons as elusive now as they seem to have been to many at the time. Of three varying accounts in the *Anglo-Saxon Chronicle*, that most clearly sympathetic to Harold related: '. . . Earl Aelfgar was outlawed on the charge of being a traitor to the king and the entire nation. He admitted his guilt before the assembly, though the confession escaped him unawares.' Of the others, one saw him as 'almost without guilt', and the other as 'quite guiltless'. (If so, it is strange that Leofric appears to have accepted his son's banishment.) Like Harold before him, Aelfgar took refuge in Ireland where he hired ships and Viking crews and, after a spasm of raiding along the west coast of England, joined forces with Gruffyd on the Herefordshire enterprise.

Encouraged by the strength of Aelfgar's mercenaries, the lightly-armed and mobile Welshmen poured down from the hills, ravaged the border, then struck through the Wye Valley for Hereford itself. Above the trees on the river-bank rose the cathedral church of the

---

[1] Probably the same assembly that approved Tostig's preferment. It has been speculated that Aelfgar opposed the appointment.

diocese, the minster of St Ethelbert, a former king of the East Angles whose enchanted remains dwelt within. Around the minster clustered the homes of the blind and aged prelate, Aethelstan, of his spiritual partner, Bishop Tremerin, a Welshman, and of the canons, craftsmen and citizens of the city. Dominating both town and river, the fortress of Earl Ralph, later known as Ralph the Timid, stood guard on the Wye. Though Ralph seems not, by nature, to have been a soldier, as a Norman he cherished pretensions of military superiority and was presently engaged with the ambitious notion of teaching English thegns and ceorls to fight on horseback. It appears that he saw himself sweeping his enemies before him at the head of a glorious and omnipotent force of cavalry. Perhaps for this reason, Ralph allowed the Welsh to come within a mile or two of the city where he could engage them, his horses fresh, on flat ground. Were it not for its tragic consequences, the cavalry 'charge' at Hereford must have rated as one of the great comic scenes of early English history. Ralph's army indeed charged in the most spectacular fashion. Unfortunately, however, it charged in the wrong direction. Accustomed to do battle with their feet planted firmly on the ground, the men of Hereford had no heart for these new-fangled tactics. Nor, in all probability, had their mounts, for these were not fiery war-horses but shrewd little hill ponies, suited neither in stature nor temperament to being driven on to axes and spears. Whether the decision was theirs, or their riders', can only be guessed, but Ralph's cavalry took one look at the fearsome Welsh and Irish host before it and retired in no leisurely manner. The chroniclers did not mince words. '. . . before a spear was thrown, the English fled,' wrote one, 'because they had been made to fight on horseback'. Wrote another: 'and many were slain in that rout'.

Gruffyd and Aelfgar entered Hereford the same day, unopposed. The rest was sheer horror. The whole place was sacked and fired while those of the people who had not escaped were murdered or led away to suit the pleasure of their captors. Seven priests, according to one account, made a desperate attempt to defend the door of the minster, but they, and others sheltering inside, were cut down mercilessly by the raiders, after which the church trappings were plundered and the building put to flames. Bishop Tremerin and the blind

Aethelstan escaped the massacre, both to die, broken-hearted, within a few months. Having destroyed Ralph's castle with equal relish (unhindered by the earl, who had wisely abandoned it), the Welshmen retired. King Edward, wintering at Gloucester, was close enough to the border to be shaken; appalled at the desecration and shamed by his nephew Ralph's ineffectuality. Something had to be done about the Welsh, and done promptly. Harold took over. Now, for the first time, he was to be seen as supreme commander of an English army. 'Then levies were called out from all the neighbouring districts of England; and they assembled at Gloucester and went a little way into Wales, remaining there for a time while Earl Harold had an earthwork built around Hereford' (*ASC*). With the hard weather settling in, Harold contented himself with camping his army threateningly on the Welsh side of the border while he supervised the restoration of the ravaged city, providing for its defence a rough wall which could be improved on later. Burghers were appointed, both by the king and by Harold, and made liable to military service against the Welsh; mints were established, and Harold's chaplain, a priest named Leofgar, was made the new bishop and strong man of the community. Harold respected a worldly type of clergyman, and the chroniclers noted, with a hint of disapproval, how Leofgar 'wore his moustaches during his priesthood until he became bishop. After his consecration he forsook his chrism and his cross, his spiritual weapons, and seized his spear and his sword...'

The morale of the area thus refurbished, Harold split the opposition. Instead of attempting to pursue the now reticent Gruffyd on to his own ground (terrain eminently suited to the practised guerrilla tactics of the Welshman), he offered Aelfgar pardon and peace, a gesture not only calculated to divide the alliance that had vanquished Ralph, but to further his own reputation for fairness and moderation throughout the country. The bait was taken. Abandoning Gruffyd, Aelfgar paid off his mercenaries, presented himself to the king and was duly restored to his earldom of East Anglia.

But Gruffyd, if weakened, remained unsubdued. With Harold's retirement from the immediate scene, the Welsh king soon appeared on the border again, now squaring up to Leofgar, Hereford's battling bishop. Unlike the unhappy Ralph, Leofgar's attitude to warfare

was neither hesitant nor unduly pretentious. Strapping on his sword
and calling his priests to do likewise, he went out to avenge the
earlier murder of his brethren, supported by the sheriff, one Alfnoth,
and his militiamen. Like Ralph, however, the bishop was no tactician.
Eight days before midsummer, 1056, the skilful Gruffyd inflicted
a second humiliation on the men of Hereford. Leofgar and Alfnoth
walked straight into disaster and went down fighting. By the time
reinforcements arrived, bishop and sheriff were dead and Gruffyd
had gone. It seems that the Englishmen, in their fury, pressed hard
after the Welshmen, but whether the campaign proved more harass-
ing to Gruffyd, or themselves, remains doubtful. According to an
Abingdon writer, 'it is hard to describe the distress, and all the
marchings, and the camping, and the toil and destruction of men and
horses which the army of the English endured . . .' It was not until
Harold appeared on the scene once more, this time accompanied by
Earl Leofric, that Gruffyd was brought to terms. With no great
magnanimity, he agreed to surrender a small portion of his territory
west of the Dee (apparently part of the present shire of Chester) and
to be 'a loyal and faithful under king to king Edward' (*ASC*).
Gruffyd kept the promise until the moment it suited him to do
otherwise.

★

Leofric's co-operation with Harold on the Welsh front was to
provide an agreeable conclusion to a life that had often been spent
in opposition to Godwin's house, though with relatively little
apparent bitterness or violence. The good old earl of the Mercians, as
one historian called him, was so seldom charged with excess, so
frequently commended for moderation and reason, that it is gratifying to think that he lived long enough to see a like-minded man at
the helm of the country. Not that the forbearance of Leofric, the
'dear ruler' [1] should be judged outside the context of his time.
According to Florence of Worcester, he crushed a revolt in Worces-
tershire with such savagery that the shire town was depopulated,
while the propagators of the Godiva legend, whose writings date

[1] Leo = dear + ric = hero or ruler.

from the beginning of the thirteenth century, had no difficulty in seeing him as the sort of man who would have his wife ride naked through a market-place before he would relax his heavy tolls on the people. The St Albans historian, Roger of Wendover, writing some time before May 1237, believed that

The Countess Godiva, true lover of the Virgin Mother, longing to free Coventry from its heavy bondage and servitude, frequently begged and prayed her husband that, for the sake of Jesus Christ and His Mother, he would release the town from its burdens. The Earl [Leofric] repeatedly refused, sharply rebuking her for asking what was so much to his damage, and forbade her ever again to speak to him of the matter. Godiva, however . . . never ceased to worry her husband, until finally he answered her thus: 'Mount your horse naked and ride through the market of the town from beginning to end when the people are assembled, and when you return you shall have what you ask.'

At least there is credit for Leofric at the end. 'Then the Countess . . . attended by two soldiers . . . mounted her horse naked, letting down the tresses from her head so that her whole body was veiled except her lovely legs, and no one saw her as she crossed the market. The journey completed, she returned to her husband rejoicing, and he, full of admiration, freed Coventry and its people from servitude . . .' It has been suggested that the story was first encouraged by the monks as a means of deriving Christian propaganda from the old Saxon predilection for fertility rites in which a naked maiden paraded in the village centre by a sacred tree or bough, sometimes accompanied by a male animal.

No doubt the glowing terms reserved for Leofric by most monkish chroniclers owed much of their inspiration to the considerable benefits he and his wife conferred on the Church. The Benedictine monastery founded at Coventry in 1043 by 'the praiseworthy earl of happy memory' and 'his wife, the noble Countess Godiva, a worshipper of God and devoted lover of St Mary', (Roger of Howden), was described by contemporaries as the richest in all England. (Among other things it owned the alleged arm of St Augustine, acquired in Pavia for 'one talent of gold and 100 talents of silver' and mounted in a silver case), probably owning many scores of dwellings and giving home to a good proportion of the town's estimated 1,200 or more inhabitants. Otherwise Coventry was a simple agricultural town. There is no indication that Leofric had a palace there or that he or his wife spent very much time among the community at large. They had a hall at King's Bromley, Stafford-shire, and probably interested themselves in a number of churches throughout the earldom. Leofric was closely linked with the legend of Edward's saintliness by the king's twelfth-century biographer, Abbot Ailred of Rievaulx. Fable has it that the earl and Godiva were attending mass with King Edward one day when they experienced a vision of the holy child holding his hand out to the king. Leofric, under the impression that the king had not seen it, was about to 'pray him to be certified of the living saint' (Humphrey Burton's MS), when Edward interposed, exclaiming: 'Stay, Leofric, what thou seest I myself see.' Leofric died the year following the peace with Gruffyd, at Bromley, and was buried at the Abbey Minster of Coventry, supposedly in the porchway. 'He was very wise in all things, both Godly and worldly; a blessing to this nation,' com-mented the *Chronicle* with touching simplicity. Godiva outlived him by many years, still holding part of the family estates, but hardly consoled by the behaviour of her son and grandsons who turned out to have few of Leofric's better qualities. The death of the last of the great earls of Canute's time signalled a reshuffling of the main regional governments of the country. Aelfgar vacated East Anglia to succeed to Leofric's Mercian earldom, nine broad shires from the Wash to the Dee; part of East Anglia went to Harold's brother, Gyrth, the fourth of Godwin's sons, while a new earldom embracing Essex, Bedford, Hertford, Kent and Surrey was created for the fifth son, Leofwine. With Tostig established in Northumbria, Harold and his younger brothers now dominated the whole of England save Mercia: the more so since Ralph of Hereford died a month or two after Leofric, leaving a child son, and it seems that the Earl of Wessex took personal responsibility for the vital Welsh border area.

Bishop Leofgar, Gruffyd's battle victim, had been replaced in his command at Hereford by the former Bishop of Worcester, Ealdred, Sweyn's old intermediary at the court of Edward. Like Leofgar, Ealdred had no scruples about bearing arms, nor of using them, but it was as a sort of roving ambassador, a courier extraordinary, that he had gained his considerable reputation as a man of affairs and was to earn the probable distinction of being England's most-travelled diplomat. Several years earlier, Ealdred had been assigned a remarkable mission on the Continent that was to bear strange, and short-lived, fruit in the year of Ralph's and Leofric's deaths. In 1054 a resolution had been passed (seemingly by king and witan; and presumably approved, if not actually proposed by Harold, with a view to off-setting the bogy of Duke William) to invite the son of Edmund Ironside, Prince Edward the Exile, to return to England. Edward the Exile, then a man of forty, had lived most of his life in Hungary since his childhood banishment, where he had married a lady of royal descent named Agatha, a kinswoman of the Hungarian queen, and similarly of Emperor Henry III, by whom he possessed three children, Edgar, Margaret and Christina. The Exile could have known little of England, and that country less of him, but, as King Edward's nephew, and the son of a former English king, he was an obvious, if not pressing, candidate for the succession. Bishop Ealdred was summoned and briefed for his mission: to deliver the invitation. It seems he was given a great reception by the Emperor, who was then at Cologne, and by Herman, the Archbishop at that city, and, after lingering a year there, finally managed to fulfil his assignment. In the spring of 1057, long after Ealdred had returned, and more than three years since the invitation had first been mooted, the travel-worn Exile disembarked in England, only to die before he could meet even his uncle, the king. No causes were recorded; no accusations made. Perhaps he simply succumbed to an obscure illness contracted on the journey. He was buried in St Paul's cathedral, London, to a soulful chord of perplexity and anti-climax.

With Prince Edward the Exile dead, the problem of succession remained open. His son Edgar was little more than an infant. The clear possibility that King Edward might die before the child had grown up must have made the chances of a new royal line now seem very real indeed, and, some time from this point in developments, Harold appears to have been at least tacitly conceded unique status in the country: if not '*subregulus*', as Florence visualised him soon afterwards, he was undoubtedly very much a super-earl. When, in the following year, Aelfgar again had the temerity to quarrel with him, the Mercian was promptly outlawed by a witan significantly dominated by Harold's supporters. Once more, Aelfgar pinned his hopes on his only close ally, Gruffyd ap Llewellyn, the alliance being re-established more firmly than ever about now by the Welsh king's marriage to Ealdgyth, Aelfgar's sister. 'In this year Aelfgar was banished from the country, but soon returned with violence through the aid of Gruffyd,' declared a contemporary writer, who also reported the arrival of some Norwegian ships which, according to another account, co-operated with the rebels. The information is scant. 'It is tedious to tell how it all happened,' wrote the chronicler. Harold appears to have repeated his earlier accomplishment of talking sense into Aelfgar, who was 'inlawed' not long after and re-united with his earldom. At any rate, Harold's dogged restraint in his dealings with the Mercian seems to have paid off, for there is no record of more trouble from Aelfgar before his death, probably in 1062, when his eldest son, Edwin, was allowed to succeed peaceably to his father's earldom.

But Gruffyd was another proposition. Too inveterate a raider to be reasoned out of his habits, he was soon back across the border, reputedly even plundering beyond the Severn, and this time Harold resolved to deal with him for good. His initial plan was a daring one. Setting out from Gloucester with a compact and highly mobile assault force, probably of mounted housecarles, about Christmas 1062, he crossed the entire neck of Wales to the Dee, aiming to surprise the Welsh king at his winter quarters at Rhuddlan, in what is now Flintshire. Gruffyd, lulled into unreadiness by the close of the customary campaigning season, and reckoning the English commander a hundred hilly miles away, was very nearly caught by the manœuvre. But luck was with him. He received just enough warning to escape his loot-filled palace on the Clwyd before Harold could surround it. The earl had to content himself with burning the palace, destroying Gruffyd's ships and tack and commandeering what treasures he could find. He did not stop long in the hostile Welsh vale. According to one authority, he commenced the return march to Gloucester the same day.

The second phase of operations was on an altogether different scale. This time the Earl of Wessex called in his brother Tostig to help with a powerful two-pronged offensive against Wales. Harold visualised a combined sea and land invasion, mounted simultaneously from north and south, with the intention of bludgeoning these fiery descendants of the ancient, and once ubiquitous, Britons into submission. By spring he was ready. In the last days of May ('towards Rogation days'), Harold hoisted sail at Bristol with a strong seaborne army to attack the coastal areas of Wales, while Tostig, leading a great mounted column across the Pennines and on to the flats of Cheshire, struck south-west to tackle the Welsh interior. Little as can be known of the tactical details of the campaign, it is certain that it established Harold's reputation among his countrymen as a general of hitherto unrecognised brilliance. To Englishmen of the time, a campaign in the uncharted fastnesses of Gruffyd and his dreaded warriors must have been a matter for much the same sort of superstitious pessimism that, centuries later, accompanied their pioneering descendants into 'darkest Africa'. Its success was a psychological as well as a military revelation, and it is easy to imagine the wonder which nourished its tales and traditions: tales of marvellous snow-clad mountains, of grim skirmishes across strangely-misted moors, of wild enemies who emerged like phantoms from the hillsides, and, inevitably, of the taming of resentful, ferine women. The general delight in giving the raiders a dose of their own medicine, was emphasised in the popular tradition (developed by Giraldus) that Harold taught his soldiers to live and fight like Welshmen, discarding their mail and heavy armour for leather jerkins and javelins, and to subsist on the lean fare of the highlands. To be sure, the Earl of Wessex struck hard and repeatedly, descending on community after community to claim submission and hostages from the chieftains, or to lay waste with fire and sword. So great, in fact, was the terror inculcated by Harold and Tostig that, before the end of summer, Gruffyd's power over his people was broken. 'The man who had once been invincible was now left in the glens of desolation,' wrote a Welsh chronicler. Could the Welsh king have held out until winter, he might have gained respite, but there were men in his following who were not prepared for the massacre and destruction to continue so long. At Worcester, the nearest English chronicler recorded the end thus: '. . . on 5 August [1063], king Gruffyd was killed by his own men because he persisted in struggling against Earl Harold. He was king over the whole of Wales. His head was brought to Earl Harold, who took it to the king [Edward] together with the figure-head of his [Gruffyd's] ship and the adornments with it.'

On the bizarre image of the devout Edward gazing with gratification on the severed head of the Cymric warrior, the last of Harold's Welsh campaigns closed. Once for all, it established that Harold, so practised in negotiation, could also be appalling effective in a fight. It is eloquent of the mark the episode made in men's minds that, a century later, writers then conditioned to the disparagement of Harold's politics were, nevertheless, still extolling it as a classic of exemplary generalship. Harold himself, perhaps mindful of the precedent of the conquering Canute, eventually took Gruffyd's widow, Ealdgyth, daughter of Leofric and Godiva, in marriage, no doubt presuming a closer diplomatic relationship with both Mercia and Wales. According to one version of the *Anglo-Saxon Chronicle*, King Edward entrusted Wales to two chieftains, Bleddyn and Rhiwallon, apparently brothers of Gruffyd (perhaps the instigators of his death), who duly swore the customary oaths of fealty and offered hostages and tribute to the English king. If either Edward or Harold needed a lesson in the inadequacy of armed suppression, it came almost exactly two years later. In the summer of 1065, Harold ordered the building of a grandiose lodge at Portskewett, Monmouthshire, in the south-east of the newly-conquered territory, where he had staked claim to a wide estate with excellent hunting. His intention, on the word of the Worcester chronicler, was to invite King Edward along for the sport. The Welsh, however, got their sport in first. For several weeks they watched the elaborate construction and stocking of the buildings with mounting interest until, on St Bartholomew's day, 24 August, one Caradog, a son of Gruffyd, led them on a wild and rampaging treasure hunt. When their fun was over, most of the workmen lay dead: nothing that was movable remained of the lodge.

7

Peace and War in England and Normandy

To Harold's contemporaries, not least King Edward, his victorious emergence from the benighted hills of Wales must have seemed a convincing demonstration of his grace in the eyes of their god. Such favour, above all things—above even the respect of friends and the fear of enemies—was invaluable to a man of princely ambition. It is hardly possible to over-emphasise the superstitious nature of the times, nor the heartfelt need among men of all classes for supernatural protection in a world bursting with magic, both good and bad. Accounts of witches, demons and devils were common, and attested by people of the best education. William of Malmesbury, for instance, repeated with great detail and assurance a story he had heard 'from a man of such character, who swore he had seen it, that I should blush to disbelieve'. It involved a witch who lived at Berkeley. Her son was a monk and her daughter a nun. Approaching death, and wishing to avoid the summons of evil spirits, she called her children to her bedside and entreated them to sew her corpse in the skin of a stag, place it in a stone coffin bound with three iron chains 'of tremendous weight' and topped with a heavy stone. On the fourth day after her death, all being well, she declared, they should bury her. Psalms should be sung for fifty nights and masses be said for as many days.

They did their utmost to comply, but alas! vain were pious tears, vows or entreaties; so great was the woman's guilt, so great the devil's violence. For on the first two nights, while the choir of priests was singing psalms round the body, the devils, one by one, bursting open the church door despite its being secured with a huge bolt, broke asunder the two outer chains; the middle one, being more sturdily wrought, remained intact. About cock-crow on the third night, the whole monastery was shaken to its foundations by the clamour of the approaching enemy. One devil, more terrible in appearance than the rest, and of taller stature, broke the gates to shivers by the violence of his attack. The priests grew motionless with fear, their hair stood on end and they became speechless. He proceeded, as it appeared, with haughty step towards the coffin and, calling the woman by name, commanded her to rise. When she replied that she could not, because of the chains, he said, 'You shall be loosed, and to your cost', and immediately broke the chain which had defied the efforts of the others with as little exertion as though it had been made of flax. He also beat down the cover of the coffin with his foot and, taking her by the hand, before them all he dragged her out of the church. At the doors appeared a black horse, proudly neighing, with iron hooks projecting over its whole back; on this the wretched creature was placed, and, immediately, with the entire devilish party, vanished from the eyes of the beholders; her pitiable cries for assistance were heard, however, for nearly four miles. No person will deem this incredible who has read St Gregory's Dialogues. . . .

White magic was hardly less common than black, while miracles of all sorts were esteemed with charming innocence. For the great mass of people, exceptional talent and accomplishment were often understood more readily in terms of supernatural power or assistance than as the result of special human endeavour; great warriors owed success to divine intervention in battle, healers might derive their capability from the saints, and so on. By the same token, formulae existed for invoking heavenly aid in a whole range of domestic troubles. To prevent bees swarming away from home it was considered efficacious to cast earth from the right hand under the right foot, throw gravel on the swarm and to recite a short jingle to the bees commencing with the flattering supplication, 'Alight, victorious women, descend to earth!' Other magical remedies, curiously blending Christian and pre-Christian elements, were more intricate. The treatment for unproductive pastures, perhaps those harmed by sorcery or witchcraft, for instance, involved in the first place digging four sods, one from each side of the field, before daybreak. A collection had then to be made of products from the domestic creatures on the land (milk, honey, etc.) plus part of every tree and herb (except, for some reason, hard wood and burdock), on which holy water was sprinkled and allowed to drip three times on the bottom of the sods. After this, the sods were taken to church and placed green-side towards the altar while the priest sang four masses over them. Finally, four crosses were fashioned of aspen wood, with the names Matthew, Mark, Luke and John inscribed on the points of each, and the sods replaced before sunset in their original positions with the crosses buried beneath them. All this was interspersed with incantations and paternosters and concluded with the farmer or landowner facing to the east, bowing nine times and reciting a special prayer.

The most potent and versatile of Anglo-Saxon antidotes for bodily injury or infection appears to have been the so-called nine herbs charm. Dating from the days of heathen worship, and later revised with Christian overtones, it was professed to avail against 'nine evil spirits . . . nine poisons and . . . nine infectious diseases'— everything, in fact, from battle wounds and snake bites to nettle-blister and the touch of 'a fiend's hand'. The nine 'herbs' were crushed and combined with a mixture of water, ashes and egg, and the salve was applied to the body after the appropriate jingle had been sung into the patient's mouth, ears and wound. Even more curious was one piece of enchantment for use against dysentery. Apparently it was believed that during an outbreak of dysentery in Rome an angel had come to the aid of the people bearing a magic message in code. The cure was to fix round the neck of the sufferer a piece of parchment on which was inscribed this same strange formula: *Ranmigan. adonai. eltheos. mur. O. ineffabile. Omiginan. midanmian. misane. dimas. mode. mida. mamagartem. Orta min. sigmone. beronice. irritas. venas quasi dulap. fervor. fruxantis. sanguinis. siccatur. fla. fracta. frigula. mirgul. etsihdon. segulta. frautanur. in arno. midoninis. abar vetho. sydone multo. sacculo. pp. pppp sother sother. Misere. mei deus deus mini deus mi. AΩNY Alleluiah, Alleluiah.*

Despite Christian teaching, and sometimes with its tacit or even open approval, supernatural power was attributed to many earthly objects in Harold's day. Some trees and wells, for example, were regarded as magical and closely connected with fertility (they are still remembered in maypoles [once sacred trees] and wishing wells), certain cross-roads had a mystical and more sinister relevance, while

few fetishes were regarded as so potent and awesome as the bones or
other remains of a saint. The most sought after of wonder-workers,
these were treasured immensely in the churches and cathedrals that
housed them, while zealous priests were not above packing a limb,
or a head, in their luggage when transferred from one place to
another. According to Lanfranc's biographer, Eadmer, the famous
Roman-Saxon cathedral at Canterbury, which included among a
fine collection of relics the bones of St Dunstan, the head of St
Furseus and the head of the blessed virgin Austroberta, had gained
the head of St Swithun in this way when Archbishop Aelfheah
moved from Winchester to Canterbury. The great Christian centres
of the East did a brisk trade with pilgrims in allegedly holy remains,
and, a little after Harold's time, William of Malmesbury could write
of England: 'You can scarcely pass a village of consequence without
hearing of some new saint, apart from numbers of whom all knowledge has perished through want of records.' Boundless faith was
placed in the beneficial properties of their bones; catastrophe
promised those who abused them. The universal power of an oath
sworn on sacred relics derived not so much from the obligation
imposed by honour, deeply though this might be felt among men of
good faith, as from the terrible and unholy consequences of breaking
it. Throughout Christendom the oath was used commonly in the
sense of a modern legal contract, and it is not surprising that an oath
was to play a crucial part in Harold's future.

*

During the period covered by the Welsh wars, work finished on a
project which casts an interesting light on Harold as a god-fearing
man. Some thirteen or so miles north-east of London Bridge,
between the Lea and what is now Epping Forest, stood the small
township of Waltham. Waltham had once belonged to Canute's
lieutenant, Tovi the Proud, the lord at whose wedding feast Harthacnut had died, and Tovi's rule had inspired yet another of those
mysterious legends so acceptable to the age. Tovi, so the story went,
had been obsessed by a strange dream in which it had been revealed
to him that a crucifix was buried beneath a hill at Lutegarsbury (later

Montacute, Somerset), another of his estates. Dutifully, Tovi had
begun to excavate. Deeper and deeper his men had burrowed until,
no less than forty cubits down (a cubit approximated to the length
of a fore-arm), their tools had struck an enormous boulder. Beneath
it was the promised crucifix and, among other smaller items, a book
of the gospels. The book and the cross, or rood, were taken to
Waltham where, on the low grassland beside the Lea, Tovi built a
church to house his miraculous find. Whatever its origin, the holy
rood of Waltham had soon become another object of popular
worship and pilgrimage; the church and forest settlement, an
embryonic town. After Tovi's death, Waltham was confiscated, for
some uncertain reason, by the Crown, and was granted, eventually,
by Edward to his brother-in-law, Harold, then Earl of East Anglia.
It was Tovi's sanctuary, enlarged and transformed, that was to stand
through history as a monument of the great earl's faith and prestige.
Harold's vision embraced a rebuilt church, secured to Tovi's endow-
ment, filled with precious gifts, surrounded by its own lands, and
served by a dean and twelve canons plus various inferior officers.
Unlike the king, who was himself sponsoring a new abbey on
Thorney island at the time (the famous West Minster), Harold
favoured the installation of secular priests to monks, and there was to
be a college or seminary at Waltham where students could be trained
for the priesthood.[1] The choice of a continental scholar named
Adelhard, of Lüttich, as chancellor, gave rise to yet another mysterious fable. According to Edward's biographer, Adelhard was a
physician who first came to England to treat Harold for some form
of paralysis, perhaps gout, but who, on failing to cure the earl,
recommended the powers of the holy rood at Waltham. The
miraculous cross did the trick and Harold, having founded his
college, put Adelhard in charge of it.

If the same writer can be believed, Harold collected some of the
relics for Waltham during a pilgrimage to Rome. For two centuries,
Englishmen of devotion, both humble and distinguished, had gone
on the long and hazardous trail across the Alps to worship at the
tombs of the apostles. The poor or the penitent travelled austerely,

[1] Waltham was not to become an abbey in the true sense until the reign of Henry II, who
refounded it as an Augustinian monastery.

often barefooted and carrying their entire possessions on their backs, begging hospitality at churches and monasteries en route. Journeying in bands for protection and armed with little more than a clubbed stick, many perished on the way, and more still on the way back. By comparison, the noble and rich were often well equipped, travelling with heavy bodyguards and smoothing their way with gold.[1] All the same, the road was excruciatingly rough and their fate unpredictable, while their very eminence begged the attention of the unscrupulous. Tostig, for instance, whose pilgrimage to Rome is better authenticated than Harold's, appears to have been attacked by bandits in the early stages of his return journey. The main object of the assault seems to have been to take the Earl of Northumbria and hold him to ransom, but this was thwarted, according to the story, by a thegn named Gospatric who quick-wittedly announced himself as the earl. He was carried off by the robbers but released when they learned their mistake. Meanwhile, the rest of the party, including Tostig and a number of English churchmen, had fled back to Rome bereft of all but the clothes on their backs. Here, they were reimbursed from the papal treasury and eventually renewed their journey to England.

At a time when to travel across a single country or state involved risking injury or death from wild animals, desperadoes, professional robbers and the war-parties of feuding nobles, among other hazards, a journey across a continent not only increased such perils immensely but added others, particularly in the form of alien diseases. Moreover, for a man of political responsibility, obvious dangers were created at home by his absence. The whole of Normandy had been thrown into chaos by Robert the Magnificent's insistence on visiting the holy land, and it seems that Malcolm of Scotland took bloody advantage of Tostig's trip to Rome by ravaging and looting Northumberland while its earl was away. Against such a background, the alleged pilgrimage of Harold, England's premier earl and statesman, comes as a dramatic statement of the force of spirituality on mediaeval

[1] Influential men could rid themselves of the austerities of penitence, which included not only going barefoot but forgoing good food, beds and warm water, by inducing others to share their obligations. Thus King Edgar explained how a powerful magnate might write off seven years' penitence by getting 852 men to fast for him for three days on green herbs, bread and water.

politics and a useful warning against analysis based on modern-day materialism. There was, however, another factor.

It will be remembered that Godwin's restoration had led to the election of his friend and accomplice, the careerist bishop Stigand, as Archbishop of Canterbury in place of the Norman archbishop, Robert. This appointment had not received papal blessing and, at the time of Godwin's death, the prelate was still unacknowledged in Rome. Harold thus inherited in Stigand a somewhat mixed blessing. The man was a wily politician and an assiduous promoter of Godwin's house, but his uncanonical status provided an item of propaganda with which enemies might readily taint his connections. It has been suggested, therefore, that the possibility of persuading the pope, in person, to give Stigand his blessing could well have crossed Harold's mind and might, indeed, have weighed heavily in favour of a journey to Rome. As it happened, Stigand actually received the pallium from Rome in 1058 ('In this year Pope Stephen passed away and Benedict was appointed in his place,' it was stated in the *Chronicle*. 'This same year he sent the pallium to Archbishop Stigand'), and it has been speculated that Harold carried the pallium home from Italy himself. If so, it was a wasted effort. Unfortunately for Stigand's cause, Benedict X, as the new pope styled himself, was driven from office after less than a year and his reign pronounced false. Whether it would have been worse not in fact to have received the pallium at all, than to have received it from an anti-pope, remains one of the episode's finer points.

Interestingly enough, when Harold's church at Waltham was consecrated two years later, on 3 May 1060, the day of the 'Invention of the Cross', Stigand was not called to officiate as might have been expected; instead, the hallowing was performed by Cynesige, Archbishop of York. It seems that Harold regarded the profound and mystical ceremony at Waltham beyond the scope of the Archbishop of Canterbury. It must have been a great occasion. Pilgrims from near and far had gathered to see the fabulous holy rood in its new setting and, as they rested on the spring-bright banks of the Lea, or joined the feasting in the streets of Waltham, Harold's personal guests—handsomely accoutred nobles with their ladies, thegns and retinues—rode in from all parts of the land to join them. Among others of distinction, King Edward and Queen Edith were present, but, primarily, it was Harold's day. Henceforth, Waltham Minster, with its bulky stonework and cool shadows, was to be his special sanctuary. Now, done at last with the mason's chisel, it glittered with the gifts of its founder: gorgeous silverware, jewelled tapestries, burnished wall brackets of gilded brass glowing and sparkling in shafts of sunlight or reflecting candle-flames. At key points, shimmering reliquaries of precious metal protected their hallowed and magical contents. Above all rose the famous rood of Waltham, the local relic, raised to fresh eminence by Harold's devotion. Already the fame of the 'Holy Rood' was extensive, and now it was spreading. It was to give the earl's warriors a war-cry that would not only chill the hearts of opponents from the Welsh hills to the banks of Stamford Bridge, but rally their own to the limits of mortal effort in the most momentous battle of early English history.

*

In Normandy, William's struggle to maintain power had reached its climax some years earlier. The capture of the eyrie-like castle at Arques, accompanied by King Henry's humiliation while trying to bring aid to the Count of Talou, had provided the duke with a very short breathing space. The rebel fortress had fallen to him at the end of 1053, probably some time in December, and by the following February he was faced with one of the greatest crises in the history of the duchy. Henry of France was now determined to put Normandy and its upstart duke in their place once for all. According to William of Poitiers, it was the monarch's complaint that this land, granted by a king of France to Rollo the Viking against the express obligation of homage, had become very nearly a kingdom unto itself, a realm whose lord flouted the king's wishes and challenged his personal command. That much the same might have been said of Flanders or Aquitaine, among other vassalages, made the pill no less bitter: none rankled the Parisian king so immediately as this pirate province astride the western lifeline of the Seine, especially since it could be claimed that its ambitious lord owed his survival to Henry in the first place. Nor was fear and envy of the Norman duke lacking elsewhere, and there seems to have been no shortage among the French fiefs of those who contemplated gain in an all-out onslaught on Normandy. On top of this there were many discontented Norman barons, both in exile at the French court and in various parts of Normandy itself, who were in no sense averse to contributing to William's discomfort. Even before Arques had fallen, a number of them had risen in open rebellion, particularly in the south-west where Geoffrey the Hammer had enlisted their support. The Norman town of Moulins was actually handed over to Geoffrey's ally, Guy-William of Aquitaine, by its inhabitants.

Henry's offensive was planned under two commands. One, under the personal banner of the king, with troops drawn broadly from north-western France, was to invade by way of Evreux and fall on that area of Normandy to the west of the Seine. The force included men from such parts as Blois, Sens, Touraine and Anjou and was perhaps accompanied by Geoffrey of Anjou himself. The other command, under Henry's brother, Count Odo of Blois and comprising arms from the north-eastern fiefs, was to invade to the east of the Seine. By a simultaneous advance, Henry intended to crush Normandy in a devastating embrace. Caesar himself, wrote William's panegyrist, might have quailed at the prospect of such an attack; a prospect which caused peaceful men throughout Normandy to tremble for the safety of their families and possessions. Feudal warfare, even less than the wars of most ages, was not waged for the benefit or protection of humble people. To the peasant in the field, disputes among dukes and kings were of little moment; all he asked was to be left in peace to scratch a meagre livelihood from the soil while trying to avoid the worst burdens which might be imposed upon him by his landlord. At the approach of an army, a wise man took his wife and children, his pig and his fowls to the woods and prayed that his hovel would still be intact when the scavengers had passed. Whether it was a foreign army, or native to the country, made no great difference. All armed hosts lived by denuding the land and 'protectors' were often as ruinous as their enemies.

In any case, William could hardly have protected every one of his subjects. For one thing, the summoning of an army took time; for another, it seems reasonable to suppose that his force, at the best, was

outnumbered, and that a direct challenge to pitched battle would
have left Henry with every advantage. Thus, while the two prongs
of the grand assault swept into Normandy leaving terror and
destruction in their wake, the duke took stock of his resources and
waited. In fact, the response to his call-up was heartening. This time
his cause had been espoused not only by veteran loyalists, and knights
whose estates were immediately threatened, but by magnates from
many quarters of the duchy, some by no means sympathetic in the
past. At last the freebooting barons of Normandy seem to have
joined cause as a reasonably cohesive body, their own best interests
identified with those of Duke William. His tactics were wily. No
attack was to be made on either main body of the enemy unless the
occasion was entirely propitious; instead, the Normans would
shadow the invading columns, wherever possible cutting off strag-
glers and foragers. William himself led one group to meet Henry's
advance through the Évreçin, while Odo's incursion east of the Seine
was met by a force under the lords of that area.

It appears that Odo had entered Normandy by way of Beauvais,
sweeping north bent on ravaging the northern frontier-lands.
Hidden among the trees, in a bottom between two hills, the small
township of Mortemer commended itself to the invaders as a
pleasant headquarters from which the surrounding countryside
could systematically be raided and plundered. It seems they anticipated little organised opposition. So far, progress had been impeded
only by such diversions as burning villages, driving in cattle and
murdering or ravishing such sections of the populace as had been too
stubborn, or too slow, to get out of the way. The sport was good and
the risks appeared negligible. All the signs must have pointed to an
excellent campaign. By all accounts Mortemer, with accommoda-
tion for the French lords and shelter for their men, was made the
point of some celebration, wines, foodstuffs and prisoners being
brought into the place by day while the night was given over to the
excesses customary in the circumstances. This was exactly what the
Normans had waited for. Guided by the local lord, Roger of
Mortemer, the businesslike levy from north-eastern Normandy
converged swiftly through the woods and lanes and fell on a dissi-
pated and vulnerable enemy.

No reliable details of the battle have survived, but the tradition was colourfully established by Wace in the epic *Roman de Rou*. The island poet conjured up a vivid image of Mortemer in flames, Frenchmen tumbling bleary-eyed from burning billets to grope in the smoke for horses and bridles while vengeful Normans waited grimly at the exits of the town. Wace postulated a massacre in which the majority of French losses were sustained in attempts to escape the environs of Mortemer itself. However, since all versions gave the battle as strongly contested and lasting the best part of a day, events were probably more complex, if equally dramatic. Without doubt, the initial surprise achieved by the Normans led, eventually, to a complete rout of the French. Odo escaped, but the Norman victory was so decisive that when the news reached Henry beyond the Seine he struck camp and led his army not on towards Rouen but back to Paris and safety. A romantic story popular with most Norman chroniclers told how, when the result of the battle of Mortemer was conveyed to William, he despatched a messenger to announce the tidings in a novel fashion to the French king. Concealing himself, under cover of darkness, by the French camp, this man startled the invaders from their sleep with a grim and stentorian message. Thus Wace: '*Franceiz, Franceiz, levez, levez, Tenez vos veies, trop dormez; Alez vos amis enterrer, Ki sunt occiz à Mortemer.*' At all events, Henry's retreat was hasty and seemingly unhindered by William who had once more avoided a direct conflict with the king.

Three years later, in August 1057, bolstered this time by the certain presence of Geoffrey of Anjou with his men, the King of France marched imperiously upon Norman soil yet again. As before, William mustered his forces, this time near Falaise, and waited. If his tactics during the earlier incursion had suggested a tendency to conserve his own strength at the expense of the country, the invasion of 1057 underlined it more starkly. Indeed, William showed no inclination to risk himself or his knights in any effort to keep Henry's horde from the villages and towns of lower Normandy, not even from his own home province. His policy, it seems, was to let the wolves gorge to the full before lifting a hand.

Thus, while the duke's army held itself ready at Falaise, Henry and Geoffrey marched unopposed to the very rim of the sea, turned inland again to sack Caen, then made to cross the river Dives. The spot chosen for the river crossing was a ford near the village of Varaville, a natural bottleneck approached across flat, marshy land on the west bank, and overlooked by wooded slopes on the east. (There is now a bridge at the spot, but the writers of William's time mentioned only a ford.) Here, William decided, at last, to put in an appearance. Surrounded by his knights, and a levy of armed peasants from the district, he moved swiftly north from Falaise by Bavent and took the French column from the rear in the very process of crossing the river. According to William of Poitiers, he arrived just in time. Henry, Geoffrey and the van of the invading force were already on the far bank; the rear of the French command was still on the near bank, delayed by the incoming tide which rendered the ford impassable. The duke's strategy was consummate. Before him lay the tail of an army, irretrievably cut off from its head, reduced to a rabble by a campaign of unrestricted pillaging, unprepared for opposition and leaderless. For this William had waited. The so-called battle of Varaville resulted, on the word of Norman writers, in so complete a destruction of Henry's rearguard that the king and his Angevin allies forthwith retired from Normandy at top speed.

While there is room to wonder how much comfort the stricken populace of Western Normandy derived from Varaville—the tradition of Varaville as a national triumph was not established until the next century—it certainly added a further flourish to William's military reputation and has been seen as the crowning event in his early struggle for authority. Neither Henry nor Geoffrey invaded Normandy again. In 1060, Henry of France died. and both sides were ready for peace. Amnesty between France and Normandy was finally completed about the time of the king's death, though an improving relationship between the countries was to rest on less flimsy foundations than a formal treaty. As it happened, the new French king, Philip I, son of Henry's Russian wife Anne, and a juvenile at the time of his accession, had been placed by his father under the guardianship of Baldwin of Flanders who, for the time being, became Regent of France. The political utility of William's marriage now became increasingly evident. A father-in-law with such influence at the French court was no small advantage. Furthermore, the year of Henry's death rid William, too, of his most powerful southern rival. The later years of the Count of Anjou had been beset by ill fortune; his campaigns had turned sour and, eventually, disillusioned by the limitations of the sword, Geoffrey the Hammer had entered a monastery to seek the peace he had so persistently denied others. He died, according to Angevin chroniclers, the day after donning monastic habit. Thus William, seventh Duke of Normandy, victor of Val-ès-Dunes, Mortemer, Varaville and interminable sieges, had not only overcome his enemies within the duchy, but had also survived the two main threats to his power from without. Ahead stretched new vistas of opportunity.

★

In particular, the fertile but hitherto dangerous marches of Maine beckoned enticingly on Geoffrey's death. When the Hammer had occupied Le Mans in 1051, William had undertaken to back the exiled grandson of Herbert Wake-Dog, Count Herbert II of Maine, on condition that Maine passed to Normandy should Herbert die childless. In March 1062, Herbert's death brought the Norman duke to the border brandishing his claim. At the same time, a group in Maine had put forward their own candidate for succession in the person of Walter of Mantes, count of the Vexin and husband of Wake-Dog's daughter Biota. Despatching part of the forces at his disposal to create a diversion in the Vexin, William promptly led the rest into Maine and began the systematic destruction of every property and crop in his path. His plan was to take Le Mans, where Walter and Biota were established, intact, with the minimum of bloodshed, and to this end he avoided a direct assault on the capital. Instead he busied himself with the smaller towns and villages, reserving the gem of the province for later.

Doubly desirable both as a military centre and as the mercantile heart of a broad and flourishing province, Le Mans *was* Maine, a glittering symbol of wealth and power beside which all other Cenomannian towns were of small account. Yet the Norman duke also realised how much the well-being of its citizens depended on the surrounding lands and their trade. The key to such a community was not the battering-ram but economic isolation. Denied the sources of their livelihood, it could only be a matter of time before the people of Le Mans forced Walter and Biota to resign their claims or clear out; meanwhile, William continued to lay waste to the country. When, inevitably, the capitulation came (some time in 1065), it seems there was indeed much relief in the city. The Norman chroniclers wrote of the duke's '*joyeuse entrée*', telling enthusiastically how the populace burst forth through the gates, led by priests chanting hymns and swinging censers, to welcome the prince of Normandy as their rightful lord and master. As the crowd parted, subservient and applauding, before the triumphant approach of his knights, William, at last truly the Conqueror, must have gazed down on the flushed necks of the city's churchmen, factors and merchants and allowed himself a cynical smile. If they loved not the Duke of Normandy so much as their own interests, it was a sentiment William, better than most, knew how to reciprocate. Before the end of the year, he had consolidated Le Mans as a Norman stronghold. Walter and Biota, at first placed in custody, died soon afterwards in unknown, but not unsuspicious, circumstances.

8

A Confrontation of the Rivals

During the closing years of Edward the Confessor's reign, possibly in 1064, with Harold and William firmly established as the dominating powers in their respective countries, there occurred one of the most perplexing episodes in the whole story of the impending struggle over England. Its historical importance was to turn upon it being the only peaceful meeting between the earl and the duke to survive on record: its fascination on the fact that, due largely to its detailed treatment in the Bayeux Tapestry, posterity was enabled to follow the sequence of events almost step by step, yet could only guess at the motives. Was the meeting intended or fortuitous? Behind the strange ritual of respect, even comradeship, which surrounded it, was either participant, or were both, engaged in a double game? Had either an inkling of the epoch-shattering collision in store for them? The Saxons left no guide to the episode; the Norman writers were neither impartial nor always consistent. No real evidence was to survive as to whether or not these two men, so exceptional in their own ways and so dramatically fated, had ever met before. It has remained for generations to gaze in wonder at one of the most exciting picture-stories ever created, and to deduce their own theories.

Worked within living memory of the scenes it depicts, the Bayeux Tapestry is 230 feet long, 20 inches wide and includes among other things in its design 626 human figures, 190 horses and mules, 35 dogs, 506 other animals, 37 ships, 33 buildings, plus a verbal key in letters an inch high. While its origin is debatable, it was possibly commissioned by Bishop Odo of Bayeux for display in his cathedral at that town, and designed and worked to his wishes by English artists, perhaps from the school of Canterbury. One uncontestable feature about the Bayeux Tapestry is that it is not, in fact, tapestry but embroidery, being worked in coloured wools on linen. That so fragile an object should have survived almost intact down the centuries seems an almost incredible blessing to art and history. After coming within an ace of destruction in the French Revolution, careful steps were taken to preserve it during the threatened Prussian invasion of Normandy, 1870, and during the two world wars of this century. The Nazis demanded to inspect it on several occasions during their preparations for an invasion of England in 1940. Unfortunately the early stages of its narrative, dealing with Harold's meeting with William, can be checked only against Norman sources since the *Anglo-Saxon Chronicle* makes no mention of this episode.

As far as the designer of the Bayeux Tapestry was concerned, the tale began with Harold taking leave of the bearded Edward, presumably at the royal palace at Westminster, whence the tall figure of the earl, with flowing hair and mantle, rode to Bosham to embark on his mysterious adventure. Harold was depicted travelling in the style of a rich nobleman, mounted on a handsome stallion and with a hawk on his wrist, while his dogs ran ahead and his retainers brought up the rear. Beside the quiet creek at Bosham, once the scene of his brother Sweyn's treachery to Beorn, he was shown calling at the church to pray for the success of his voyage, and feasting at the family manor, then, with hawk and hounds stowed safely aboard, setting sail for a destination which, despite his eventual arrival in Normandy, is now unknown. On the reason for the journey, the artist was silent. According to Norman writers, Harold was carrying confirmation to William of King Edward's alleged promise that the Norman duke should succeed to the English throne. Another account concerned hostages supposedly exchanged by Godwin and Edward at the time of their reconciliation. Edward was purported to have sent Godwin's hostages, Harold's young brother Wulfnoth and a nephew, Hakon, to Normandy for safe keeping, and it was suggested that Harold was now bent on arranging their return. Yet the story of the hostages is not confirmed by any Saxon account of Godwin's eventual triumph over Edward. And, even if Harold's attitude to Normandy represented a mellowing of his father's antipathy, many historians have found it hard to believe that, with so much to lose, he would have placed himself, voluntarily, in William's hands.

Instead, they have preferred to assume an intended voyage to some other place, maybe no more than a fishing expedition, from which he was inadvertently cast on the French coast. The idea of a storm, or the sort of high wind which would have rendered an eleventh-century ship unnavigable, seems to be borne out by the fact that almost all accounts, including the tapestry, placed Harold's landfall not in Normandy itself but to the north-east, on the coast of Ponthieu.[1] By local customary law, the contents and survivors of all wrecked ships automatically became the right of the ruling lord in the land, and Harold's eminence and consequent value at ransom would soon have been recognised and notified to Count Guy.

From this point, the tapestry consigned the earl, spurless and with a now somewhat dejected-looking hawk on his wrist, under mounted escort to Guy of Ponthieu's castle a short distance inland. William of Malmesbury asserted that Harold was held here in fetters, but, if so, it was not in all probability for long, for news of the wreck had also reached William in Normandy who acted, it seems, with characteristic speed and vigour. The chance to bring the Earl of Wessex into his camp in circumstances which would make the Norman at once benefactor and 'protector' must have struck William as an infinite blessing. His generosity was ostentatious. Though Guy was ill-placed to resist his formidable neighbour and liege-lord's demands, it appears that William paid handsomely for Harold in money and land, every sou and vergée adding to the Englishman's obligation.

Guy handed Harold over at Eu, and it was at this stage that the creator of the tapestry confronted Norman with Saxon for the first time in his narrative. While Guy, depicted astride a sleek and elaborately-saddled mule, did the honours, the two warrior-magnates were shown facing each other, eye to eye, stiff-backed and inscrutable on their chargers. It would be hard to miss the drama implicit in the simple stitchwork outline. Both men were of an age, in their prime, powerful, active and hardy. In William, Harold faced one who could be described by a monkish contemporary as 'great in

---

[1] This would not be inconsistent with a storm en route for Flanders, a more likely destination, in the opinion of some historians, than Normandy.

body and strong, tall in stature but not ungainly. . . . In speech he was fluent and persuasive, being skilled at all times in making known his will. His voice was harsh, but what he said always fitted the occasion' (Monk of Caen). Here was a man who conceived his schemes daringly and executed them dynamically, who 'never allowed himself to be deterred from the prosecution of an enterprise by the labour entailed' and who was 'undaunted by danger' (*ibid.*); a man so committed by his own nature to the pursuit of power that another contemporary could write, 'he was too relentless to care though all might hate him' (*ASC*), and of whom it was bewailed, 'Alas! that any man should bear himself so proudly and deem himself exhalted above all other men!' (*ibid*). In William could be seen perhaps a caricature of the paradoxical elements in all men; brutal, ruthless and sanguinary when it suited his own ends, yet so addicted to order and temperance that his subjects marvelled at the lawfulness he established: a man who dealt with murderers, where he found them, as severely as Rollo had, who punished rapists by the simple expedient of castration and who blinded those who dared kill his deer and hares. William of Normandy was much hated, not infrequently admired but seldom loved. In short, he was dangerous; and not least of all, in the present circumstances, for his ability (again noted by the Monk of Caen) to 'appraise the true significance of events' and to take advantage of 'the fickle promises of fortune'.

In Harold, the duke was faced with a fundamentally different proposition. Where William verged on the neurotic, the English earl was as firmly balanced, it would seem, as any man of his time. Unlike the Norman, he had been neither terrorised in childhood nor forced to fight, at any stage, for his virtual existence. Brought up in as much security as the times allowed, his early privileges unchallenged, Harold could afford a more patient and tolerant view of life. To Godwin's political astuteness and flexibility, he added a degree of forethought and sensitivity which sometimes made the most self-interested of moves seem akin to philanthropy. Edward the Confessor's biographer, who was perhaps all the more reliable in the matter for seeming closer to Tostig than Harold, portrayed the latter as a great warrior and leader, capable of sustaining his men through the most testing of campaigns and battles, a civil ruler of much knowledge and wisdom. As far as history allows judgement, Harold was to emerge as a man seldom motivated by vengeance; a man capable of seeing more than one side to a question, shrewdly aware of the advantages of compromise; a man whose actions not infrequently suggested that the gaining of a friend was worth more than the defeat of an enemy. It is tempting to take as Harold's text the verse from Proverbs, 'He that is slow to anger is better than the mighty . . .', yet if so it was the text not of an altruistic but of a practical man. While Harold's methods and motives varied from William's, it would be unwise to regard him as less ambitious or determined. Beneath tolerance often lies rock-hard stubbornness. Those who understand the other point of view can deploy their own the better. Harold was by no means contemptuous of might.

In Harold, then, William had a potential rival at a disadvantage, but one it would have been very foolish to underestimate. Superficially, there was much they could share in common. The Earl of Wessex was no stranger to Norman culture and language, for these prevailed at Edward's court, and the two men had a topic of mutual interest and respect in their military achievements. A great charmer when it suited him, William could tempt the Englishman with prospects of superb hunting, a fine range of entertainers and lavish hospitality which, though he was relatively abstemious himself, would have done full justice to the Saxon taste for good liquor. William's efforts to bring the English duke, as the tapestry designated Harold, under his influence, were nothing if not comprehensive. The earl was subjected not only to the blandishments of William but to the charm of the Duchess Matilda and her children, especially the child Agatha who appears to have been held out as a potential wife for Harold.[1]

Earl Harold's reaction is as much a mystery as the rest of the adventure. No doubt his safest course was a prompt return to England, but, matters of courtesy apart, was he free to leave had he wished to do so? In all probability, such a course would have been tricky indeed. Life as William's guest might have been considerably

[1] This would possibly place the visit before Harold's marriage to Gruffyd's widow, Ealdgyth, the year of which is uncertain. A romantic tradition, based on Orderic, that the duke's daughter fell so heavily for Harold that she later refused to marry another is hardly compatible with the fact that she can have been no more than a child at the time.

more gratifying than life as Guy of Ponthieu's prisoner, but it was life, after all, on William's terms. 'His fetters were gilded,' Edward Freeman wrote of the earl's dilemma, 'but he was still in fetters.' Surely, it needed less than Harold's intelligence and caution to prompt discretion, for the duke's temper when thwarted cannot have been a secret, and accidents were so very easily arranged. From now on, William's exploitation of his advantage was masterly. For some time Normandy had been troubled by the hostile activities of her Breton neighbours and, in particular, one Count Conan, son of Alan of Brittany. In Conan lay a potential hindrance to a future Norman move towards England, and already the duke had succeeded in whipping up resistance to the man among certain Breton chiefs on the border. When one of the rebels, Riwallon of Dol, now appealed for help against the counter-measures of Conan, William readily invaded Brittany, taking Harold with him.

Harold's participation in this rather obscure Norman campaign was coloured with a picturesque irony. In Norman eyes, the Bretons appeared as unruly and barbarous a race as the Welsh appeared to Harold and his English contemporaries. William of Poitiers depicted Brittany with a shudder, as populated by a polygamous, fast-breeding people with altogether unholy propensities. They had, he declared, little aptitude for arable farming, living instead off cattle and the proceeds of plunder. Approached perhaps as a vaunted opponent of the Welsh, the Earl of Wessex was induced to accompany William against these distant kinsmen of the ancient Britons, rather as he might have been invited to a hunt. For all their alleged barbarity, it seems that the Bretons, through their prince and leader Conan, had had the civility to inform William of the time at which they intended to commence hostilities. With finer sophistication, William resolved to strike first.

It was autumn as Harold and the duke rode side by side beneath the sea-girt hulk of Mont St Michel to surprise Conan and his men at Dol. In the image of the tapestry, William travelled light in a quilted tunic wielding a cosh-like mace while Harold, bareheaded, carried a spear. Behind, on horses with flowing manes, came heavily-armed knights in hauberks and conical helmets; others, in full-length tunics, shouldered long, kite-shaped shields, some carrying lances with pennants. Conan did not stand to face the Norman barons at Dol. Abandoning his siege of the truculent Riwallon, he retired with his force towards Rennes, leaving William's men the pick of the land. Before long, the people of Dol were begging their Norman saviour to remove his forces before they did more damage than Conan. Little good, however, it served them. When the duke complied, Conan returned to take revenge on the Breton rebels and Riwallon was lucky to escape into exile.

William's plan to disrupt and weaken Brittany was soon in full swing. With Harold still soldiering beside him, he pushed on relentlessly, raiding deeper into Conan's province. At the hill-top stronghold of Dinan, the defence was more vigorous than elsewhere and, when direct assault had been abandoned, William employed his unrivalled knowledge of siege warfare. Beating back several Breton sorties, the Normans swarmed forward with torches of flaming pinewood and fire-baskets glowing with tinder and pitch to burn the defenders out. At least part of the town's defences were of wood (the Bayeux Tapestry suggested a timber palisade), and with the outer wall fired it needed only a stiff breeze to ignite the more combustible dwellings inside. The smoke must have given the rocky heights above the Rance a volcanic appearance. Like vultures awaiting the fugitive creatures of a forest fire, the Normans swooped for the kill. In the tapestry, the ultimate surrender of Dinan was symbolised by the handing over of keys on the tip of a lance.

It is not possible to know how many expeditions were involved in the Breton campaign, nor the exact extent of Harold's role, though Norman propagandists conceived it as a prominent one. Perhaps it was no small part of William's shrewdness to realise that while the Earl of Wessex accompanied him much in the spirit of an honoured guest, it would not be hard to confuse such a guest-role in the feudal mind with an act of vassalage. The effect was not diminished by portraying the Englishman as a hero. While crossing the estuary between Normandy and Brittany, part of William's force had got into difficulty in the water. The tapestry made a significant point of the episode. Soldiers wading into the current with shields held high above their heads were in danger of being swept away, horses fell, riders were dragged under. At this point, Harold, by prompt action, gained a brave reputation. Plunging into the water, it seems that he saved several Normans by hauling them to dry land. In the tapestry he was shown actually carrying one man on his back. His feat was heightened by the presence of quicksands. For this, and possibly other acts of heroism, Harold was now invested by William as a knight. Again, there was an element of ambiguity. The investiture could be presented as an honour to the Englishman; to others as a sign that the earl was the duke's man. At last, the Breton war concluded, William and Harold returned to the duchy to celebrate their achievements and to perpetrate the final, and perhaps most significant act in the whole puzzle of their short but memorable fellowship.

For a graphic representation of what followed, history turns once more to the tapestry. The ceremony in which Harold swore a sacred, and now famous, oath to the duke, was one of the key scenes in the work, and one the craftsmen depicted with most care and beauty. It appears to have been set in the open, William, majestically seated on a claw-footed throne, watching the earl perform the appropriate rites. Harold, portrayed with bowed head and reverent expression, was placed, in flowing cape, between two shrines or coffers, his arms extended to touch each at the same time. Both were raised on draped stands, one in the shape of a conventional reliquary; the other, a portable model, shown with handles not unlike those of a sedan chair. They contained, it appears, some of the most potent relics in the land, maybe including portions of Rasyphus and Ravennus, British saints who were martyred in France. Later traditions to the effect that Harold swore under duress (this based on Eadmer), or that he was tricked into taking an oath on concealed relics (the authority for this was Wace), had no foundation in the earlier chroniclers, who admittedly varied in their own accounts. Orderic placed the ceremony at Rouen, William of Poitiers at Bonneville-sur-Touques while the tapestry based it firmly at Bayeux. More important was their variation on the nature of the oath itself. According to most accounts, Harold undertook to marry one of William's daughters, some added that he promised a sister of his own in marriage to some Norman noble, others that he swore complete fealty as William's vassal. But on the most vital issue of all, few left any room to doubt that Harold understood William's intention to press his claim as Edward's heir and at least undertook not to stand in his way. William of Poitiers was quite positive, asserting Harold's promise to accept the duke, on Edward's death, as king of England, and meanwhile to further William's interests in that country, even to the point of maintaining garrisons in favour of the Norman at Dover and elsewhere in the island.

Whatever the precise nature of the oath, or, for that matter, of any of the events suggested in the parable of the Bayeux Tapestry, the effectiveness of the episode as Norman propaganda can hardly be doubted. In due course, the listening posts of the Continent would receive the news that the most powerful man in England had enjoyed the intimate hospitality of the Duke of Normandy, had distinguished himself in war beneath the Norman banner, had accepted arms from his host and confirmed his support in a form of pledge which all Christendom regarded as sacrosanct. In a few short months William had turned one of the most considerable stumbling blocks to his ambition into an instrument for its furtherance. It is impossible, however, to believe that Harold acted in all this as a dupe. On the contrary, even his admitted share of the game was by no means paltry and he may well have reserved one or two tricks up his sleeve. No peaceful Norman accession to England could be accomplished without the co-operation of the Earl of Wessex, and William must have been willing to pay expensively for this. The rewards mentioned included honours, grants, the highest position in William's favour and even a fifty per cent cut in the kingdom. At this rate, Harold's status might have seemed secured while the Duke of Normandy took the risks and responsibilities of the crown. It was the sort of arrangement greatly favoured in the past by the house of Godwin and it must still have seemed a good one, though William could hardly have been expected to prove as amenable as Edward. Perhaps, above all, it offered one advantage big enough even to transcend considerations of personal or family benefit. As the virtual marshal of England's defence, Harold's greatest danger lay not in the south but the north-west. Harold's England had inherited no tradition of invasion from France; for generation upon generation its enemies had descended from Scandinavia and the fortunes of Harald Hardrada

had increased the ever-nagging Viking threat. Under such circumstances, some sort of partnership, some alignment of interests with
William, was not altogether inconsistent with security. It could even
have been envisaged as a form of deterrent.

That the Earl of Wessex would not lightly have sworn an oath on
sacred relics seems as certain to most historians as anything is certain
in this highly problematical episode. To the patron of Waltham and
the devotee of the holy rood, all Normandy in arms was less formidable than the untold furies of supernatural vengeance. At the same
time, the phrasing of an oath, like the wording of a latter-day legal
document, was important, and it is not inconceivable that Harold's
undertaking to William, whatever it represented, might have contained some ambiguity which the earl could fall back on as a let-out.
Again, time, in an age when death struck mysteriously and savagely,
could provide its own release. Edward the Confessor, despite his
advanced age, apparently enjoyed good health when Harold left
England. He could well have been expected to reign another decade.
Duke William, on the other hand, might ever have died suddenly
and violently. All considered, Earl Harold appears to have played his
hand cautiously, even wisely. Starting out a prisoner, he had escaped
with life, limb, land and wealth intact, having had his ransom paid
for him; he had gained a first-hand introduction to Norman military
tactics and resources from the duke himself, and he had psychologically, perhaps even effectively, strengthened his defences against the
north. At the worst, he had taken an oath which guaranteed him
status and dominion should the greatest prize in England eventually
go to another; at the best, he had tricked his Norman rival.

One way or another, he must have been glad to see the shores of
Wessex once more. The creators of the Bayeux Tapestry caught the
mood of homecoming touchingly, the crew of the shield-lined long-
boat standing to the sail, the earl peering intently landward where
eager faces were displayed in the windows and on the balcony of a
fine Saxon hall. Cloaked and astride a suitably virile stallion, the son
of Godwin proceeded to London, accompanied by an escort of
mounted spearmen, where he was ushered by the palace housecarles
into King Edward's presence. Anxious to hear the earl's news, the
veteran monarch, magnificently robed and wearing the crown of

state, received the traveller from a long, couch-like throne ornamented with wolves' heads. And here the first episode of the tapestry story ended, as it began, with a tantalisingly dumb charade. On the face of an eloquently gesticulating Harold Godwinson, the embroiderers stitched the bare trace of a smile.

9

The Death of the Confessor

The Oxford of Harold's day, a busy rural and river-trading centre on the Mercia-Wessex border, loosely scattered amidst tall trees and water meadows on a stony terrace between the upper Thames and its offshoot, the Cherwell, was a relatively youthful township. The Romans had ignored the site, and, despite traces of early Saxon inhabitation nearby, there is no evidence of a town there before the ninth century. Of several colourful legends to grow around the embryonic stage of the city, one at least contained a germ of historical fact. It concerned a girl named Frideswide, the daughter of a local chief, and her unwanted suitor Algar, a fellow of some substance, it seems, from Leicester. One balmy day, as the geese and ganders dunked amorously in the Cherwell and oxen nudged each other flirtatiously in the ford,[1] Algar, hot and fidgety with impatience, puffed into sight to claim his beloved. Frideswide, warned of his approach, hitched up her shift and ran. At last, unable to throw off her impassioned admirer, she darted into a pigsty to hide. According to the story, as Algar drew abreast of the hiding place he was stricken, suddenly and miraculously, with blindness; though it might be imagined, in the circumstances, that the diminution of his ardour would have related more to his nose than his eyes. In gratitude for her escape, Frideswide, having prayed for the restoration of Algar's sight, founded a nunnery wherein she lived, died and was hallowed as a virgin saint.

Whatever the demerits of this fascinating story, St Frideswide was more than a myth. The remains of the saint were to linger among the most sacred possessions of the church later raised on the founda-

---

[1] The city arms show oxen crossing a ford, hence Oxford, while Gosford, on the Cherwell, suggests a shallower crossing place for geese.

tion she was said to have started (now Christ Church cathedral), and doubtless the shrine was a potent influence in early Oxford. Nevertheless, for a good while the town was of lesser ecclesiastical importance than nearby Abingdon (not to mention Dorchester) whose abbey exacted tolls on boats travelling between Oxford and the downstream ports. On the other hand, its military importance as a frontier town between Saxon and Danelaw England was considerable, and in at least four attacks during the reign of Ethelred its wooden buildings were put to fire. In the infamous massacre of St Bricius's Day, ordered by Ethelred, St Frideswide's minster was burnt to dislodge the Danes who had taken refuge there. From such anguish, however, Oxford survived to become, by the same token of its location, the venue of some of the most important political gatherings in eleventh-century England. At an historical concourse in Oxford, Canute had proclaimed his intention to bring all England together under one law; at Oxford a divided witan had debated the matter of succession following Canute's death; at Oxford Harefoot had been crowned, and had died. And now to Oxford in the autumn of 1065 rode Harold Godwinson to face the most explosive convention since his accession to the earldom of Wessex.

Old wounds had been festering for some time in the far north, where Tostig's appointment had never been popular. The establishment of a son of Godwin as Earl of Northumbria could hardly have proceeded without difficulties, especially since heirs survived from the two great local families, the houses of Siward and his predecessor, Eadwulf, but such difficulties might well have proved surmountable given a wise and dedicated ruler. Tostig did not match up to the need. Despite a certain reputation for piety, and more obvious talents as a soldier and courtier, he was a harsh and uncompromising man, intemperate as a governor, merciless as a collector of taxes and too frequently absent when proper leadership was needed. When his greatest efforts were demanded in the north, he was away hunting, or otherwise socialising at Edward's court where, it seems, he was a greater favourite with the king and Queen Edith than his brother, Harold. Edward's biographer, who was also Tostig's apologist, claimed that the earl's detractors in Northumbria were offenders carping against his firm justice. Just how far such justice degenerated into tyranny must be judged by the charges levelled against him. The *Anglo-Saxon Chronicle* said that the men of his earldom were 'unanimous in repudiating him' because his law was unfair, because he deprived those who could not defend themselves of land and life, and because he 'robbed God'. A slightly later authority, Florence of Worcester, added the charge of intolerable taxation, and reported more specific accusations. If they were true, Tostig shared much the same weaknesses as his late brother Sweyn. 'In his own chamber in York he slew by treachery Gamel, son of Orm, and Ulf, son of Dolfin, who had come to him under sworn safe-conduct.' Orm and Dolphin appeared as landowners in Domesday. Presumably their families had proved troublesome to Tostig, who perhaps considered them too strong to tackle in the open. He was also accused of procuring the murder of a thegn named Gospatric, son of one Arkell, while the former was a visitor at the king's court; a crime committed, if Florence's sources were accurate, with the connivance of the queen herself.

Shortly after Michaelmas 1065, Yorkshire and Northumberland had risen in open insurrection against Tostig, who was away hunting with the king in the south. At a tumultuous assembly in York, two hundred thegns from all over the earldom, headed by three influential landowners, Dunstan, Gamelbeorn and Glunieorn,[1] enthusiastically declared Tostig an outlaw, electing in his place Morcar, grandson of Leofric and younger son of Aelfgar, thus drawing to their cause Edwin, Earl of Mercia, his brother. Though their action was hardly constitutional, it is easy to understand their reluctance to appeal to a king who thought the sun shone from Tostig, and who, in any case, had never set foot in Yorkshire or Northumberland in his life.[2] Intoxicated by their own audacity, the rebels broke into the earl's palace, filling their pouches with his gold and silver, arming themselves with his weapons and slaughtering as many of his followers as could not get away. Two Danish officers of his houseguard, Amund and Reavenswart, were among those captured while attempting to

---

[1] The names suggest both English and Danish blood among the leaders.
[2] There is no record of Edward the Confessor travelling further north than Gloucester throughout his reign.

flee the city and put to death beyond its walls. Still in the full flush of exuberance, and determined to oust Tostig not only from Northumbria but from England, the insurgents turned south, enlisting Lincoln, Nottingham and Derby to their colours. For Morcar, now at the head of an unwieldy but cock-a-hoop host, it was important to extract sanction of his irregular appointment from Edward before the emotional impetus of the movement faded and the tide began to subside. He pressed on rapidly, therefore, to Northampton, in which region he was joined by his brother Edwin with Mercian reinforcements and a force of Welsh auxiliaries.

Hereabouts, too, he was met by a greater lord, Harold of Wessex, With 'half England in confusion' (Edward Freeman), it appears that the king was cursing its infidelity from his pleasure grounds in Wiltshire, while Tostig, at least the catalyst if not the entire cause of the trouble, was at his side prompting his maledictions. It was left to Harold to face the problem objectively, to probe possibilities, to try to smooth ruffled tempers. Accordingly, he rode to meet the northerners not at the head of a challenging army, with threats and abuses, but alone with intent to bring crown and rebels to negotiation. One aspect of the crisis at least was made clear at this preliminary meeting. The Northumbrians had no argument with the king. If Tostig were banished and Morcar's election confirmed, they would return happily and loyally to their homes. If Tostig were forced on them, however, the king would know their enmity. They had no intention of compromising. It was a straight ultimatum. From Harold's point of view, the family loss of Northumbria to Morcar could be anticipated only as a considerable snag to his ambitions. With the two vast northern earldoms in their grasp, the combined power of Aelfgar's sons would almost equal his own. Yet the alternative, a clash of armed strength between north and south, held gloomier prospects. If a large enough army could be raised in the south to face both a winter campaign and a popular insurrection (a combination calculated to induce lethargy in all but the most belligerent), if that army could then be brought to battle with another army of Englishmen (and the abortive marching and counter-marching of 1051 was a very poor precedent), moreover, *if* the southern command won (which was not a foregone conclusion), then the balance of charges could still prove disastrous. Towns, villages, cattle and provisions over wide areas of country would be destroyed in the war (the rebels were already laying waste to the countryside around Northampton), and the defences of north and south reduced by mutual annihilation. Not only would England be wide open to invasion; the goodwill of Edwin and Morcar would be hopelessly alienated and anything resembling a united kingdom based on tolerance and common advantage would be gone once more.

Everything that was prudent in Harold's nature must have warned him against such a course, even at the expense of sacrificing his brother, and giving ground to his rivals. It would not be the first time Harold had scored in the long run by giving ground graciously, and it seems reasonable to believe that he held Tostig greatly to blame for the whole affair in any case. He was too much of a statesman to emulate his father's calamitous adherence to Sweyn by backing a relative regardless of reason and cause. Having failed to reconcile the two interests, therefore, the Earl of Wessex returned to report his findings to the king. Faced with the rebel ultimatum, Edward could procrastinate no longer. Leaving his hunting, he called a meeting of his immediate counsellors at his lodge at Britford, near Salisbury, to debate the crisis. A detailed account of this witenagemot put on record by the king's biographer, though uncorroborated by contemporary chroniclers, suggests a scene of heated recriminations and passions. Tostig, openly accused by some speakers of tyranny and avarice, allegedly hit back by charging Harold with the instigation of the rebellion on the grounds that the Earl of Wessex was jealous of his (Tostig's) influence at court. Perhaps Tostig had expected his brother's support willy-nilly and was provoked by Harold's impersonal attitude into wild accusations; perhaps Harold's level and calculating approach seemed sufficiently bloodless in the stormy give and take of the moment to warrant a malevolent explanation. There is no evidence of earlier animosity between the two men, who had co-operated in the recent Welsh campaign with notable success, while, on the score of relative influence in the kingdom, jealousy might have dwelt more aptly in Tostig than Harold. At all events, Harold seems to have dispelled the charge by denying it on oath, whereupon the assembly, doubtless strong in Harold's supporters, turned to the more urgent problem of how to handle the rebels.

According to Edward's biographer, the king, shocked by the inescapable fact that events were not conforming to his own notions of divine order, lapsed into a state of violent irascibility that cannot have been improved by the realisation of his virtual impotence. Bursting to wreak vengeance on those who defied his favourite, he cast about for his general, his captains and his army. But Edward had relied too long on the strong shoulders of Harold, and now they showed no response to his wrath. The king might fume and call upon heaven to punish his unrighteous subjects, Tostig might protest and urge him to action, but, when it came down to actuality, they both depended on the one man with the influence to implement their politics, and that man went his own sweet way. Such was the tradition, and if Harold's ultimate treaty with the rebels, who had now moved into Oxfordshire, was formally backed by full royal authority, Edward had no option but to accede to the witan. Harold rode to Oxford with what amounted to Edward's blank cheque.

Here, in the town that had grown so much in importance since the days of Algar and the reluctant Frideswide, the centre of many a discussion between north and south, the Saxon earl called a great conference to witness the settlement and reconciliation. In fact, the rebels were to get their demands, but Harold was too shrewd a stage-manager to leave it at that. The whole country should know of his 'magnanimity'. When the fighting prospects were poor, the time was ripe to advance as a great peacemaker. On the appointed day, 27 October, the Festival of St Simon and St Jude, the concourse at Oxford found itself not merely witnessing the confirmation of Morcar's election and Tostig's outlawry, but standing-in on what suddenly looked less like a regal capitulation, the legalisation of a massive smash-and-grab raid, than the birth of a bright new epoch. Forty-seven years earlier, the mighty Canute had called the warrior lords together at Oxford to reconcile north and south, Dane and Saxon, under the peaceful laws of Edgar. The north, in particular, looked back on Canute as a hero. To all England, his shade towered as a sort of father-figure, stern, wise and patronising, of the past. It cannot have been without solemnity and some real sense of achievement that the witenagemot of Oxford, the Earl of Wessex presiding, 're-enacted there the laws of Canute' (*ASC*).

Tostig had no option but to quit the country. Sorrow mingling with bitterness, he and his wife, Judith, made their farewells of the royal couple and, accompanied by their children and some supporters, set sail for the shores of Flanders where Baldwin once more gave his son-in-law shelter. Harold's thoughts on his brother's departure are anyone's guess, but perhaps, since Tostig's inadequacy had torn a great hole in the otherwise unassailable position of the family, necessitating the complete rethinking of a decade's painstakingly laid plans, the Earl of Wessex was not loath to see him go. Edward, on the other hand, was grievously upset. His biographer affirmed his sorrow on the occasion, and this seems to have worsened to a state of morbidity as the full shock of his own incapacity took effect. The whole affair, from the York rising to Tostig's exit, was over in a month. Though Edward was now in his sixties, there was no suggestion that he was unfit before he received news of the rebellion. He left the last sparks of his fitful vigour on the Wiltshire chases, returning to London a chronically depressed man.

*

'King Edward came to Westminster towards Christmas and there caused the minster to be hallowed which he himself had built to the glory of God and St Peter and all God's saints, and the hallowing of this church was on Childmass day. . . .' (*ASC*). But the king was too ill to attend the consecration. Although the date, 28 December 1065, had been brought forward in the knowledge of his failing health, the event he had dreamed of for years finally eluded him. Edward had become attached in a special sense to Westminster through his reverence for the Apostle Peter who, in turn, had legendary connections with the Thames-side foundation. Tradition had it that when Saberht, the first Christian king of the East Saxons, had founded the church in honour of St Peter, the bishop Mellitus refrained from consecrating it on an intuitive warning that the saint had already hallowed it in his own honour. By the middle of the tenth century, the lands of Westminster seem to have extended west from the river Fleet (itself the western boundary of London city) to a line running roughly north from the Thames to the present site of Marble Arch. The church of St Peter, commonly known as the West Minster in relation to St Paul's, the East Minster, stood on Thorney or Bramble Island, an area of dry ground somewhat less than a mile in circumference flanked on one aspect by the Thames and the others by the marshlands of the Tyburn delta. Though at least one king, Harold Harefoot, and a prelate, Abbot Wulfnoth, had been buried here in the past, the foundation appears to have been less fashionable for a long time than its rival within the walls of the city. Edward the Confessor conceived it his duty and special interest to turn the poor relation of St Paul's into something altogether more splendid: the temple for his own sepulchre and, thereafter, the sacred crowning and burial place of his successors.

In 1050 work had started on a new church of St Peter, designed on the latest Continental pattern and probably a good deal larger than any church yet standing in England; certainly more pretentious in most respects than Harold's edifice at Waltham. Edward's Westminster Abbey was planned on a cruciform basis, with a long nave to the west and its main tower, topped by a wooden cupola, above the junction of the western limb and the north and south transepts. Two lesser towers completed the building to the west, while the short eastern limb contained the high altar. The site chosen was conveniently close to the royal palace at Westminster (itself allegedly founded by Edward though there was already a palace thereabouts in Canute's time) and handy for London, yet sufficiently detached from the hubbub and turmoil of the city for the purposes of dignity and meditation. Rising gradually amidst the river haze and marshy vapours, the hulk of the great church and its surrounding buildings were already a familiar sight. It is a measure of the ambitiousness of the project that by 1065, fifteen years after it was started, Edward's tribute to St Peter in Westminster, which had lacked neither funds nor enthusiasm, was still undergoing construction.[1]

[1] Though the shrine of Edward the Confessor remains at Westminster Abbey, little of his building stays with it. Henry III commenced rebuilding the church in 1245, and alterations have continued, with intermissions, into modern times. Westminster Palace, also altered and extended by subsequent monarchs, was used as a royal residence until its damage by fire in the sixteenth century, and gradually developed as the venue for meetings of Parliament.

No doubt the work was rushed forward with great urgency as the king's health failed dramatically towards Christmas, and it may be that the church eventually was consecrated before its absolute completion. If so, these expedients served at least one of Edward's purposes. The object of so much of his life's concern was to be ready, in the nick of time, for his funeral. The Christmas witenagemot, by precedent set at Gloucester, was this year called to Westminster for the long-awaited hallowing of St Peter's. If the lords and prelates of the assembly had not already realised the full import of the meeting, the king's absence from the ceremony on 28 December can have left them in little doubt. Edward the Confessor was dying.

The portentousness of the moment was not lost to the propagators of legend. Within a generation, the climactic events of 1066 were to be rationalised in the bizarre context of Edward's death-bed hallucinations. According to the king's biographer, the dying man prophesied the impending doom of the realm. Two saintly monks, appearing to Edward in a vision, had informed him that for a year and a day following his death England would be chastised at God's wish by fire and sword because of the wickedness of its people. When he had replied that he would warn his subjects to repent, he was told not to waste his time. The English would not repent, nor would God show them mercy. Edward's magic powers of prophecy became the subject of a number of fables. One other, contrasting with this somewhat slanderous piece of hindsight by its charity and charm, was appropriate, it is nice to think, to this stage of the story. It told how, when the king was attending a dedication of the church of St John at Clavering, Essex, a beggar had asked alms of him in the name of the patron saint. Having no money to hand, Edward offered the man a valuable ring off his finger. Shortly afterwards, so ran the legend, the apostle John revealed himself to two English pilgrims in the Holy Land, giving them the ring to return to their sovereign with a promise: thanks to his good and holy life, within six months the king should join St John in Paradise.

New Year, 1066, found Edward very close to his final destination. For seven days following the consecration of St Peter's he lay in Westminster Palace growing weaker and weaker, and on the eighth day, 5 January, he died. The traditional account of the king's last hours is based on the contemporary *Life*, the relevant passages of which, if not largely imaginary, must have been based in turn on the evidence of one or another of a small clique of highly interested individuals. Among those mentioned as keeping vigil at the death bed were Harold, Archbishop Stigand, Queen Edith, who was portrayed in a state of abject grief, and a high official of Edward's household, a man of Breton birth, Robert son of Wimarc. A few of the king's chosen friends were called to his chamber to bid him farewell, but the writer did not name them. He did assert, however, that in one of his last moments of clarity, Edward raised a feeble hand towards Earl Harold and commended to his care the queen, the royal household and, particularly, the Norman and French elements in the court circle. Whether this was meant to imply the king's approval of Harold as a successor, or whether it harboured nothing less obvious than the fact that the Earl of Wessex was the most powerful man available at the time, is not clear. A rather doubtful testimony in the *Anglo-Saxon Chronicle* (it described Edward as 'noble in armour', the 'protector' of his realm, and claimed that in all times Harold had faithfully obeyed him in word and deed) averred that 'the wise king committed his kingdom' to Harold. But it is possible that the chroniclers were swayed by subsequent events. In any case, the king's designation of a successor was not final, as Edward, of all people, must well have known. It was the duty of the witan to decide his successor, and, with good warning of the looming crisis, in all probability it had already done so.

It was Thursday, the eve of Epiphany, when the reign of Edward the Confessor, son of Ethelred and Emma, the reputed descendant of Woden and last king of the house of Cerdic, came to a hushed end. The biographer, describing him at rest, likened his cheeks to the rose and his beard to the lily. Edward the Simple, as William of Malmesbury preferred to call this strangely uninspiring sovereign, was on his way to sainthood. Before long, a miracle-avid public would be seeking cures at his tomb; meanwhile it seems to have pleased those around him to bury him with the customary alacrity of the times. With little further ado, the earth was opened before the altar of St Peter in the new temple on Thorney Island, and orders given for the funeral. For one night the king's body, washed and dressed in full regalia, lay at the palace, then next morning, Friday the 6th, it was borne in state to the abbey accompanied by the same earls and thegns, prelates and priests, abbots, monks and bell-boys who had so recently attended the church's consecration.

★

Harold Godwinson's moment had arrived. He required no poll of opinion that day to assure him the crown was his for the taking. Coming away from the funeral service, the eminent men of the witan, who would next assemble and formally declare their choice of the new king, no doubt watched the partisan southern crowd hailing its strong earl, noticed the loyalty of the soldiers on duty to the hero of the Welsh wars, and wondered what chance any proposal other than a prompt acknowledgement of Harold's candidature would stand in the present circumstances. The lords of Wessex, they knew, were overwhelmingly for Harold; East Anglia, his old earldom and his spiritual home in Waltham, looked on him kindly; to the west, Hereford and elsewhere in the borderlands regarded him fondly as the scourge of the Welsh. Only the north, as far as England was concerned, could have been looked to for concerted opposition, and even the Northumbrians had been pacified, at least for the time being, by Harold's impartial handling of Tostig. In any case, northern representation at a winter assembly in London was inevitably in a minority.

True, there were weak points in Harold's candidature. Among other things, he represented a break in an old and familiar dynasty. He was also compromised to some extent abroad by his dalliance with William in Normandy and Brittany, and by his connection with Stigand. Even allowing for one or two of Edward's French courtiers in the assembly, however, foreign influence on the witan was too weak to give overseas attitudes much weight in the election. As far as the ancient dynasty was concerned, the only kinsman of Edward with a candidature, Edgar the Atheling, was a mere child, little known to the English. The chances of a successful juvenile reign cannot have been rated highly, especially when the choice was liable to be challenged by force. Moreover, though Harold was not of royal blood, he was of a house that had presumed to hold royalty in its hand. King-making was not an illogical preliminary to being made king. In more personal terms his position was iron-clad. No witan could deny that he was a shrewd and experienced politician. As an administrator, his record was of firmness modified with tolerance and understanding. Militarily, his proven ability to plan and execute successfully a full-scale international campaign rendered him unique in the country. Not only was he the only Englishman palpably capable of holding the reins of the kingdom; his adherents could reasonably argue that during the long years of Edward's declining political influence Harold had in fact done no less.

The single contemporary mention of Harold's election to survive clearly stated that he succeeded to the kingdom 'as he was chosen thereto' (*ASC*). Later versions, based on varying degrees of loyalty and hostility, ranged from a hotly partisan Waltham tradition that Harold was elected unanimously, to the outright animosity of William of Poitiers who denied that there was an election at all. Between the two extremes came a body of opinion, to some extent exemplified by the views of William of Malmesbury, and more or less tainted with Norman influence, that the witan was divided between Harold, William and the child Edgar, but that Harold's party prevailed. While it is not unreasonable that there should have been some feeling for perpetuating the royal line in Edgar, Harold's election by a large majority of those present at the London witenagemot must be without doubt.[1]

He was, in fact, crowned the self-same day as Edward was buried. Such urgency has sometimes been connected with charges of irregularity, but haste in confirming the succession was by no means unprecedented in the history of English kings. Regardless of the method and merits of the selection, a *fait accompli* was still the most desirable argument.

The details of Harold's coronation are unknown. According to Florence of Worcester, the newly-elected king was crowned by

[1] It is perhaps interesting to note from among the chronicles of other nations that while Scandinavian tradition seems to have accepted the fact of Harold's election, the Welsh, not altogether surprisingly, preferred to believe he acquired his sovereignty by harsher means. Both schools, as it happened, were prone to dramatic inaccuracy in dealing with events in England, 1066.

Ealdred, that remarkable prelate whose devotional and diplomatic travels to the lands of the Rhine, the Tiber and the Jordan were at present recollections amid his duties as primate of the North. His supervision of the ceremony presumably would have offered fair token of northern allegiance. It would also have underlined Harold's continued reluctance to accept the ministrations of Stigand who, as primate of all England, should now rightfully have discharged the highest duty of his office.[1] But even the venue is obscure. Edward Freeman, the great champion of Harold among Victorian historians, plumped for St Peter's rather than St Paul's, and his reconstruction of the ceremony, based on the coronation office of Ethelred, is still the stateliest piece of speculation on the subject:

Earl Harold, the King-elect, was led by two Bishops, with hymns and processions, up to the high altar of the minster. . . . The hymn sung by the choir in that great procession prayed that the hand of Harold might be strengthened and exalted, that justice and judgement might be the preparation of his seat, that mercy and truth might go before his face. Before the high altar the Earl of the West Saxons bowed himself to the ground, and while he lay grovelling, the song of Ambrose, the song of faith and victory, was sung over one whose sin at Porlock, whose atonement at Waltham, might well make him seem another Theodosius. The Earl then rose from the pavement, and for the last time he looked on the crowd around him, the Prelates and Thegns and the whole people of England, as still one of their number. . . . Once more the voice of Ealdred demanded of the English people, in ancient form, whether they would that Earl Harold should be crowned as their Lord and King. A loud shout of assent rang through the minster. Chosen thus by Prelates and people, the King-elect swore with a loud voice his threefold oath to God and to all his folk. . . . He swore to forbid wrong and robbery to men of every rank within his realm. He swore to enforce justice and mercy in all his judgements, as he would that God should have mercy upon him. And all the people said Amen. The Bishops then prayed for the ruler whom they had chosen. . . .

And now came the sacramental rite itself which changed an Earl into a King, and which gave him, so men then deemed, grace from on high to discharge the duties which were laid upon him. The holy oil was poured

---

[1] William's apologists asserted that Harold *was* crowned by Stigand, and he was depicted at the scene of the ceremony by the creators of the Bayeux Tapestry. Norman interests, however, were clearly served by this interpolation.

by Ealdred upon the head of Earl Harold. And while the symbolic act was in doing, the choir raised their voices. . . . Again the Primate prayed that, as of old Kings and Priests and Prophets were annointed with oil, so now the oil poured on the head of God's servant might be a true sign of the inner unction of the heart, a means of grace for His glory and the welfare of His people. And now Harold, the Lord's Anointed, the chosen of the people, the consecrated of the Church, vested in the robes of royalty and priesthood, received in due order the insignia of his kingly office. The sword was placed in his hand, with the prayer that he might therewith defend his realm, and smite his enemies and the enemies of the Church of God. The King then bowed his head, and the Imperial diadem of Britain was placed by the hand of Ealdred on the head of the King of the Angles and Saxons, the Emperor of the Isle of Albion. God was again implored to crown his Anointed with glory and justice and might, and to give him a yet brighter Crown in a more enduring Kingdom. Then the sceptre crowned with the cross, and the rod crowned with the holy dove, were placed, one after the other, in the royal hands. . . .

Grandiloquence apart, Harold had reaped the reward of thirteen years of watchfulness and political dexterity. How readily, or with what misgivings of conscience, he reconciled this with his earlier undertaking in Normandy, perhaps nobody but himself could ever know. In a less problematical field, he now had to arm against William or risk being vanquished. Legend had it that the duke heard the news some three days later at his Quévilly estate near Rouen. Wace, with unfailing imagination, visualised the Norman's reaction as that of a man momentarily demented, agitatedly lacing and unlacing his cloak, rocking from one side of his seat to another, pressing his head against a pillar, speechless with anger, too terrifying to be approached by his followers. Perhaps the description was not out of character. Nevertheless, for Harold the first moments of anxiety were over. When dusk fell on 6 January 1066, the old dynasty had finally crumbled. The last king of the house of Cerdic was in his grave; the son of a 'self-made' Englishman stood in his place.

10

Harald the Ruthless

Adam of Bremen, historian, geographer and authority on the north, who was writing in 1066, expressed the fascination and awe with which people in many other parts of Europe regarded the remote and mysterious lands of Scandinavia.

Having passed beyond the islands of the Danes, a new world opens in Sweden and Norway, which are two kingdoms of broad extent in the north and hitherto almost unknown in our world. Of them the learned king of the Danes told me that Norway can scarcely be traversed in a month, and Sweden not easily in two. . . . On the northern borders of the Swedes and the Norwegians live the Lapps [*Scritefini*] who are said to outpace the wild beasts in their running.

For more than two centuries the roving Scandinavians had explored the waterways to their south, yet relatively few southerners, since the folk-wanderings of older times, had pursued their chances in this 'unknown' world of the north. Of those who had, most had restricted their travels to Denmark and the southern part of Sweden. They took home stories of great lakes and swamps, many of which have since disappeared, and of woodlands of birch, beech, ash and alder more profuse and less penetrable than those of today. But it was the visitor who pushed northwards up the huge rocky peninsula of Norway and Sweden, with its gradual easterly fall to the Baltic and the Gulf of Bothnia and its sudden westerly plunge to the Norwegian Sea, who returned with the most gripping image of these dreamlike yet daunting Scandinavian kingdoms. Here, where the deciduous forests gave way to fir, pine and spruce, where the mountain lakes of Sweden spilt seawards through long, twisting rivers, where the melting glaciers of Norway cascaded from towering cliffs into the 'drowned valleys' of the fjords; here was the heart of the North.

To the southerner, this world of continuous winter darkness, of brief but glorious summers, of strange celestial twilights, of the eerily beautiful aurora borealis must have seemed the playground of potent, if fickle, wizardry—of a people who bleached their beards yellow, hung jewellery on their ears, travelled in wheelless carriages drawn by reindeer and who carved dragon heads on the front of dwellings which might include in their construction transparent panes of the membrane from newborn calves and a framework of whalebone. Though their communities, small and often isolated, were clannish, the reception for travellers, in peaceful times, was friendly. The winter hazards of exposure and danger from wild animals, especially in parts where towns were far distant and wayside inns unknown, made private hospitality a common and practical virtue. According to Adam of Bremen, no act was more shameful in Sweden than the refusal to shelter a traveller. Indeed, in some regions it was obligatory in law to provide food for such a person and his horse, and fair prices were fixed for the service. In Norway, where the population was more thinly spread, rough huts containing dry wood and straw were often maintained on the trails, with a legal proviso that those who used them moved on after three nights if the demand for shelter was greater than the space. Regardless of legality, hospitality was regarded generally as a desirable social grace.

The life shared during the bleak season was austere, though not without its compensations. The single-room dwellings, perhaps of wattle or whalebone and sod (or of log, stone and even fashioned timber, depending on the class of inhabitant), were often tarred or topped with moss to keep out the elements, and, in some places, dug into the ground basement-fashion for additional warmth. Many of the long hours of darkness were spent round open fires where the women prepared food, the men drank ale and exchanged stories of hunting, fighting and exploration. Perhaps some older member of the family would enjoy a perspiration bath in front of the flames while the children or servants rubbed his body and sought out the vermin which infested the majority of European people at the time. Another cleansing process, the steam-bath, was a popular winter pastime for which separate bath-houses were constructed with elevated ledges where the bathers could recline. Water was sprinkled on hot stones to build up the steam. Families often bathed happily together without segregation of sex, switching each other, or themselves, with clusters of twigs to stimulate perspiration and tingle the flesh.

In many ways, these northerners were a direct, uninhibited people. Sex relationships considered improper and practised furtively under later moralities were engaged upon openly and unashamedly, little or no stigma attaching to 'natural' marriage, to the progeny thereof, or to the candid maintenance of slave, or otherwise contracted, mistresses. Nevertheless, the Northman's strong urge towards independence, to head a home and family of his own, usually led sooner or later to full legal marriage, the wife of such a marriage normally holding an honoured position in her husband's life. So, it must be allowed, did his drinking cup. For hard drinking, largely of native-brewed ale, appears to have been part of the northern way of life, particularly in the southern regions of Scandinavia. An Arabian traveller of the tenth century, Ibn-Fahdlan, who observed the Northmen in Russia, reported that they frequently dropped dead while intoxicated at their revels, a state of affairs corroborated in the ancient Scandinavian reflection that 'Carousing and ale have brought men grief, death and curses.' Alcoholic excesses, however, were probably confined mainly to the trading and fighting classes, and were not unknown at the time, after all, in many other parts of Europe.

Apart from his appreciation of beer, the northerner had a special taste for rancid butter, a type of porridge called *graut* and for sour whey, sometimes kept for several years and mixed with water to make a refreshment known as *blanda*. He also ate a variety of meats, including horse, a large quantity of fish and many kinds of cheese made from cow, sheep and goat's milk, often with vegetable flavouring. Farmers gave priority to the crops that would ensure the livelihood of their stock. In some places the scarcity of fodder became so critical in winter that cattle and horses were fed fish bones boiled to a soft pulp. Meats, fish and eggs were preserved for human consumption in the hard months when the poorer families, with smaller 'pantries' and stock yards, took to snow-shoes and skis to track down their food across the frozen countryside. Elk, deer and other wild animals were hunted inland with arrow and spear; seal and walrus in the coastal regions with harpoon and club. Though whales were hunted at sea with much daring from small boats, the elements sometimes provided a welcome bonus by stranding these highly-prized creatures on the coasts. If such a whale were of a good size, the ruler of the kingdom on which it was stranded held automatic rights to the major share, though smaller whales, together with other stranded ocean denizens, were commonly divided between the finder and anyone with claim to the coastland. Eggs were collected not only from the normal range of farmyard poultry but from the nests of seabirds on cliffs and the small coastal islands. Indeed, so valued was this harvest that coast dwellers frequently took pains to establish their ownership, by law, to specific nesting colonies which they 'cultivated' as carefully as the farmers tended their sheep and cattle.

Winter was the time of drinking and reminiscing in the halls, of working in the long boat-houses by the rivers and the sea, building and repairing ships, of fashioning implements, utensils, shields and weapons, and, for some, of pursuing the dark business of the blood feud which thrived on the code of private retribution and family justice. If winter was exceptionally harsh, the Scandinavian summer was correspondingly welcome and uplifting. The sun shone generously (in the more northerly lands for almost twenty-four hours of the day), and with it came a great surge of outward-bound energy. Round the coast, ships were launched and fitted for journeys to foreign parts. Farmers set off with their herds for the mountain pastures, sometimes taking the whole family along for a change of environment. Men of rank strapped shoes[1] and richly decorated bridles and saddles to their favourite white horses and rode off to visit distant relatives and friends. They went to the traditional summer markets and fairs, great conglomerations of skin booths and tents which made an annual appearance in certain parts of the land, usually on the well-used highways. Here they could watch their favourite entertainment, the horse fight, and indulge a pronounced

---

[1] Nails were not used for the shoeing of horses. The shoes were made to overlap the side of the hooves, and strapped.

gambling instinct at the same time. They went to the towns, the small but busy trading centres of Scandinavia with their stone and earthen walls and wooden watchtowers: towns such as Roskilde on Seeland, the ancient capital of Denmark, and Schleswig, home of one of the earliest Danish mints; Uppsala, the political capital of Sweden, and the nearby commercial centre of Sigtuna; and, in Norway, the old towns of Tunsberg and Vigen in the south and the young town of Nidaros in the west. They went, too, to sacrifice and pray at the public temples with their armour-clad images of Thor the Thunderer, Odin the All Father, and many other gods, for although Christianity had already made inroads on the north, there was still much paganism, and even converts tended to regard Christ as yet one more addition to a formidable list of deities. They went across the seas to the east, to the west, to the south. In the season of the sun, which their ancestors had not surprisingly worshipped, the Northmen set sail to explore, trade and plunder.

The stark seasonal contrasts of the Scandinavian environment seem to have found odd reflections in the contradictory nature of the people. For a breed moulded to severity and harshness by the long winter struggle for existence, these northerners showed remarkable creative vitality. Ships, houses, wagons and sledges—almost anything incorporating a lump of wood—appear to have presented an irresistible challenge to their skill at sculpting and carving. The same ornamental flair, often making use of intricate patterns and animal forms stemming from primitive times, was displayed in stone and metalwork, particularly in superbly-wrought weapons and such items of personal adornment as brooches and bangles. Hard-headed and practical, perhaps a technical craftsman rather than an artist, the northerner still loved to dress in bright colours, load himself with jewellery and dye his flowing locks red or yellow.

Self-reliance and decisiveness flourished alongside a profoundly fatalistic philosophy, elaborate laws and legal processes could co-exist with countless blood feuds and murders while, despite a powerful sense of public order, 'private' disorderliness was rampant. Feasts and other social gatherings ended, perhaps more often than not, as drunken brawls, women throwing lengths of material over their sozzled menfolk in the attempt to prevent them killing each other.

Clever strategy in war and patient bargaining in commerce were thinly separated from an apparent propensity to frenzied rage (*berserksgangr*) which was, indeed, cultivated as a soldierly virtue, soldier and trader often being the dual role of the self-same man. Perhaps it was the flexibility of the northerner, this strange blend of the primitive and the civilised, that provided his main strength as a voyager and helped him to adapt so readily to the challenge of foreign environments.

That he was a man of action is unchallenged, and Adam of Bremen found him inhibited in the display of softer emotions. According to Adam, the Scandinavians cried over neither their sins nor their dead. But any attempt to generalise about the characteristics of a people so widely spread can be charged with over-simplification. The lowlanders of Denmark must have differed from the mountain-dwellers of Norway, just as the people of the Norwegian fjords would have differed from the lake-dwellers and river folk of Sweden, or their Scandinavian brothers in Iceland. Some Northmen grew up in the tradition of islanders, others as plainsmen; some were reared in isolated homesteads, some amidst the comparative bustle of the trading ports. Moreover, there were inherent racial contrasts. Though a characteristic Norse type, tall, fair and businesslike, had long since dominated the survivors of a swarthier, stockier race (more brooding and emotional, according to some, than their later visitors, the Teutons), examples of both were represented in the lands of the north, plus the various shades resulting from assimilation.

In the mythological *Lay of Rig*, type and class were unequivocably linked. The story told how a god called Heimdall, assuming the name of Rig, wandered the earth and begat three sons by three different women. From these three, Thrall, Karl and Jarl, descended the three traditional classes. 'Thrall was swarthy, with wrinkled hands, gnarled knuckles, thick fingers, ugly face and long heels. He utilised his strength binding bast, making loads and lumping home faggots throughout the weary day. His children occupied themselves building fences, dung spreading, tending swine, herding goats and digging peat. Their names were Sooty and Cowherd, Clumsy and Lout and Laggard...' (*The Rigsmal*). The thralls, or slaves, in Scandinavia at the beginning of the Viking Age were probably, as the legend suggested, mostly descendants of the short, dark people who had preceded the Teutons into the north. To these, however, the Vikings had added many recruits bought or captured outside their own territories, Irish Celts from the West and Finns and Slavs from the east being among the most common. Some were people of high birth in the lands of their capture who had failed to realise an expected ransom. The wives and daughters of foreign nobles, if not kept by their captors, sold well as slave-mistresses. Although reasonably treated by individual owners,[1] the thrall had meagre rights under law, could be maimed or killed by his master, was often left to die of exposure in an open grave when too old or ill to work and was sometimes put to death on the funeral pyre of the owner. Slaves, however, formed a minority fraction of the people. The majority was free and by nature independent.

'Karl was red and ruddy, with twinkling eyes, and he fell to breaking oxen, building ploughs, timbering houses and making carts' (*The Rigsmal*). At the top of the scale, his descendants were freeholders of some substance and importance, with influence in the political assemblies, the *things*. As well as prosperous yeomen farmers, or *hauldar*, proud owners of ancestral soil, this strata provided master-craftsmen, lawmen, poets and priests, forming the middle class, as it were, of Scandinavian society. At the other end of the scale was the cottager, or *kotkarl*, and the paid labourer, whom, though less privileged, shared the legal rights of other free people and had protection under law against unjust employers. Since, however, the same law allowed a master to whip truculent or recalcitrant employees, it would be unwise to regard the statute as unduly protective. Indeed, in a society based at rock bottom on family solidarity and the bond of common blood, the root of security was in kinship rather than in any modern concept of legality. Bare, it was said, was the back of the brotherless, and the desirability of fraternal ties sometimes led to a form of artificial brotherhood in which unrelated men ceremoniously cut themselves to let their blood mingle while swearing to undertake the duties of kinship on each other's behalf.

---

[1] Some became very close to their owners. It was not uncommon for an infant of well-to-do parents to receive a slave child of the same age as its teething gift, the latter becoming playmate, attendant and perhaps the lifelong companion of its owner.

Karl had been swathed in linen; they wrapped Jarl in silk. 'Light was his hair, rosy his cheeks, his eyes as keen as a young serpent's. His business was shaping the shield, bending the bow, casting the javelin, flourishing the lance, riding horses, throwing dice, fencing and swimming. He began to make war, to redden the field, to fell the doomed' (*The Rigsmal*). Jarl of the myth was an ideal, dedicated to battle. In fact, the Viking Age *jarl*, a development from an ancient ruling class called *jarler*, was concerned not merely with military leadership but with the general political control of a district. Socially superior to the rest of the nobility, and in some cases regarded almost the peer of kings, his prestige, like that of all *tignarmenn*, or men of rank, was measured largely by the strength and richness of his personal retinue, his houseband, sword-takers or housecarles. Sworn followers to the death, bound by the tradition of centuries, these were the men who shared the food, the ale and the entertainments of his hall, who stood by him through the rigours of his travels and campaigns and who expected reward from his tribute, his treasures, his loot. The greater the *jarl*, or the king, the greater their bravura, the more opulent the barbaric splendours of their rough and adventurous life. In the *Lay of the Raven*, a creature regarded with some awe by the northerners, the knowledgeable bird was made to describe the warriors and minstrels who cast dice and otherwise occupied themselves at a royal court. They had red cloaks elegantly fringed, ring-woven shirts or *sarks*, silver-mounted swords, gilt trappings, graven helmets, bracelets and gold rings. 'They are endowed with wealth and fine weapons, with the ore of the Huns, and with maids from the East.' Such pleasures were not won by sitting on their backsides. 'They are pleased to have tidings of battle, preparing themselves in hot haste, plying the oars, snapping the oar-thongs and cracking the tholes. Fiercely they churn the water with their oars at the king's bidding.'

*

Harald Hardrada (the Stern or Ruthless) of Norway, son of a wise but minor king, Sigurd of the Fairhair clan, and his pushing, ambitious wife Asta, was about fifty when Edward the Confessor died and had reigned some twenty-one years, nineteen of them as sole king. Despite this long period of comparatively settled government, he seems to have been more feared than loved by his people. Snorri Sturlason, the celebrated Icelandic historian, writing rather more than a century after Harald's death outlined the man succinctly and with commendable objectivity:

King Harald was stately and good to behold, with fair hair, a fair beard and a long moustache. One eyebrow was somewhat higher than the other. Five ells in height [Harald reputedly stood well over six feet tall] he had large hands and feet, though these were not unshapely. Towards his foes he was cruel and, when withstood, revengeful. . . . King Harald greatly loved power and all worldly advantages, but towards his friends and those who pleased him he was very bountiful. . . . King Harald never fled from battle, but often used cunning when the odds were against him. Those who followed him in war agreed that his decisions, when hard-pressed or obliged to act quickly, were generally right.[1]

Snorri also quoted a contemporary of Harald as finding the king vigorous of mind, valiant, masterful, overbearing, haughty, fond of possessions and power and quick to chastise, yet religious and not disregardful of honour. He 'harried for renown and dominion, bringing under his yoke all people that he could bring under it', added the same source.

Bold, resourceful, level-headed and widely-travelled, Harald had much in him of the Viking spirit, that inexorable force born of character and circumstance which had impelled the first scattered sea expeditions of the Northmen and had led, in time, to their whole-sale migrations. The great expansion of racial experience resulting from this outward-bound urge had contributed valuable attributes to Harald's heritage, gifts of observation, reasoning and self-assurance, plus the power, perhaps born from the group instinct of small, isolated communities, to utilise such gifts co-operatively. In a sense, the homestead unit had gone adventuring in a boat; it had returned contemptuous of its old limitations and fears, its world no longer hedged by invincible trolls and monsters but by the boundaries of its own capabilities. This emphasis on things practical and reasonable,

---

[1] 'The Saga of Harald Hardrada' from *The Heimskringla*.

and the desire to push them to worldly advantage, had produced a craftsmanlike attitude to life. The age of the Viking has been generalised both as barbarian and heroic. History is now beginning to recognise it, perhaps more aptly, as a technological era.

The design of Viking ships, for instance, was in advance of any others of their time. Vessels some 80 feet in length, their bottom-planking fined down to no more than an inch in thickness, their keels so fashioned to make it possible to sail close to the wind, were capable of ocean speeds in excess of eleven knots, and reputedly averaged nine on some journeys of several days' duration. Trips from Greenland to Oslo and from Jutland to England were recorded in six and three days respectively. The traditional day's sailing of larger ships, fully manned and equipped, was a hundred miles at four knots. Viking craft, designed both to be sailed and rowed, to cross seas and to probe far up shallow rivers, had a symmetry of proportion, a functional grace, breathtaking even to the modern beholder.[1] They have been classified into three main types: the swift *skuta* used on the fjords and home rivers, carrying from 10 to 15 pairs of oars and from 20 to 50 men; the *snekkja*, often used as a coastal raiding vessel, with up to 20 pairs of oars and a length of from 70 to 100 feet, which might carry between 50 and 100 men; and the larger and later *skeid*, well-known by Harald's time, with up to, sometimes above, 30 oars a side, measuring between 100 and 150 feet in length, designed to sail the high seas in search of trade and conquest. The largest and most famous of these were sometimes recalled by their names in the sagas. Harald Hardrada's half-brother, Olaf the Thick, had a ship known as the *Bison* after the carved likeness of this animal's head on its prow. The renowned *Long Serpent* of the warrior king Olaf Tryggvason was in the region of 150 feet long

[1] Among the most beautiful surviving examples of Viking ship building are the Gokstad and Oseberg ships, so called after the locations where they were discovered, preserved in clay, having been used as burial vehicles. Now at the Viking Ship Museum, Oslo, they belong to the medium-sized class of Viking vessel. The Gokstad ship is about 77 feet overall, beam 17 feet, hull draught 3 feet with a freeboard amidships of 3 feet 9 inches. It is an oak ship with 16 overlapping planks a side. The Oseberg ship, also built of oak in the same 'lapstreak' method, is 80 feet overall, and has similar proportions to the other. Each was originally fitted with a mast amidships, a square sail of linen or woollen cloth held by ropes made of skin, a series of short, light oars (16 a side on the Gokstad specimen, 15 a side on the Oseberg) and a large steering oar aft on the starboard.

and carried 34 pairs of oars, while the mightiest of all recorded long ships or 'dragon boats', that of Canute, was said to have had no less than 60 oars a side, presumably carrying a complement of several hundred fighting men.

The war vessels of Harald's time had a full-length deck below the gunwale and additional short-decks at stem and stern, the former being occupied by the most formidable warriors in sea-battle, the latter by the helmsman. A tent roofing, supported on poles, was sometimes raised amidships to provide some shelter for the crew from the weather. Though the Viking ship was often a dual-purpose craft used for fighting and for trading (sometimes both on the same voyage), regular merchantmen were stripped of maindeck and boarded over on the frame-ribs to give an open hold, perishable cargo being protected from rain and spray by sailcloth and skins. Larger vessels carried windlasses, conventional iron anchors, ship's boats and rudimentary aids to navigation, including a board with holes and pegs on which to chart progress and, probably, some form of sun-compass.

Viking weapons also demonstrated a great pride in craftsmanship and no mean technical knowledge. According to Arabic writers, the swords of Scandinavian settlers in Russia (country familiar to Harald in his youth) were wrought from laminations of soft and hard metal, a composition suited to use in extremely cold conditions. It seems probable that the northern smiths also knew how to produce damascened, or serpent-marked blades, by an intricate process of pattern-welding somewhat analogous to the method now used for putting the lettering in seaside rock. Even in Viking art and litera-ture there was the same workman-like precision, the same liking for a neat and dexterous job. If the themes were simple and unsophisti-cated, the treatment was full of technical complexity. In the visual arts, primitive animal and human representations often formed the excuse for a riot of intricate geometrical designs. Poets revelled in a form of figurative circumlocution that made their lines read like the clues to a crossword puzzle. Harald was quite familiar with this poetry. Indeed, Snorri reported the strong tradition that King Sigurd's son, the man England was to regard as 'the last of the Vikings', even composed verse of his own amidst the fury of battle.

Since Viking expansion was inevitably dependent on war and conquest, violence was a favourite theme of early Scandinavian literature. The treatment was nothing if not exuberant. 'The sword in the king's hand cut through the weeds of Woden [mail coating] as though through water, spear-points clashed, shields were shattered, axes rattled on the heads of the warriors.' 'Wound-fires [sword blades] burnt in the bloody wounds, halberds stooped to take the life of men, an ocean of gore dashed on swords'-ness.' 'The gory spears flew, the destroyer of the Scots fed the steed of the witch [the wolf], the sister of hell trampled on the supper of eagles [corpses].' 'The lips of the wound-mew [the barbs of the arrow] were not left thirsty for gore. The wolf tore the wounds and the wave of the sword splashed against the beak of the raven.' 'The grey web of the hosts [the intestines of the enemy] is raised up on spears; the web we, Woden's friends, are filling with red weft.' 'The shaft shall sing, the shield shall ring, the axe shall fall on the target.'[1]

A great impression seems to have been created by a particularly uninhibited class of warrior known as the *berserker*,[2] a wild, rough type readily provoked to *furor*, in which state he abandoned almost all self-control, howling like an animal, gnashing his teeth and generally running amuck amongst the enemy. When the frenzy ended, he was utterly exhausted, but during the transformation he was believed to be twice as strong as normal, even impervious to swordthrust and spear. A striking physical description of this condition was provided by an Irish-Scandinavian story-teller dealing with the legendary hero Cuchullin. When the *berserksgangr* came upon Cuchullin, one eye bulged and the other contracted, his mouth was wrenched sideways, the sinews of his neck and forehead tautened, his heart beat like the barking of a chained dog, his limbs and joints shook like a tree in a storm and every muscle protruded like a clenched human fist. When he exerted himself in this rage, blood-drops gathered at the roots of his hairs, sucking them into his head; he revolved like a millstone and expanded his chest to such proportions that a man's foot could have been placed between his ribs.

[1] Random extracts from the *Corpus Poeticum Boreale*.
[2] *Bär* = bear + *sark* = shirt; the name was perhaps thus derived from the bearskins worn by athletes and professional strong-men.

Doubtless the *berserker* element in the Viking force was a useful one, especially for its psychological effect on the enemy, but it can hardly have been dominant, for planning, co-ordination, discipline and guile repeatedly emerge as the real keys to the striking military success of the Northmen. It was not lack of control or intemperance that appealed to rulers of both east and west when they chose Scandinavian mercenaries for their personal bodyguards. It was strength, discipline and a strong code of loyalty. The famous Varangian guard of the Byzantine emperor in Constantinople, a select body of several hundred Viking warriors, was held in such esteem by its employer that the Greeks called its members the emperor's 'treasures'. The Varangian guard was an exceptional group, but they shared a common tradition with many Northmen in that, for at least some part of their lives, they depended for their living on aggressive and predatory skills. Professionalism was no small part of their strength.

Harald Sigurdson's early Viking ancestors had soon learned to exploit their maritime advantages. At first they must have approached foreign lands with some apprehension of naval interception, but, on discovering that theirs was virtually a monopoly of sea-power, they had soon settled to helping themselves. The word Viking derives from the Old Scandinavian *vikingr*, or sea-rover, and before long it had become an accepted part of the young northerners' ambition to make his *vikinge*, his sea-voyage, to 'go abroad with the Vikings . . . steer a good bark to the haven and cut down man after man there'. While trading was by no means out of character (it seems that the commercial instinct was so strong in the Scandinavian that he not infrequently threw in his wife to clinch a hard deal), his ability to choose a landfall unmolested, to descend by surprise and make a getaway at will, was extremely conducive to aggressive methods. Monastic communities on the off-shore islands of Britain were a typically enticing target. The raiders were particularly attracted by loot of high value and small bulk, the sort of valuables to be found in churches and monasteries, and they had a shrewd eye for the line of least resistance.

Monkish writers, like most early chroniclers of Viking behaviour, had good reason to be hostile in their portrayals. Especially during

the earlier raiding periods, the Northmen were barbarously unheed-
ful of life, slaughtering old and young, male and female with equal
promiscuity. Killing was often preceded by torture. One of the
more repugnant Viking habits involved pulling a victim's lungs
through incisions made at his ribs while he was still alive (the so-
called 'blood eagle'), though such treatment seems to have been
reserved for particularly hated enemies. One ancient story told how
the Vikings tossed alien children on their spears, giving a warrior
who objected to the practice the nickname of Barna-Karl, or child's
friend. It would be difficult, however, to establish that the Vikings
were more, or for that matter less, cruel than the people of the lands
they attacked. Much as today, a large number of people, regardless
of race or religion, tended to psychopathic behaviour under conditions of organised hostility, and certainly no one nationality had a
corner in arrant brutality. Perhaps a more significant element in
the Scandinavian attitude to death and personal injury was the strong
vein of fatalism in its philosophy. For the true believer in the gods,
the time and place of death was inexorably appointed. Since life
could not be prolonged by avoiding danger, nor fate provoked by
courting it, there was a premium on living adventurously, if not
violently. Many a Northman made the most of it.

By the end of the eighth century, regular Viking raids were taking
place on the European coast. At first, these were summer excursions
with no attempt at settlement. It was not until the 'first wintering'
in a foreign country that the invaders developed the concept of
conquest. Such winterings had commenced in the west by the middle
of the ninth century. Before it closed, the ubiquitous dragon-boats
had penetrated most of the major waterways of Europe and were so
feared by the native populations that a special prayer, 'From the fury
of the Northmen deliver us', was inserted in the litanies of Christendom. But if the seas could not stop the Northmen, prayers, it seems,
did not. To the west, they reached Greenland and possibly even the
North American mainland; to the south, they raided Spain, penetrated the Mediterranean to plunder Italy and attacked the North
African coast; to the east, they sailed the Gulf of Finland, founded
Garðariki, or Russia, and followed river routes to the Caspian, the
Black Sea and thence to the Bosphorus. Well before Harald was

born, the long ships of the Vikings had girdled the whole world, as it was then known to Europe.

★

Harald Sigurdson's childhood is lost to history. Snorri took up his biography at the battle of Stiklestad, Norway, in 1030, when his subject was a youth of fifteen. It was at Stiklestad that Harald's half-brother, King Olaf, overshadowed by the influence of Canute, perished in a vainglorious attempt to reassert his will on the chiefs and bonders of northern Norway, and Harald, wounded fighting beside his kinsman, was forced to flee to Sweden. From here he took ship with his band of supporters to Novgorod, the Holmgard of the sagas, a city-state founded by Vikings and enriched by lucrative inland-water connections with Constantinople and the middle east. There had been no Russian empire before the arrival of the North-men, but the great slow-running rivers of the country, wending north and south from the central plains, had proved an irresistible challenge to the long ships and, decades before Harald's time, a regular trade route had been established via the Dvina, Lovat and Dnieper with the Bosphorus. For the Varangians (as the Northmen were known in these regions) the odyssey began at Novgorod, their commercial centre on the Volkhov, just above Lake Ilmen; the city renowned in Russian history as 'My Lord Novgorod the Great of the North'. In this rich cosmopolis, 'where merchants were kings' and the citizens very much controlled the government, many northern adventurers had served a worldly apprenticeship. The main conurbation, with its busy streets and minor waterways, its crowded docks and colourful markets, lay on the left bank of the main stream. On the right stood the new cathedral of St Sophia and the palace of its builder, Yaroslav, grand prince of the Varangian dominion.

Young Harald Sigurdson must have been received well in Nov-gorod (his late half-brother Olaf had once been well known in the city) for within a relatively short period he was holding an honoured office in Yaroslav's guard, with all the privileges conferred by such a post. The household troops of the Varangian princes were largely Scandinavian, and their captains, the élite of soldier-traders, formed a class of immense authority, an aristocracy providing not only war leaders but state councillors, governors for the fortified trading stations on the rivers and so on. But, like many of his countrymen before him, Harald was to find the lure of the south beyond his resistance. In Novgorod there were opportunities in plenty to learn of the splendours and scope for enrichment that awaited a strong and personable young Viking in the service of the Byzantine monarchy, and it was only a matter of time before Harald had made suitable arrangements to terminate his service with Yaroslav and was setting out to seek his fortune with the tough, heavily-armed merchants of the *austrvegr*, or eastern way. For safety against the wild tribesmen of the plains, the long ships travelled from Novgorod in convoy, laden with cargoes of furs, waxes, honey and slaves. Their journey was arduous in the extreme. To begin, they followed the north-flowing stream to the watershed of the Valday plateau, a huge tract of marshy land in which the ships were caught in a porridge of clogging bog-growth and stagnant water. Whether it was possible to haul them through on the oars, or whether they had to be portaged to the headwaters of the south-flowing rivers is uncertain. Either way, it was an unenviable task, and Harald and his crews must have been relieved to find themselves, in due course, on the Dnieper, heading for the major water-junction and trading centre of southern Russia, Kiev.

Here local boats and those from adjoining rivers swelled the convoy, all lured by the same bait—the rich southern markets. Beyond Kiev came a series of seven rapids. Where possible, the ships were dragged round on rollers, but, where the ground was not suitable for this manœuvre, they had to be unloaded and carried. Having survived swamps, rapids and the almost constant danger of attack by tribes of fierce nomadic horsemen, the Scandinavians faced their final danger in the Black Sea where treacherous storms might swamp their small craft with little warning. As a precaution, the captains kept close to the west coast, ready to beach at short notice. At last Harald's convoy nosed into the fabled haven of the Golden Horn.

Already capital of the Eastern Empire for seven centuries, Constantinople, the blending bowl of European and Asian culture, represented a depository of exotic wealth beyond northern calculation.

Seven times crowned by its historic eminences, complemented by the shining waters of the Marmora, here was a giant of architectural brilliance and civic compass that must have had Harald and his band of adventurers rubbing their eyes in disbelief. After the simple towns of Scandinavia, it is hard to imagine what they made of the glories of Byzantium: the dazzling palaces, marble towers, bronze-coated obelisks, golden gates, the sunlit domes and breathtaking mosaics, the royal harbours, arenas, churches, baths, basilicas and porticoed markets. Perhaps above all, as strategists and warriors, their admiration was taken by the sheer scope of the fortifications, vista after vista of walls set with scores of towers, enormously tall and thick—ramparts which had defied barbarism for seven hundred years and were to hold their own against the East for another four centuries.

It seems that the young prince from Norway took personal service under the formidable Empress Zoe who, notwithstanding her advanced years at the time, had an eager and appreciative eye for a strong male. Time and again he led her Varangians to victory, raiding deep into the Mediterranean, falling on Italy, Sicily, perhaps parts of North Africa and even Jerusalem, and always returning laden with booty. This he despatched, periodically, under trusted lieutenants to Novgorod, where it was held for him in safe deposit. 'Exceeding wealth did he collect together there, not surprisingly, for he was pillaging in that part of the world richest in gold and costly things,' asserted Snorri, claiming that Harald and his Greek and Viking followers captured no less than eighty towns in their campaigning.

Snorri's account of these Mediterranean exploits was hardly less fantastic than the Arabian Nights. In one instance, Harald allegedly set about capturing a walled town by snaring sparrows from the thatched roofs of the buildings when the birds flew abroad in search of nesting materials. By attaching lighted shavings of pinewood, soaked in wax and brimstone, to the sparrows, and turning them loose to fly back to their nests, he set the town ablaze. Its occupants surrendered. Obtaining entry by trickery seems to have been Harald's forte. Unable to force the defences of one loot-worthy stronghold, he set his men to play games within sight of the walls.

Ostensibly unarmed, they carried swords concealed in their cloaks. When the sentinels obligingly opened the gates to watch, the 'players' whipped out their swords, improvised shields by wrapping the cloaks round their arms, and successfully charged the bastion.

But the best story of all involved Harald's feigned death. His men were attacking a particularly well defended town.

So strong was it that they had given up hope of taking it by assault and settled round it to starve out the inhabitants. Now it chanced that Harald fell sick after a while and took to bed, causing his tent to be placed apart from the others for the sake of quiet. Backwards and forwards went his lieutenants seeking his counsel, and this was noted by the townsfolk who rightly deduced that something had befallen the Varangians, so they sent spies to find out what it might be. Their intelligence, on returning, was that the chief of the Varangians was so sick that his force had hesitated to advance on the town. . . . Then went the Varangians to speak to the townsmen, telling them of the death of their chief and praying the priests to grant him a tomb in the town. On hearing the news, many of the religious leaders of the community cherished hopes of obtaining the body for their own churches, knowing well that the place of burial would be greatly endowed; thus, donning their vestments, they sallied forth from the town in solemn procession bearing shrines and holy relics. Likewise, the Varangians formed a mighty funeral train, bearing aloft the coffin covered with a rich pall and, above it, many banners. In this manner the procession entered the town gates and the coffin was put down within the city. Then did the Varangians blow a war-blast on their trumpets, and drew their swords, the remainder of the force charging fully armed from their tents towards the town roaring battle-cries. The monks and priests in the cortège who had vied with each other to be the foremost in receiving the offering, now vied twice as urgently to be the farthest off, for the Varangians slew everyone within reach be he clerk or layman. In this manner they went through the whole town, putting men to the sword and pillaging the churches, whence snatched they exceeding great wealth.

Such anecdotes should be regarded warily for they were popular ones among ancient literature, the various ruses being attributed to different commanders at different times. Thus, while Harald might indeed have been a student of military history, the likelihood of traditions becoming confused in the saga is not improbable. Nevertheless, his career in the south clearly was a brilliant one and must have included innumerable adventures which escaped the record. He emerged from it a leader of considerable reputation, a general quick to perceive enemy weaknesses and to exploit a fortuitous advantage, an audacious and ruthless raider, a courageous man yet by no means an incautious one. Harald was not above holding back from a fight in which the result seemed too open, especially if it stood to confer any glory on an allied commander. Under such circumstances, 'Ever said he that he would take good care that he did not lose those of his own company; but when he and his men alone were opposed to an enemy, so fierce was he in battle that they must win the day or die.' Given so blatant a policy of self-aggrandisement, it is hardly surprising that he seems to have fallen out at an early stage with the military establishment at Constantinople, subsequently conducting most of his campaigning on an individual basis. All the same, he must have retained the favour of the empress, for he stayed in the royal service about ten years, qualifying on three occasions, if Snorri was correct, to participate in the *polota-svarf*, the periodic right of the palace guards to help themselves from the treasure-house of the Byzantine emperors to as much as they could carry away without help.

Meanwhile, there had been political changes in the north. Canute had died; so had his ill-fated offspring, Harefoot and Harthacnut. Magnus, son of the vanquished Olaf of Stiklestad, now found himself king of Norway and Denmark. The news can hardly have failed to impress his wandering half-uncle. Life as a soldier of fortune, an empress's favourite, was all very well, but it was not in Harald's nature to be unresponsive to the greater accomplishments of others, especially his kinsmen. It was time to be going home; to be paying his respects to the family. The circumstances of Harald's departure from Constantinople appear vague and confused. For some reason he was thrown in prison when his plans to retire became known, tradition maintaining that he was rescued by a wealthy woman devotee of his dead half-brother who had appeared to her in a vision. According to the story, a chapel was afterwards built and consecrated to King Olaf near the prison, but no record of such a chapel exists in the city. Nor was the mysterious woman, who allegedly rescued Harald by means of ropes, identified by name.

'It has been said by Varangians who were then serving in Constantinople,' wrote Snorri, 'that those in the know averred that Queen Zoe desired to have Harald for her husband, and therein lay the cause of his difficulties when he wished to leave the city, though people may have been told otherwise.' Apparently one of the things they were told was that Harald had misappropriated booty taken while campaigning on behalf of the empire, a charge with a highly plausible ring. A more dubious story connected his imprisonment with the empress's jealousy over a girl he had once sought to marry, a certain Maria, 'the daughter of the brother to Queen Zoe'. At least the relationship was wrong, for Zoe had no brothers. One way or another, Harald and his followers made good their withdrawal from the city, together with considerable treasure, avoiding apprehension in the Bosphorus, and sailed north on the eastern way. At Novgorod Harald found that the wealth he had forwarded for safekeeping was indeed intact; a hoard which, added to the valuables he had brought with him from the south, was possibly unequalled in the entire north. Yaroslav was impressed; sufficiently so to give his daughter Elizabeth in marriage to his former captain of the guard. The first phase of Harald's career could hardly have ended on a brighter note. Together with his royal bride, and a fortune in gold, the prince sailed west for his homeland.

★

A year after they killed him at the battle of Stiklestad, the Norwegians dug up the body of Olaf, gave it a place of honour beneath a gold-embroidered canopy in Clement's Church, Nidaros, and proclaimed him a martyr. Such belated popularity was eloquent of a widespread dissatisfaction with the Canute family régime in the country. Olaf's remains became a form of political barometer. The greater the resentment felt for the government, the more miraculous the powers attributed to the dead king. Not only had his corpse refused to decompose, it was rumoured, but his hair and beard persisted in uncanny growth. The spirit of Olaf the Thick, now Olaf the Holy, began to influence the most prosaic of affairs. Eventually, the situation developed into a movement to reinstate the blessed house in the person of Olaf's exiled son Magnus, and, when Canute died in 1036, it was this youth and his supporters who challenged Harthacnut for rule of Norway.

For a while the customary clichés of war-talk hung in the air, but neither side seems to have been anxious to match them with action, and agreement was reached on the basis of co-existence. Under its terms, Magnus took the crown of Norway, Harthacnut that of Denmark. Peace was sworn between them for the duration of their lives with the proviso that if either should die without a son the other should inherit the kingdom of the deceased. Upon Harthacnut's death in England shortly afterwards, Magnus was left to assume the crown of Denmark. Theoretically, the clause opened a further claim, for since Harthacnut died the king of England as well as of Denmark, Magnus was virtually the pretender to Canute's entire empire.

That he failed, ultimately, to assert a claim against the lawfully elected Edward the Confessor with force was due perhaps less to his own lack of conviction than to the oblique efforts of a singularly ill-starred yet resilient man, Sweyn Estrithson, a nephew of Canute and grandson of the redoubtable Viking Sweyn Forkbeard. Handsome, charming and not a little lacking in reliability, Sweyn Estrithson had a fatal talent for winning popularity. Magnus, having succeeded Harthacnut as king of Denmark, appointed Sweyn *jarl* of that country, entrusting its government to this smooth young aristocrat. He was to spend the rest of his life regretting it, for Sweyn soon attracted sufficient supporters to proclaim himself king and Magnus was forced into a prolonged and disconcerting series of wars against the usurper. In each one, Sweyn was defeated; repeatedly, he fled into exile; indefatigably, he came back. Time and again, charm won him fresh adherents and, in the long run, sheer perseverance triumphed. He reigned, on and off, for the remarkable period of thirty years, outliving the greatest of his enemies.

Sweyn was at Sigtuna, Sweden, with his cousin the king, when Harald arrived from Novgorod with his new wife. Elizabeth was also related to the Swedish monarch. As an outcome of this apparently convivial family gathering, Harald sailed for Denmark with Sweyn, ostensibly to join the fight against Magnus. Perhaps it was his intention to provoke his nephew into making him a better proposition than Sweyn could offer. If so, it succeeded. It says a great deal for Harald's reputation as an aggressive force, even at this stage, that Magnus apparently offered to share his kingdom with his returned uncle rather than face an alliance between Harald and Sweyn. The invitation was too good to dismiss and, forgoing his farewells to the wrathful Danes, Harald slipped away from his anchorage in Denmark and sailed jubilantly for Norway. According to tradition, Sweyn had had wind of secret negotiations between Magnus and Harald and attempted to pay off his defaulting ally by lodging an axe in the captain's berth of Harald's long ship one night before it set off. Harald, however, had bunked elsewhere in his wisdom, and the axe supposedly cleft into a wooden dummy. The story also maintained that Harald shared his hoard of eastern treasure with Magnus as part of their contract. After Magnus had bestowed on his uncle half of the Norwegian power, Harald reputedly invited the king to his tent. The centre was clear except for animal skins spread on the ground. There, in the company of the chief lieutenants and guards of both men, the treasures were disgorged, measured and apportioned between the two leaders. True or not, Harald lost nothing on the bargain. Magnus died prematurely while the partnership was still young, and, in 1047, Harald became sole king of Norway.

He appears to have developed into something of a tyrant. 'King Harald loved power,' wrote Snorri, 'and this grew as he took root in the land; so much so that in the case of most men it was useless to speak against him or bring forward matters other than those on his mind.' As evidence, the biographer quoted the verse of a fellow-Scandinavian, Thiodolf the Skald:

> The men of the war-willed chief
> All humble have to sit or stand
> In place wherever the harsh king desires;
> Many men bend before this filler of ravens,
> And few in truth will not do in all things
> Whatever the king may bid.

The overlordship of Denmark remained in dispute. In his dying hours, Magnus is supposed to have bequeathed it to his enemy

Sweyn, perhaps responding to a final glow of magnanimity, or maybe to a mounting distaste for his uncle. Though Harald nevertheless managed to induce the Danish *thing* at Viburg to proclaim him king, it was no more than a temporary success. His powers of persuasion had been backed by a Norwegian army, and when this retired Sweyn quickly reasserted his old influence. For some time, Harald busied himself consolidating his position in Norway, restricting himself to summer excursions to the coast of Denmark which he ravaged with an animus surprising even his most hardened followers. But these operations smacked rather of a reversion to his earlier raiding form than of a determined attempt to overthrow his rival. Indeed, Danish loyalty to Sweyn probably hardened in consequence. On at least one occasion, Harald's ships were put to hasty flight by an intercepting fleet of Danes. They escaped only after distracting their pursuers by casting plunder and prisoners overboard. At last, in 1064, a peace treaty was arranged on the Gotha River and ratified between the two countries, though not before Harald and Sweyn finally clashed in a head-on sea battle at Nisaa, to the south.

Harald reputedly commanded some hundred and fifty vessels, sailing himself in a specially constructed flagship of thirty-five rowing benches, lavishly decorated and accoutred with the customary dragon's head at its golden prow. Sweyn's fleet, if tradition may be relied on, was considerably larger. Such forces would not have been unlikely. The Scandinavian kings maintained sizeable war fleets at their call, Harald's turn-out on this occasion representing perhaps about half his potential force. In Norway, the coastal regions 'as far inland as the salmon swims' were apportioned into ship-raths under a royal ship levy in which each *rath*, or district, was obliged to supply and maintain a number of warships for the king's disposal in defence and military enterprise. This method of ship finding, among others, was in evidence wherever Scandinavian influence spread. As the outstanding maritime peoples of the western world, the northerners frequently chose to settle their disputes by fighting on water, and the normal procedure for the set-piece sea battle, usually located in an estuary or otherwise close to the coast, was for each side to fasten its major vessels together at the bows, providing their fighting complements with a kind of floating fort. From this the marine warriors fired arrows, hurled volleys of stones and cast spears at their opponents, hoping so to weaken the other side that its craft could be secured by grappling hooks, boarded and cleared. At the same time, ships not employed in the 'fortress' manœuvred on the flanks of the enemy formation harrying crippled vessels or taking those with depleted crews. Some, equipped with iron beaks, were used for ramming their opponents.

With their bigger craft lashed together in two heaving piers, the water slurping and splashing about them, the fleets of Harald and Sweyn must have presented, by modern standards, an astonishing sight. Slowly the clumsy platforms converged. 'Then did either side join combat, and the struggle raged fiercely, both kings lustily shouting on their warriors. . . . Stones and arrows streamed across the short space between the hosts, and the sword drew blood, depriving of life the men of either force.' Of the ships faring loose from the tangled mass, Snorri observed drily, 'each captain placed his as far forward as he had courage for; but this was exceeding varied'. After several hours of hard fighting on the slippery and gory planks, Harald appears to have asserted supremacy. The Scandinavian tradition, with pleasing matter-of-factness, accorded it no dishonour to Sweyn that he abandoned his shackled flagship once the outcome was clear, retiring with those of his vessels as could still make a getaway. 'To my mind, the courageous Sweyn went not from his ship without good cause, and empty did his craft float. . . .' But though Harald allegedly captured some seventy Danish warships, the battle was not politically decisive. The subsequent armistice left Sweyn on the throne of Denmark.

Harald of Norway was left to look elsewhere for conquest. Having tasted the rich pleasures of the Mediterranean, having won a major kingdom in Scandinavia, according to Adam of Bremen, this amazing Viking leader next steered north across the polar sea. His motives are unknown. Elizabeth, his queen from Novgorod, had given him two daughters, Maria and Ingigerd. But the king had also taken a mate named Thora, daughter of Thorberg Arnison, a member of a powerful trio of Norwegian magnates, the Arnison brothers. And Thora had done better than Elizabeth. She had presented Harald with two sons, Magnus and Olaf. Now they were young men and would want lands of their own to control. Perhaps Harald hoped to reach fresh dominions via the Arctic waters: if so, he was unlucky. He seems to have reached an impasse. Returning home, he concentrated once more on strengthening his hand in Norway, waiting for some new opportunity to present itself.

It came, perhaps not unexpectedly, on the trading ships from England; the news of Edward the Confessor's death. Harald's Viking blood must have stirred. Had not his nephew Magnus inherited a claim to the English throne from Harthacnut? And had not he, Harald Sigurdson, inherited his title from Magnus? The history of his Viking ancestors told repeatedly of brave deeds and rich bounties in the mild lands of Britain. Was he, after all, a lesser man than Canute the Great? If Harald had doubts (and he had never been a man of foolhardy enterprise), he was soon to find an ally who removed them: none less than the favourite of Edward himself, the brother of the new king of the Isle of Britain. Snorri made no bones of Tostig's message to Harald: 'If you wish to conquer England then I can arrange that many of her lords will be your friends and supporters, for I lack nothing against my brother save the title of king. . . .

'All England lies at your hand.'

II

An Invasion Fleet

With ominous rapidity, the creators of the Bayeux Tapestry shifted their story from the business of Harold Godwinson's enthronement to a picture of Norman woodmen felling trees, accompanied by the caption, 'here William orders ships to be built'. In fact, the simplification omitted a critical sequence of procedures which, while later evidence was to leave some doubt about their timing, must have tested the organisational capacity of the duke to the utmost. Set on a venture only matched in its perils by the sheer fervour and daring of his vision, William called up the full range of his persuasive and administrative resources. If the crown of England was to be his, he now had no option but to take it by force. So much was clear to him. Perhaps he suspected, even at this stage, that he might not be the only challenger in the field. At all events, he wasted few hours before making his first move. On the evidence of William of Jumièges, an official protest was sent immediately to Harold's court. Its terms are uncertain, ranging in varying Norman accounts from an outright demand that Harold should abdicate, to an insistence upon other forms of compromise in William's favour. To such, Harold's reply, though now equally obscure in character, was effectively negative. Not that the duke could have forecast otherwise. The object of the act had simply been to formalise the issue; to stimulate the aura of legality in which, as he realised shrewdly, he could best enlist European sympathies for his attack.

High among William's considerations was the increasingly potent influence of the Church on public conscience. As the year proceeded, a spate of grants and endowments was showered on the religious houses of Normandy, not only by the duke and the duchess, but by many of their supporters, great and small. At Avranches, Caen,

Fécamp and Rouen, among other places, churches felt the warm touch of ducal or baronial generosity. With the subtle Lanfranc to advise him, William pushed his bid for ecclesiastical backing further. Some time in the spring, or perhaps early summer, a mission was despatched to Rome under an experienced diplomat, Gilbert, arch-deacon of Lisieux, to obtain a judgement against Harold of England from the pope. Overtly William's case rested upon Harold's sacred oath and the legal and moral aspects of its violation. A number of supporting charges were probably thrown in for good measure. For instance, the house of Godwin was vulnerable on the subject of Alfred the Atheling's murder in 1036. The manner of certain ecclesiastical appointments in England following the return of God-win, and the flight of Archbishop Robert, in 1052, could also be charged, by association, to Harold's account. But William was too much of a realist to base his hopes on the power of moral argument. He had better reasons for expecting a favourable judgement. In the first place, Rome had nothing to gain by upsetting so strong and self-willed an adherent as the Norman duke, and little to lose by the chastisement of the more stubbornly independent elements in the English Church, particularly Stigand. The religious exploitation of political aggression, a concept to be expressed less deviously later in the 'crusade', was not novel in 1066. Moreover, there was obvious appeal to papal authority in the underlying suggestion that Rome should have a say in the disposal of the crowns of Christendom. The incumbent pontiff was Anselm of Lucca, who reigned as Alexander II, but the driving genius of the papacy was already the brilliant and radical Hildebrand, later to rule as Pope Gregory VII. As William and Lanfranc must have realised, Hildebrand would not be slow to appreciate the advantages of a Norman bridgehead for his reformist zeal in England. Fourteen years later Hildebrand was to admit by his own hand that a faction of the conclave had baulked at sponsoring armed intervention. But such qualms were no match for his per-suasion and ambition. Harold seems not to have been asked to submit a defence. In any case, he could hardly have done so without conced-ing the game to Rome, if not William. The duke had it in the bag. For the greater right, as Hildebrand saw it, the pope was prompted to sanction a spot of bloodshed.

Among those whose blood would be involved, however, there was less enthusiasm for the project than the archdeacon had raised in Rome. Not a few among the noblemen of Normandy regarded the risks related to an attack on England as excessive. The old Viking tradition of amphibious warfare had died with their ancestors. These knights were accustomed to fight on horseback, and horses were not at home in the Channel. Furthermore, Harold was reputed to command a large fleet, manned by experienced English and Danish sailors. A Norman armada could be cut up before it ever reached the shores of England. The survivors would be faced by a prolific army led by the conqueror of Wales, the long-haired warrior-prince of Wessex who had displayed his personal courage all too clearly alongside William in Brittany. Then there was the question of economics. Wars cost money, especially one for which scores of ships would have to be built and equipped. Failure in such a desperate gamble could ruin Normandy; a state currently enjoying rare peace and security. Finally, by the reckoning of the cautious, it was no part of the feudal obligation to follow one's liege lord overseas. The establishment of such a precedent might lie heavily on their descendants. According to Norman tradition, all these arguments, and more, were voiced at a great council of magnates called by William at a castle he had built at Lillebonne, above the remains of a Roman amphitheatre and swept, appropriately, by sea-breezes from the Seine estuary.

Backing William's enterprise against the doubters was a powerful clique of barons and churchmen long since associated with his ascent to power, among them his half-brothers Robert of Mortain and Odo, Bishop of Bayeux; his admirer William fitz Osbern, son of his childhood guardian; such eminent heads of houses as Ralph of Tosny, Richard of Evreux, Robert of Eu, Roger of Beaumont, Hugh of Grandmesnil, Roger of Montgomery and Walter of Longueville, and those memorable campaigners Walter Giffard and William of Warenne. William fitz Osbern was singled out by later writers for his forceful advocacy of the duke's venture. 'What are you waiting for? He is your master and requires your services. It is your duty to come forward with a good heart and honour your obligations. Fail him in this and it will be the worse for you in the end. Now is the time to prove your loyalty', ran the gist of fitz Osbern's message as cited by Wace. Wace, who painted the knight in striking colours, developed the scene with a picturesque, though totally unsupported, anecdote of fitz Osbern's loyalty. During the course of the meeting he was allegedly deputed by some of the barons to explain their doubts to the duke. Instead, the knight took it upon himself to stand up and proclaim the support of the whole assembly for the projected operation. According to Wace's imaginative interpolation of tradition, the meeting broke up in confusion.

Whatever the extent of the opposition, however, it was totally overwhelmed, both at Lillebonne and at meetings elsewhere in the country, by William's single-minded drive and plausibility. Caution apart, the spirit of the project was well suited to the aggressive and expansionist instincts of Norman nobility. It was William's concern to harness this old and potentially disruptive force to his new and superbly integrated offensive. According to William of Malmesbury, the duke 'negotiated individually' with many of his magnates. Having subjected each to the full force of his personality, he extracted from him a promise of soldiers and ships. In some cases a specific reward of possessions or status in England was agreed by return. Thus an ambitious monk of Fécamp, who promised twenty men and a ship, appears to have been staked for a bishopric across the Channel in the event of God's granting victory to the Norman cause. Other contributors sought land, treasure and even well-to-do English brides. With characteristic thoroughness, William had each bargain committed to ledger, keeping a businesslike eye on what has been called the memorandum of his Joint Stock Company of conquest. Contemporary detail of the agreed armaments has not survived, but later testimony put the offers of Robert of Mortain, 120 ships, Odo of Bayeux, 100 ships, and William, Bishop of Evreux, 80 ships, among the highest bidders. William fitz Osbern, Roger of Montgomery, Roger of Beaumont and Hugh of Avranches were said to have pledged 60 ships each, Hugh of Montfort 50, 'Fulk the Lame' and 'Gerald the Seneschal' 40 each, Walter Giffard and Vougrin, Bishop of Le Mans, 30 each and the duke's kinsman, Abbot Nicholas of St Ouen's, Rouen, 20. Such figures, however, are probably misleading, even if accurate, since they do not distinguish between variously sized vessels. This variation is distinctly suggested by the apparent generosity of some ship quotas, and the relative meanness of others, compared with the number of knights claimed for respective contingents. Hugh of Montfort, for example, seems to have supplied a mere 60 knights with his 50 ships against 100 knights from Abbot Nicholas with only 20 ships.

With support and enthusiasm spreading through Normandy, William cast his recruiting net further afield. Such were his reputation and the alluring rewards he held out that volunteers began to gather from many parts of Europe. They came not only from the feudal dependencies, from Poitou, Maine and Brittany, but from central France, Flanders, Aquitaine and even from the Norman colonies in Apulia, southern Italy. For the most part they were land-less knights and footloose mercenaries, armed adventurers eager for good pay and the prospect of a share in the spoils of foreign victory. But there were also men of established rank among them. The chance to extend their estates and affairs to a new country was appealing, while papal approval had lent dignity to a speculation they might otherwise have shunned as somewhat disreputable. It had also helped to check the potential opposition of their various imperial overlords. If few of the neighbouring princes of Europe could find much con-solation in William's scheme to invest himself with yet more power, albeit for the moment in a seaward direction, the elevation of the exploit to something approaching a crusade at least bound them to the semblance of benevolent neutrality. In Germany, those govern-ing in the name of the young emperor, Henry IV, were actually induced by the duke to offer help were it needed.

The next task was to secure the welfare of the duchy itself during the time its ruler, and many of its warriors, would be overseas. In this context, the Duchess Matilda was to deputise for her husband in association with their son Robert, then fourteen years of age. Though Matilda's father, Baldwin of Flanders, was too prudent to commit himself to one side or another before the impending struggle, it seems that William visited him at Lille and was doubtless satisfied that his wily and powerful father-in-law would keep a protective eye on his diminutive daughter. At the same time, in case the duke should not survive the expedition, the boy Robert was solemnly declared heir to the duchy on the proclamation of his father, and oaths of fidelity exacted from the leading men of the state. One tradition had it that the young King Philip I of France, the same age as Robert, honoured this ceremony with his presence; another that Philip, or perhaps rather the hardened French counsellors around him, viewed William's intentions with distrust, actually refusing him aid at a meeting at St Germer, near Beauvais. The precise relationship between William and Philip (and, indeed, between the two and Baldwin) at the time, is now hard to unravel. In effect, however, the French court appears to have been among those who resolved conflicting emotions in the posture of official neutrality.

But William's memories of his own youthful dealings with a French king, not to mention the disastrous antics of the Normans themselves following his own father's death, were too vivid to allow him to leave Matilda and Robert to the mercy of outsiders. A number of his strongest and most loyal adherents were granted personal exemption from the call-up in order to stiffen the government, and to help protect Normandy in his absence. Prominent among them were Roger of Beaumont, whose son Robert was to sail with the duke, and, according to the writing of Orderic, Roger of Montgomery, William's trusted comrade since the early struggle with Geoffrey Martel. They must have been considerably relieved when at least one persistent source of anxiety was removed late in the year by the death of Conan of Brittany, especially since a strong sample of the pro-Norman Breton party had joined William's invasion contingent.

Thus, while William juggled with the political complexities of the case, the mercenaries and plunder-seekers attracted by his propaganda converged on an excited Normandy to assemble alongside the local magnates and their armed underlings who formed the nucleus of the invasion force. With summer urging the land to fruition, the duke faced the first great danger in his programme, that of harbouring a perilously miscellaneous and eager fighting host on his own soil. Some of its members were the traditional enemies of others, many were natural spoilers and most, if not all, would be prone to high-handed behaviour where the local peasantry was concerned. The problem was an explosive one. Both economically and from the immediate standpoint of control, delay of embarkation could amount to a crisis. And delay, as William knew, was inevitable. The wheels of medieval logistics were beset by many ruts.

Nevertheless, his talent for dominance and leadership proved up to the task. The discipline and patience he was able to exact from his rough feudal troops and their hired allies before they ever set sail for England, plus the organisation he must have contrived to supply them, was perhaps the most brilliant tribute to his generalship, and a crucial contribution to the coming campaign. Writing of the accomplishment, William of Poitiers drew attention to the fact that during a whole month of waiting at Dives-sur-Mer, about fourteen miles north-east of Caen, the army was 'forbidden any form of pillage', the duke finding provisions 'at his own expense'.

He provided generously for his own knights, also for those from other parts, but he did not permit them to help themselves by force. The herds and flocks of the country people grazed securely throughout the province. The crops remained intact for the sickle, neither trampled by the knights in their arrogance nor plundered in greed by the forager. A weak and unarmed man could behold the armed host without fear, and go as ever he would, singing behind his horse.

Even allowing for exaggeration, the point made was a remarkable one. The Duke of Normandy must have prayed that his polyglot band of adventurers would behave as obediently when the mainland had dissolved in their wake and unforseeable perils opened before them.

★

By late spring, the first vessels destined for the invasion fleet were beginning to appear along the river and coastal strands of Normandy —sleek double-enders in the Viking pattern, some tarred a sombre black, other striped from stem to stern in gaudy fair-ground colours. Many more were under construction. In part William's transport requirements could be met by existing Norman shipping: the duke's own fleet (probably considerably diminished since the days of his father), perhaps small flotillas maintained by other powers in the land, merchantmen and fishing vessels pressed into service. To some extent, also, he relied on craft bought or hired from maritime interests in France and Flanders. But this was only a start. The cross-Channel conveyance of an army, complete with horses, equipment and provisions, presumed a ship-building programme on a quite extraordinary scale. The makers of the Bayeux Tapestry showed woodmen felling trees with great gusto. Normandy was well supplied with oak, and the popularity of wooden forts and other structures meant that skilled carpenters and joiners were not hard to find. Teams were recruited rapidly to supplement the regular shipwrights and put to work under master-craftsmen from St Michel to Tréport, especially around the small harbours and river ports between the Vire and the Seine. It was on this stretch of coast, at the estuary of the Dives, that the whole operation was to pivot.

If the Normans had come to prefer campaigning on land to on sea, they had not lost their ancestral facility for making ships. Their efforts were carefully represented in the tapestry, where a carpenter was portrayed shaping timber into planks while others worked on the actual boats. The man shaping the timber stood astride the plank, one end of which was supported in the fork of a tree, the other on the ground, while he shaved it with a long-bladed adze. Among the tools attributed to the shipwrights were a small, narrow-headed axe, an instrument which appears to be a combination of fine axe or chisel and hammer, a form of drill for boring the oar-ports and, again, an adze. Since the Norman vessels clearly did not differ to any appreciable degree from the Viking craft of the preceding two centuries, it is possible to describe their construction in fair detail. Working mostly in oak, the shipwrights used the clinch method of overlapping planks on the hulls, fastening them on the overlap with metal rivets or bolts and either bolting or tying the planking to the ribs. The seams were caulked with a mixture of pitch and animal-hair or wool. For each ship, a single mast was fashioned from a tree trunk, probably fir or pine, to be set amidships in a keel-block with an open-ended channel or fish-tail socket to control the slide of the mast as it was raised or lowered. The completed mast was stayed fore and aft and fitted with shrouds. Meanwhile cloth-workers had been occupied turning out dozens of large square sails in linen or woollen cloth, one for every vessel. Each sail was probably woven in sections, stitched together and given brailing lines of some sort of skin.

At an advanced stage of the construction, a rudder or steering oar was secured to the starboard quarter of the Norman invasion galley by means of a pivot-chock. While capable of being raised in shallow water, or when the craft was beached, by means of forward pressure on an athwart-ship tiller, the rudder was suitably proportioned to obtain a greater depth than the keel when convenient, thus offering similar advantages to a modern centre-board or lee-board. Its position also meant that the gull-like rise of the stern in a following sea was not incompatible with its function. Another outboard device fitted to some of the vessels, according to the Bayeux Tapestry, was a shield-type anti-ramming fender at bow and stern. Too literal a translation is unwise with many of the tapestry studies, but a good proportion of the ships in the completed fleet were depicted without the familiar stem and sternpost embellishments, and it seems feasible that the craft specially built for the invasion might have been given a less ornate finish than those built in more leisurely circumstances. If so, however, such austerity stopped short at William's flagship, *Mora*,[1] a magnificent vessel presented to the duke by his wife in honour of the occasion, and fitted throughout at her own expense. At the *Mora*'s prow was a formalised lion or leopard head, and at her stern, turned to face forward, the golden figure of a child blowing a horn and holding out a miniature lance and gonfanon.

One by one, the finished ships were hauled to the water, launched and ferried to the assembly point in the mouth of the Dives. May saw the first-comers starting to muster, but building continued through June and July and it was August before the whole fleet rode at anchor.

It seems there were more than 500 major vessels in the duke's fleet, an impressive figure without the inflated reports to come later. Geoffrey Gaimar, the first of the Anglo-Norman historiographers, was writing within a century about upwards of 10,000 ships, while

---

[1] Possibly a diminutive of Matilda, though sometimes said to mean Wise.

William of Jumièges put the building order at 3,000, not to mention existing vessels and those hired or purchased outside the duchy. The alleged quotas assigned to the Norman magnates, however, add up to less than 780, the same authority reckoning the overall fleet at 1,000. And even this was undercut by Wace who, explaining that he had the number on the good authority of his father, reduced the armada to a more plausible 696. Since it is known that the fleet which eventually sailed for England was smaller than that originally assembled at Dives, the last two strengths can be reconciled to some extent by accepting a time-lag in the counts. Nevertheless, it would be unwise to ignore the probability of exaggeration even in these, the most conservative of early evaluations. It is perhaps fair, then, to concede that not less than 500 ships were to participate in William's offensive, a figure which seems more or less consistent with the transportation problem involved. Modern estimates put the number of fighting men shipped at about 7,000, of which perhaps 2,000 were mounted. This gives an average of 14 men and four horses, plus servants, provisions and equipment (including a proportion of that necessary to build temporary strongposts) to each ship.[1]

William now had everything he needed for his enterprise save a favourable wind. Day after day it frustrated him, refusing to blow from the south, and when the days turned to weeks, and August to September, without better luck, the morale of his army must have slackened accordingly. The resources of the area were not unlimited, nor was the mental fortitude of a superstitious and augury-conscious army. It would seem surprising had there not been cases of despondency in its ranks. A Norman story that Harold of England had directed his spies to the locality might well have originated in a touch of the jitters. According to William of Poitiers, one man was actually dragged before the duke during his sojourn at Dives and charged with espionage. The anecdote was used by the panegyrist to demonstrate his hero's magniloquence. 'Harold has no need to waste gold and silver buying the services of you and your kind,' the Norman leader supposedly declaimed. 'A sign more positive than he would

---

[1] It might be interesting to note in relation to this that the capacity of the Gokstad ship, a medium-sized Viking vessel, has been estimated in modern terms at rather more than 30 tons register.

wish and more certain than he anticipates, will inform him of my designs and preparations; in short, my presence in England.' As William of Pointiers had it, the alleged spy was despatched to England to transmit the boast to his master. At last, on 12 September, with the equinoctial gales drawing dangerously close, the Duke of Normandy felt compelled to make a move. The wind was now from the west. It would not take him to England, but at least it promised to shift his armada from its stale and depleted assembly area to a fresh staging post on the French coast, and one nearer its ultimate objective. The wind might even change in the course of the voyage, enabling him to proceed directly to the point of invasion. William gave orders for the embarkation.

In portraying the loading of arms and provisions, the tapestry creators were most explicit. Pairs of men-at-arms carried their hauberks, or coats of mail, between them on poles which were slipped through the sleeves rather like elongated coat-hangers. In fact, the hauberk, weighing about 30 lbs or a little less, was not an unduly heavy load, but in this manner it could be kept uncreased, ensuring that the links did not become tangled. The entire equipment of a Norman warrior, including weapons and armour, has been estimated to have weighed between 45 and 50 lbs, several pounds less than the personal load of the modern infantryman, and the men depicted in the tapestry were able to carry bundles of swords on their shoulders as well as the hauberks. A form of mobile armoury, hauled by two men in leather harness, appears to have been employed to move other equipment. This vaguely resembled a wheeled version of the sort of gun-rack used today for the vertical storage of weapons, displaying a neat row of javelins and helmets, as well as bearing on its chassis a huge barrel, probably of cider or wine. As the files moved down to the waterside, other men carried axes, spears and helmets (the latter commonly grasped by the nose-piece), miscellaneous bundles and, with generous foresight, yet more liquor, both kegs and skins of wine. These Normans and Frenchmen had no intention of neglecting their appetites. From elsewhere in the tapestry, it can be deduced that they took with them a whole range of cooking equipment, including trenchers, spits and other culinary implements. It seems probable, too, that they shipped at least some of the elements of the familiar Norman campaign fort, together with the tools necessary for its construction.

On the subject of horse-loading, the picture-makers were less clear. The wholesale conveyance of these animals within the very limited confines of narrow and shallow galleys was perhaps the biggest transport problem of the lot. It seems unlikely that any but a few of the horses had faced such an experience before, and anyone remotely acquainted with the difficulties of shipping horses, even under ideal conditions, could not fail to admire the audacity of such an undertaking. Even on a calm sea, one or two querulous animals might be expected to throw an open boat into confusion, whereas, given a heavy swell, a deck-cargo of slithering, kicking, terrified horses could turn a pitching galley into a floating hell. The situation must have been aggravated, from a temperamental aspect, by the common employment of stallions as chargers at that time. Of more than a hundred and eighty mounts represented in the Bayeux Tapestry, the majority distinguishable by sex were depicted quite clearly as stallions, this being particularly evident in the invasion scenes. Since the designer made no attempt to show how these spirited creatures were taken aboard, it must be assumed that some form of ramp was used. Once there, presumably they were secured by halters and probably leg-shackled. It is even possible that they were thrown and trussed to make the voyage as dead-weight. Unloading presented less difficulty. Eager to get back to land, the horses were most likely induced to jump the low gunwales of the vessels, as one rather awkward scene in the tapestry seems to intimate. The action of a jumping horse seems to have defeated the artist who showed it with one leg cocked up like a can-can dancer.

Neither horses nor men can have been sorry to regain a dry footing after the forthcoming run up the coast. Having completed his embarkation, William put to sea on the westerly wind, taking his fleet past the mouth of the Seine estuary, round Cap de la Hève, along the coastline of Upper Normandy and, ever reducing the distance to England, into the waters of his vassal state, Ponthieu, the land of Harold's earlier 'shipwreck'. If William had anticipated some change of wind on the voyage, his hunch was at least partially correct. The weather changed, but for the worse. Somewhere on the journey the fleet was overtaken by conditions which proved too much for a number of the heavy-laden vessels. Some appear to have foundered, while the crews of others, perhaps separated from the convoy, took it upon themselves to desert. William of Poitiers, who mentioned the losses, has been thought by some historians to have implied further damage to the Normans in actions with English vessels, but the episode is now obscure. The bodies of drowned men, he added, were buried as discreetly as possible where they were washed up. The duke had no wish to increase the alarm of his followers. Meanwhile, the bulk of the armada, somewhat the worse for its passage, dropped anchor at St Valéry, in the mouth of the Somme, to refit and wait once more for a wind from the south.

The small community of St Valéry, on the side of the estuary nearest to Normandy and standing back from the water against a setting of pastoral calm and broad woodlands, can hardly have rejoiced at the sight of the fleet. The town had risen peacefully near the older abbey of St Valéry, the shrine of the Merovingian saint, Walaric, whose wonder-working powers were of wide repute. Now the fishermen, cowmen and swineherds must have prayed long and earnestly for the safety of their homes and possessions. The last thing they might have wished, with the harvest freshly gathered, was for St Valéry to be chosen as a Norman transit camp. They added a prayer for the virtue of their wives and daughters. On the other hand, the authorities at St Valéry were not hostile. The place was linked to William by family connections. Then there was the obligation of the monastic community to assist a campaign endowed with papal blessing. William pitched camp under a banner consecrated by the pope, and wearing about his person a hair and a tooth donated by the same source, supposedly from the remains of St Peter.

Yet, despite the pleas of the army, and the greater pleas of its reluctant hosts, the weather made no change for the better. It rained and the wind blew in squalls. A week passed at St Valéry. And another. William of Poitiers told how the duke was driven to constant exhortation in his efforts to maintain the flagging spirits of his followers. According to Wace, the local monks eventually brought forth the shrine of their saintly patron, setting it upon a carpet on the muddy soil so that the Norman leader and all his host might gather round it and plead for their departure from the Somme. It was by no means their first effort to invoke supernatural assistance. Endless prayers and sacred rites of many types had been harnessed to the long, increasingly anxious quest for a fair wind. Perhaps only fate knew just how well it had served William in its stubbornness.

12

The English Army

While Harold Godwinson's enemies regarded the act of his succession as a *coup d'état*, his supporters saw it rather as the natural
sequel to a long and impressive role as the dominant personality in
England after his father's death. Between the two stood many,
neither properly hostile nor wholly in support, who, while recogniz-
ing Harold's personal attributes, could not be easy at the abandoning
of the ancient royal dynasty in favour of an upstart house. To them,
the obscurity, if not the notoriety, of the Godwin line was a real
weakness in Harold's cause. It was a weakness he could offset, to
some extent, by pointing to his affinity, through his mother, with
Canute. But, in the end, he stood to win or lose backing on his own
accomplishments. The extent to which he was able to carry English
opinion in the outcome was well suggested by Florence of Worcester, a writer of the next generation, who seems to have found no
difficulty in portraying Harold as a just and legitimate sovereign,
labouring for the welfare and safety of his kingdom. In the words of
a familiar panegyric of that chronicler, the new king set himself 'to
shun unjust laws, to further just ones, to patronise churches and
monasteries, to honour bishops, abbots, monks and churchmen of all
types, to reveal himself as pious, unpretentious and affable to all good
men, and to be the enemy of all evil-doers'. Florence told how
Harold reminded the king's officers throughout the country of their
duty to maintain public peace, while he concentrated personally on
the organisation of the national defences. The implication was that
government and administration under Harold as ruler in his own
right was, as might be expected, much the same as when England's
premier earl had stood at the sagging shoulder of King Edward.

The mud later thrown at Harold's régime by Norman writers, on the other hand, contained a whole range of abuse from charges of tyranny and rapacity to those of sacrilege and parsimony, perhaps reaching the limits of inventiveness in a claim that the responsibilities of marriage appealed less to their victim than did the abduction of the wives and daughters of his subjects. So evil were his ways, asserted the character assassins of the Continent, that the ghost of Edward the Confessor felt obliged to appear from time to time and rebuke the wayward Harold. Another accusation that, contrary to the request of the dying Edward, Harold banished all Norman and French residents from his kingdom, appears also to have been unsupported in fact. Indeed, few innovations can be attributed to Harold's government during the short spell of peace which inaugurated the year 1066. Ironically, one of the few recorded measures was the issue, from at least forty-four minting-places in England, of a new coinage bearing on one side a likeness of the crowned Harold, and, on the other, the single word PAX.

Harold's overriding consideration from the moment of taking office was the need to prepare his country for war. Nor was he backward in appreciating the importance of clerical support in this respect. It may well be that he was concerned with the profounder implications of the oath he had taken, wittingly or unwittingly, on the relics of Norman saints; but even were his anxiety of a more temporal nature, he knew William too well to underestimate the weapon his rival might forge from the incident on the anvil of Rome. If something in the nature of a holy war were to be proclaimed against him, it was vital that he should have the utmost backing of the national Church; vital to the furtherance of his own propaganda in Europe, vital to morale in England, perhaps vital to allaying the fears conjured up by a troubled conscience.

Accordingly, the early strategy of his reign was closely linked with ecclesiastical matters. The only royal writ of the period to have survived to modern times, thanks to a late copy, secured Giso, a foreign-born bishop of Wells, in all the rights and possessions of his see. At Ely, one of several places held in plurality by Stigand, Harold had a new abbot appointed, forcing the primate to relinquish such benefits as he had enjoyed there during the later years of Edward's reign. In Dorsetshire, the king won monkish approval by checking a scheme sponsored by Edward to link the county with the diocese of a German bishop, Herman of Wiltshire. Among monastic prelates who had come to regard him with particular favour, Harold could count his uncle Aelfwig, a brother of Godwin and abbot at the New Minster of Winchester, Aethelwig, a capable abbot of Evesham, and Abbot Leofric of Peterborough, a spirited nephew of the late and illustrious earl by the same name. Leofric's house of St Peter, which included Harold among its benefactors, was so rich that men came to know it as Gildenborough. The king continued, of course, to promote his own foundation at Waltham.

But it was his friendship with a churchman commanding altogether greater respect, the perspicacious Wulfstan, bishop of Worcester, that was to show the most immediately beneficial returns in Harold's reign. Wulfstan, born at Little Itchington, near Warwick, some fifty-four years earlier, and educated at Evesham and Peterborough, had first made his reputation for piety and sagacity as a tutor at the monastic school in Worcester. In 1062 he had been chosen, with much popular acclaim, as bishop, supposedly accepting preferment with becoming reluctance. Fastidious in his connections with the uncanonical Stigand, he had then sought ordination at the hand of Ealdred, Archbishop of York. Now, within a short while of Harold's coronation by the same hand, Wulfstan's thoughts turned again to the north. There can have been few hopes in court circles that Mercia and Northumbria would receive the new king as a popular choice. Florence could write that Harold had been chosen by the chief men of all England, but clearly the north had been taken at a disadvantage by the circumstances of the election, a fact in itself provocative of resentment. And feelings went much deeper than that. Traditional jealousies were enough to stir many northerners against any new king of West-Saxon blood, let alone a member of Godwin's house. Regardless of the now obscure attitudes of Edwin and Morcar, popular opinion in their earldoms can hardly have been other than hostile to Harold. Thus, threatened by mass disaffection at a time when every hope depended on a cohesive effort to thwart the dangers from abroad, Harold chose Wulfstan to accompany him on a daring mission of conversion to York.

It was a remarkable errand in several ways. Years had passed since a king of England had set foot in the north. Canute had passed through Northumbria en route for Scotland, but he had travelled surrounded by an army. Yet Harold appears to have embarked on the journey unaccompanied by any of the trappings of force. Doubtless, he took his personal bodyguard, but his purpose was to answer hostility and emotionalism with friendship and reason. And, like William, he sought to exploit the unifying influence of the Church. According to Wulfstan's biographer, the holiness of the bishop worked wonders in smoothing their path. In his presence, rugged northerners bowed their heads in reverence. Not unnaturally, the Archbishop of York was accorded less credit by this source, but, on the evidence of his earlier contacts with Harold and Wulfstan, Ealdred must have played a leading role in any entente. Just how much the royal mission did for Harold in terms of general popularity cannot be established; the important thing is that, apart from restraining any tendency there might have been in the north towards open rebellion, he seems to have convinced the powers there that his sovereignty was their best assurance against real and imminent danger. Viewed realistically, nothing was clearer than that internal strife would be fatal to all political parties at that time. If Harold had reason to fear William, Edwin and Morcar had little cause to be complacent about the hovering threat of Tostig. Harold's problem, in a sense, was to convey the realism without generating despondency.

He succeeded well enough to return to London before Easter and concentrate his full attention on the south. There is a feeling among historians that Harold's undated marriage to Ealdgyth, the sister of Edwin and Morcar, took place about this time, perhaps as a condition of the formal allegiance of the northern earls. At all events, the king now seems to have felt more secure in leaving them to themselves. Ealdgyth is as vague a character as the other women in Harold's life. Almost nothing is known of the developing fortunes of his mother, Gytha, now a wealthy and honoured widow in the south, or of Eadgyth of the Swan's Neck, the love partner of his early manhood in East Anglia. Now that their children were growing up, it is probable that Harold saw little of Eadgyth, though no doubt she was well endowed. It is possible that she was the woman, described in Domesday as a mistress of Harold, noted in that record as holding three houses in Canterbury. His sister Edith, the widow of Edward, had followed the example of that other royal widow, Emma, and moved to Winchester, where she was not prominent, it seems, as an admirer of her brother Harold. Perhaps she had never liked him much, or perhaps the antipathy dated from the banishment of her favourite, Tostig. Certainly, Harold now showed no anxiety to dwell in the city of his childhood. When the time came, he overlooked the old habit of holding the Easter festival at Winchester, gathering his chiefs at Westminster instead. London, dividing the angle between the south and east coasts and commanding the arterial roads needed for rapid movement, was the obvious point at which to hold his military councils; the nerve centre, as it were, of his anti-invasion strategy.

By Easter, the Norman threat was explicit, and Harold's mid-April gemot must have been dominated by talk of defence. The fighting strength available for this purpose through the regular channels of enlistment was considerable, as the pessimists among William's counsellors well knew. Nor were they alone in regarding the island's defences as formidable. The opinion was shared, in all probability, by most foreign observers. Indeed, far from being ill-organised and obsolete, as many later critics were to assume, the military structure of eleventh-century England, intricately developed by the hard years of Anglo-Saxon evolution, was perhaps as sophisticated as any in Christendom. In the broadest sense, it tended to operate at three levels, those of the shire, the earldom and the kingdom. Acting in defence of its territory, a shire force, led by a sheriff, a prelate or sometimes an ealdorman, might deal effectively with a localised raid, and was not infrequently called on to cope with coastal piracy. A more serious aggression could be countered by a force at earl's strength, incorporating elements from more than one shire, while a really critical threat in any part of the realm would provoke retaliation by an army drawn from a number of earldoms and led by the king himself, or an earl in his name.

Moreover, Harold could call on three main warrior classes. Of these, the most effective troops were the professional soldiers retained by the king, and other important lords, as household guards.

Exemplified at their best by the corps of royal housecarles, thought to have been introduced in England by Canute about 1018, many professionals lived on their own estates and were men of some substance. Nevertheless, they were essentially mercenaries, receiving payment in peace as well as during war, and were prepared at all times for immediate armed service. Like the Jomsviking society, after which their organisation was in some ways fashioned, the king's housecarles were a highly conformist company accepting special regulations and the jurisdiction of their own assembly, the *huskarlesteffne*, which settled internal disputes and met periodically with their employer. Loyalty to a paymaster and to each other was central in their code, and defaulters were shown little sympathy. The worst offence, treason, was punished by death and confiscation of property, while the murder of a fellow soldier could bring either death or banishment to the culprit. A man who wished to resign from the corps could do so, but only on the first day of the year. The corps of housecarles gave the king a small but efficient regular fighting force which became the backbone of a far larger army in time of crisis, when it was joined by the second class of warrior, the reservist or territorial.

This reserve force, the so-called select fyrd, was recruited on an area basis. In many parts of the country, one reservist was expected to answer the call-up from every five hides of land, the area being responsible for his pay and maintenance. Thus, it was written in Domesday of Berkshire's obligation: 'If the king sent an army anywhere, one soldier went from five hides, each hide providing four shillings towards his wages and subsistence for two months.' Duty on the reserve seems not to have been shared among the men of any such land-unit but to have remained the responsibility, perhaps the honour, of one, a thegn or a superior type of ceorl. Places such as Malmesbury and Exeter, each of which was assessed at five hides of land, owed one reservist to the select fyrd at time of war. Smaller places might bear a joint responsibility. For instance, Barnstable, Totnes and Lydford, all in Devon, represented a five hide unit in total and consequently owed a man between them. Larger towns and cities provided the select fyrd with batches of reservists, each group doubtless travelling together and fighting side by side when the necessity arose. Oxford, rated at a hundred hides, owed twenty men, as in all probability, did Cambridge, Colchester and Shrewsbury, among other places. Leicester owed twelve warriors; Warwick ten; Bath, Cheshunt and Shaftesbury probably four each; Bridport and Yarmouth probably one each, and so on.

In some cases, towns were allowed to make payments in lieu of providing territorial soldiers, the rate of commutation apparently corresponding to the hire of replacements. Under this alternative arrangement, Oxford, for example, could satisfy its select fyrd obligation by paying twenty pounds instead of sending twenty citizens to war. Since twenty shillings seems to have covered the customary hire and maintenance of a reservist for his term of service, that city, among certain others, was privileged to choose between financing its own men or paying an equivalent sum to the king. On the other hand, should reservists from a town with no commutation arrangement fail to answer the call-up, the fine imposed was much higher, seldom less than twice the price of commutation and often as much as a hundred shillings a man. Fines for defaulting were known as *fyrdwite*, and, along with commutation payments, land taxes, town taxes and other sources of revenue, helped the king to meet his defence budget, especially the large expenditure on mercenaries. In short, the territorial or reserve scheme enabled the king to reinforce his regulars with an army of select men, ready-equipped and financed, who, though subject to no special training, were imbued with a proud fighting tradition and were often experienced. While the select fyrd was not as rapidly mustered as the corps of housecarles, it was largely pony-mounted, therefore mobile. Well armed and supported, it was bound, when necessary, to sixty days' service at a stretch, though provisioning difficulties often affected the duration.

This was the force on which Harold chiefly depended for the land defence of his kingdom. The system, producing provincial units of manageable size and warranted quality, was quite capable of dealing with the type of armed threat normal to the period. In case of dire emergency, however, *every* freeman in a threatened area could be called on to take arms against the king's enemies. Such a levy has sometimes been known as the great fyrd, or the nation in arms. On the whole it was a poorly armed and unpaid peasants' or citizens' army hastily raised to add weight to the local select fyrd in defence of its specific locality. This is not to say that it was contemptible. Its members had the incentive of fighting, as it were, on their own doorsteps, and, when swords and axes were first-class weapons, perhaps there was less disadvantage than might be imagined in having to improvise arms. But necessarily the great fyrd was an awkward force to control. Most of its personnel moved on foot and their terms of service entitled them to return home at night. The commander who wished them to fight further afield was obliged to take them on his payroll as mercenaries.

As well as this threefold land force of regulars, reservists and levies, Harold had the English navy. Its composition is now uncertain, but its fame by the ten-sixties was already the best part of two centuries old. It appears to have dated from about the year 896 when King Alfred, in his wisdom, had decided to tackle the Scandinavian invaders at sea. In the words of the *Anglo-Saxon Chronicle*, he then 'ordered the building of warships to meet the Danish vessels. They [the ships he ordered] were almost twice as long as the others; some had sixty oars, some more, and they were faster, more stable and had more freeboard than the others. They were built neither after the Frisian nor the Danish design, but to that which seemed to him the most serviceable.' For some time in the ensuing period, mercenaries had played an important part in the island's naval defences, regular patrols guarding the coastal waters during the summer months. By 1050, however, Edward the Confessor had paid off most of the professional crews in an effort to reduce the strain on his exchequer, and it is probable that Harold inherited little in the way of a standing sea force. What he did inherit was a special arrangement with a number of towns in the south, later known as the Cinque Ports, whereby he could raise a strong fleet when he needed it. In return for naval service, these ports—namely Sandwich, Dover, Hastings, Romney and Hythe, though others had similar arrangements—were granted various privileges, including exemption from toll for their burghers throughout England, the profits of justice in their courts and, since their efforts were to be concentrated at sea, exemption from the customary select fyrd obligation. The naval strength available to Harold on this basis cannot be known with precision, but Dover and Sandwich were each under contract to provide twenty ships, manned by twenty-three men apiece, for fifteen days a year, and it is not unlikely that the three other main ports involved were committed to a similar extent.

Here were a hundred ships, then, readily available for the defence of the south and south-east coasts. And this was only one naval recruiting arrangement. There was also a general territorial duty throughout the country to provide sea-warriors and ships when required, very much on the lines of the select fyrd system. Indeed, where the five-hide unit was applicable, it might be required to send a man for armed service 'by land *or sea*'. The English military reservist, it seems, was expected to double as a soldier or a marine as the occasion demanded. Sixty such units constituted a 'ship-soke', that is a region or zone responsible for supplying a warship and its armed crew; rates of pay for ship-fyrd service were probably the same as for land-fyrd service, 4*d.* a day, and when the reservists took to sea they were commanded by the same leaders as on land—king, earl, ealdorman, or bishop, depending on the size of the fleet, while each ship-soke provided a suitable captain for its own vessel. Unlike the Normans, the English had kept alive the naval traditions of their ancestors. As islanders, the sea was their first line of defence, and a large number of them, especially the men of the fishing towns and sea ports, were at home on the water. Europe was well advised, on the whole, in respecting the naval power at Harold's disposal.

March had departed peacefully and April's breezes brought nothing more menacing from across the Channel than the swallows, soaring and swooping about the Kentish cliffs after their long seasonal flight from Africa. 'Airborne over rocky slopes . . . Valiant in song, they go in flocks . . . cry loudly . . . tread the wooded headlands . . .' wrote an unknown Anglo-Saxon poet. With May Day approaching, the villagers of England plucking tree-branches and spring flowers in preparation for the annual celebration, the night sky suddenly cast an unusual chill on proceedings. Towards the end of April, the recurrently visible star now known as Halley's Comet burst into earthly sight, providing an apt and avidly interpreted omen of the drama ahead. The creators of the Bayeux Tapestry, clearly impressed by its symbolism, depicted it in the form of a fiery

rocket and portrayed the awe it provoked among a crowd of star-
gazers below. It was waning, but perhaps not entirely lost to view,
when the first blow of 1066 fell upon the shores of Harold's kingdom. With a small fleet, largely manned by Flemish mercenaries,
Tostig struck at the Isle of Wight, took money and provisions from
its inhabitants, then sailed off to harry the seaboard of Sussex.
According to the English chroniclers of the time, he 'did damage
everywhere along the coast that he could, until he came to Sandwich' (*ASC*). In the great haven of Sandwich, the most important
sea base in the south of England, Tostig tried to win shipmen to his
support. It seems that he gained a number of volunteers and managed
to press others into service. 'Some went willingly, others unwill-
ingly.' But Harold was swift to move. Doubtless regarding Tostig's
activity as a precursor to the Norman invasion, he began to alert the
reservists of the south. Mobilisation was to be a far-reaching operation, aimed at marshalling 'greater naval and land hosts than any
king of the country had ever gathered before. . . .' At the same time,
he left London and headed purposefully for Sandwich.

Tostig did not wait for a showdown. He had now been joined by
a member of his old Northumbrian régime, one Copsi, who had
been lingering in the Orkneys. Copsi brought a force of seventeen
vessels which, along with Tostig's own, and those he had gained at
Sandwich, gave Harold's outlaw brother a fleet of sixty. With these,
he sailed north up the east coast intent on revenging himself on
Edwin and Morcar. While attacking the north of Lincolnshire, however, he was challenged by Edwin, at the head of a hastily raised
body of the local fyrd, and soundly beaten. At this, the greater part
of the raiding fleet deserted, leaving Tostig, with about a dozen
ships, to seek shelter in Scotland with his former neighbour, King
Malcolm, until he could be joined by a more powerful ally. Whether
or not Tostig ever went to Norway in person to seek the co-operation
of Harald Hardrada, as Scandinavian saga represented, is uncertain,
but some early liaison seems probable, and it may well be that
Copsi, conveniently based in the outposts of Hardrada's kingdom,
had acted as some kind of go-between. At any rate, Tostig was
to spend most of the summer in Scotland gathering fresh forces for
a further and less precipitate attack on Northumbria.

Meanwhile, Harold Godwinson could draw reassurance from his brother's failure. At least it showed that the north was alert and that the defensive machinery there was more than a match for a serious raid. Local hatred of Tostig would ensure that Edwin and Morcar remained alert to the danger threatening their own coast, thereby allowing the king and his younger brothers to concentrate on the defence of the south. Midsummer, the time of a lingering pagan festival then celebrated on 24 June as the Christian feast of the nativity of St John, came and went with the customary burning of bonfires and torches, but with no further trouble from abroad, and July saw the select fyrd gathered in comforting strength at strategic points along the coast of Wessex. William's fleet was still not fully assembled in the Dives, and it is possible that Harold had now received information pointing to August as the likely month of attack. At Sandwich he had supervised the mustering of his navy, embarking with a force of housecarles to take station off the Isle of Wight, a good base with a view to Channel patrol and interception. Seldom, if ever, had a king of England prepared so comprehensively against a potential aggressor. At a time when it was rare for forces to be raised in defence until violation was actually in progress, such widespread readiness was remarkable, and William's chances, seen objectively, must have looked precarious.

On the face of it, Harold's planning was as sound as it was thorough. On the first sign of a move from Normandy: (1) the patrolling English fleet would attempt to intercept the hostile armada at sea. Harold might himself join issue in a naval engagement, or he might land the crack guards he had with him and contest the enemy's disembarkation; (2) if the Normans succeeded in setting foot on the south coast, the waiting territorials would close in to contain and engage them; (3) the great fyrd of the immediate area would be called to arms to support the select reservists; (4) naval units would move to cut off the enemy's retreat by water. All was ready.

For the time being, however, the main problem lay not in organising action so much as inactivity, and in this respect the rival commanders shared a common task: the critical one of maintaining their armies in good spirits without despoiling the land on which they were quartered. The select fyrd warrior of England joined up with a two-month subsistence allowance guaranteed by his local authority, but he could not eat money, and the consumer demands of an army could soon denude markets unaccustomed to wholesale business. Shortages meant inflated prices, which in turn encouraged the mediaeval soldier in his ever-present tendency to commandeer what he wanted for himself. The passing of August led to a commissarial crisis on both sides of the Channel. The fact that Harold's militia eventually stood to arms in what the chroniclers regarded as unprecedented numbers for at least the stipulated sixty days' service, tediously waiting for a foe who failed to turn up, speaks well of their loyalty to Harold and of his provisioning arrangements. But, in the end, it was William who won the logistical struggle. By the first week of September, the English territorials were near the end of their food supplies, their term of enlistment was up and their home responsibilities were pressing. Harold's army, unlike William's, was not thick with freebooting adventurers. There was also another consideration.

Not only was the wind patently allied with England against a southerly invasion, but the premature gales which in fact hit William's fleet in transit to the Somme about this time must have convinced many Englishmen that danger from across the Channel might be forgotten until another summer. Perhaps even Harold thought that, given a bit of luck, he would be granted a respite for the winter. At all events, on 8 September, the festival of the nativity of St Mary, he dismissed his land fyrd and released his fleet from its station off the south coast. According to the *Anglo-Saxon Chronicle*, some of his ships sailed in to London, 'but many were lost before they arrived'— maybe through the weather, maybe because the crews from other ports preferred to return home instead, or perhaps because of both. Harold apparently chose to ride to his capital.

He had barely settled at Westminster once more when all hopes of a peaceful conclusion to the summer were shattered. The news was brought by men on hard-galloped ponies. The enemy had landed. But the enemy was not William of Normandy. Harald Hardrada had fallen on Yorkshire with a Viking armada of mighty proportions.

13

Fulford and Stamford Bridge

'The ocean is roused, the foam tossed; the whale mere roars, it rages loud; the surges pound the shores, casting sand and shingle hard on the high slopes,' wrote an unknown Anglo-Saxon poet. The people of the English fishing ports knew the sea in all its moods. When they were not upon it, they sat watching as their like have done through the ages, enrapt by its boundless mysteries. To such watchers, a single ship, 'moving with a cry' as another verse of the period described it, was a compelling spectacle: a fleet of several hundred in sail provided an unforgettable experience. Indeed, for the coast-dwellers of north-east England, of small brine-steeped communities like Bamburgh, Wearmouth and Whitby, the seemingly endless armada now pitching slowly and distantly southwards must have been the sight of a lifetime. Offshore, as the war dragons plunged and rose in the swell of the northern sea, spume flying over dripping gunwales to drench heavy, brightly-dyed sails, an army rode damply and uncomfortably towards the point of invasion. Huddled in the lee of their shields,[1] those warriors unoccupied at the oars nursed the freshly-ground blades of their weapons and peered through stinging eyes at the disappearing and re-appearing coastline to starboard. Each helmsman, straining on his steering oar, watched the see-sawing galley ahead, endeavouring to keep distance and line. The whole convoy was led by the great longship of Harald of Norway, 'the last of the Vikings', an impressive figure braced on veteran sea-legs, towering above his aides on the poop.

Harald had assembled his fleet off the Solund Islands, at the mouth

---

[1] The shields were not usually ranged along the gunwales of longships under sail as often supposed, but were displayed thus merely under review order or otherwise for display in harbour.

of Sogne Fjord, to sail for England by way of Shetland and Orkney. According to Snorri, the force had comprised half the fighting men of the kingdom and 'close on two hundred keels, as well as provision ships and smaller craft'. Even at this stage, it must have represented one of the most formidable amphibious operations ever mounted in the north, and several smaller fleets were to join the Norwegians before disembarkation. Harald had planned the enterprise with far-sighted optimism. Before sailing, he had placed his realm in charge of Magnus, one of his two sons by Thora. Presumably Harald, like Canute before him, intended to rule from England. Magnus, backed by his mother and her family, would mind Norway as an under-king in his father's empire. Harald's Russian wife, Elizabeth, would become empress to his emperor, and with this in view she had sailed with him from the north, as had her daughters Mary and Ingigerd, and Harald's other son by Thora, Olaf. On shipboard, too, had gone the king's treasury, reputedly including a gold ingot so massive that it had had to be carried by no less than twelve youths. Smaller items in the royal baggage, though perhaps no less valued, were some locks and fingernails apparently removed by Harald from the remains of the holy King Olaf during a farewell visit to the shrine at Nidaros. Maybe, if the detail is true, they were destined for some place of prominence at Westminster.

With the aid of the northerly wind that held William landlocked in the Somme, the Norwegian fleet had sailed, via Shetland, to Orkney, where it was joined by two leaders of this rugged Scandinavian state, Paul and Erling, sons of the wide-ranging Thorfin who had died a couple of years earlier. Here, too, perhaps, Harald was joined by the adventurers from Iceland and Ireland who were to feature in some chronicles touching on the enterprise. Tostig, with the force he had been able to raise in Scotland, appears to have made for the Tyne, and it was in this direction that Harald, having left his queen and daughters temporarily in Orkney, sailed next. Now reinforced by the sum of his allies, the Norwegian king continued south at the head of upwards of three hundred ships.[1] His manpower

[1] William of Malmesbury and Adam of Bremen supported the *Anglo-Saxon Chronicle* in putting the total fleet at this number which, allowing for additions on the voyage, is not incompatible with Snorri's estimate of the original Norwegian assembly. Florence, however, raised the figure to five hundred.

is not recorded, but a conservative translation might give something in the region of 9,000 men. Here and there on the Yorkshire coast, Harald paused briefly to assert his strength and blood his warriors. Scandinavian tradition told how, as the armada ran 'alongside England', the Norwegian king 'went ashore where it is called Cleveland and harried the countryside, bringing it into subjection without resistance.' He next attacked Scarborough, a town founded during the previous century by another Scandinavian invader, Thorgils 'Skarthi', or hare-lipped. According to Snorri, the Norwegian landing party used familiar incendiary tactics.

While engaging the men of the town, King Harald went upon the cliff there and ordered the making and lighting of a vast bonfire. When it was ablaze, his men took long forks and hurled it down into the town, causing one house after another to burn, thus leaving the townsmen no option but to surrender. The Norwegians slew many men there and took all the goods they could find. Those Englishmen who wished to keep their lives had no choice save to make submission to King Harald. Wherever he went, he brought the land into subjection. Continuing southward off the coast with his fleet he brought-to at Holderness, and there a band opposed him, and King Harald, doing battle with them, gained the day.

The English naval forces in the north, lightweight in comparison with the threatening armada, seemingly retired discreetly into the Humber and thence, via the Ouse and its tributary the Wharf, to the quiet rural centre and secondary river port of Tadcaster. Here, while perhaps safe from the larger of the Norwegian vessels, they at least held a key point on the Roman road between York and the south. Rounding Spurn Head, the Scandinavians also made inland, following the great estuary which divided East Riding from Lindsey and led to the very heart of northern England. Many of the captains would have made trading voyages to York in their time, and there cannot have been any shortage of pilots. Perhaps Tostig himself was well up with the leaders. For some twenty miles from the open sea, the first leg of the Humber took them north-west through bleak, windswept lowlands until, where the River Hull meandered into the estuary[1] across the marshy flats of the north bank, the broad waterway took a

---

[1] Here, at the end of the 13th century, Edward I was to found the commercial port of Kingston-upon-Hull.

sharp turn to the west. With curving wakes, the laden warships swung, one by one, into the natural gateway between the Yorkshire and Lincoln Wolds. Now the enclosing land was more wooded. To port, the village of Barton came in sight. It is hardly probable its inhabitants had waited for such a close view of the procession. More likely, they had retired with their beasts and chattels to watch from the safety of the slopes beyond. Harald's fleet had travelled quickly so far, but news of the danger had travelled faster.

Once past the mouth of the Trent, and through a snaking reach which led to the River Ouse, the invaders were in narrow and dangerous waters, with little scope for naval manœuvre. Here, where the water's edge was often thickly wooded, there was always the possibility of ambush, and lookouts were posted at the mastheads of many ships to scrutinise the countryside. Beneath them, their comrades fingered their weapons or made various adjustments to their armour. The best-equipped were protected by chain-mail from high on the neck to the thighs, or even over the knees. Their iron suits, some composed of as many as four layers of metal links, fitted shirt-fashion, with a hole for the head, a buckle or cord at the neck and wide sleeves to allow vigorous movement of the arms. Legs were covered with leather, and occasionally chain-mail. Heavy gloves protected the hands. The full equipment was costly and, though men of humble rank sometimes obtained it by stripping the dead after battle, it was more often sported by the scions of well-to-do families who could afford to have it made, or who inherited it along with their warrior traditions. Others made-do with tough leather jackets, or jerkins of padded linen, some of which were partially covered with mail or metal rings individually attached. The commonest form of head protection was a close-fitting conical helmet of the simplest design. Here and there a helmet was fitted with nose and cheek pieces, or, more rarely, decorated with crests and other insignia.[1]

The Norwegian armada anchored in the Ouse some three miles short of its junction with the Wharfe, about ten miles due south of

[1] The elaborately decorated helmets romantically associated with Viking warfare probably were more in the nature of ceremonial pieces, emblems of social status, than protective covering to be worn in action during Harald Hardrada's time.

York and roughly the same distance south-east of Tadcaster. The nearest reference point given in the chronicles was the village of Riccall, but, in fact, the fleet must have occupied the river for well over a mile. Harald was excellently placed. Either by accident or design, he had bottled the Northumbrian ships in an upstream tributary, leaving his way back to the sea, should he need it, free from interference. Better still, Edwin and Morcar had assembled their full land fighting strength at York. He could advance on foot towards the city with little likelihood of being cut off from his boats. It was probably about now that Harold of England received his first news of the invasion of Yorkshire, but he was two hundred miles to the south. The King of Norway wasted no time before pressing his advantage. Leaving a portion of his army with the ships, under his son Olaf and the earls of Orkney, he set out with Tostig and the main force to claim the capital of the English north.

Their path led along the east bank of the Ouse where a ridge of dry ground, giving way abruptly to the river on their left, deteriorated gradually to swampland on the right. By the military standards of later ages, the march on York would have seemed a shambles. With no idea of keeping step or formation, the warriors spread in an apparently random mob behind the leaders, though a closer investigation would have revealed that the ship's crews were still bunched together as units, and still bound to some extent by the authority of individual captains. Jostling and jabbering, the army pressed forward, each man drawing strength from the uncommon multitude about him, shields and weapons carried at all angles. Two main types of shield were in prominence. The more popular and up-to-date of the two was oblong in shape, narrower and less rounded at one end than the other, and long enough to cover the greater part of its owner. Basically of wood, reinforced with metal, these long shields were often covered with hide and decorated with such figures as dragons or ravens. The smaller and somewhat old-fashioned round shield, about two feet in diameter, had a wooden face strengthened at the rear by metal, with a metal boss at the front to protect the handle behind it. Lighter in weight than the long shield, it was also more vulnerable to heavy weapons. The shields provided a vivid advertisement for Harald's army. Many were brightly painted, predominantly in red, with blue, yellow and black as other popular colours. In the pale autumnal light, they must have stood out like beacons against the opalescent river.

Although the axe was to become accepted as the typical war instrument of the north, the most popular weapon among these warriors, as in any Viking force, was the sword. Both single- and double-edged varieties were carried, not only of Scandinavian make but also imported from the Rhine and from workshops elsewhere on the Continent. The quality varied considerably. The finest blades, on average about thirty inches long and sometimes grooved to facilitate withdrawal, often bore the engraved name of their makers. The steel was springy and supple. On the other hand, plenty of men carried swords of inferior manufacture, liable to distort or even break in action. The hand-guards were small, for the most part little wider than the pommels, but in many cases both were delicately chased, not infrequently in bronze or silver, sometimes in gold. Most hand-guards were straight, or very slightly curved, while a favourite pommel design was the so-called 'cocked hat'. Perhaps the most splendid were those of Oriental workmanship or influence. Occasionally, the handles were bound in gold wire and even set with jewels. Some warriors of repute displayed their individuality by wielding swords of exceptional size, made to be used double-handed. Harald Sigurdson allegedly fought with this type of weapon, and legend was to immortalise others quite specifically in such names as Leg-biter, War-flame, Greysteel and Venom-switch. Battle-axes were honoured, too, by individual names in some cases, and also decorated on the head with intricate and mystical patterns.

The standard axe carried among Harald's followers flared gracefully in shape from a narrow dimension at the helve to a broad, slightly convex blade. This type had done service with Sweyn Forkbeard and Canute and probably had been fashionable even before that. Nevertheless, other shapes of older origin were doubtless to be seen on the march to York, particularly the classic 'bearded axe', with its blade sharply extended at one end, well remembered in Scandinavian tradition as the Dane's axe. Like the sword, the battle-axe came in single- and double-handed varieties. Then there were spears. The cheapest and simplest to produce of the popular weapons, the unsophisticated spear was still a very useful item in the war armoury. Used as a stabbing implement, it provided the warrior with a long reach; as a missile, it was particularly effective against a close-packed defensive formation. The shaft was often of ash, carved with charms to confound the enemy, while the head, long and slender, was of iron, steel or bronze, embellished sometimes with precious metals. The casting spear was shorter and lighter than the stabbing spear, and many Scandinavians, practised as hunters, were experts at throwing it. The records mention men who could hurl two spears at once, one from each hand, and others who could catch them in flight and return them to the sender. One undoubted drawback to the throwing spear was its tendency to become a gift to the enemy, and thus, in a sense, to backfire. To obviate the process, some spearheads were made to come away from the shaft when thrown, so that while the other side might gain a projectile, there would be no immediate means of re-projecting it. Others were barbed to hinder their withdrawal from flesh or from shields. Arrowheads, too, were metallic and variously shaped, yet, though spears, swords and axes proliferated in the Viking army, bows and arrows appear to have held less appeal, partly perhaps because arming was undertaken on the basis of individual preference and the shooting of arrows seemed insufficiently relevant to the ideal of personal combat. Furthermore, the best of bows was a campaign liability once the arrows were expended, and it must have gone against the grain to discard an instrument personally prized by its most competent handlers as a means of livelihood in peaceful times.

Meanwhile, in the face of Harald's imminent approach, Edwin and Morcar had decided, with some appearance of confidence, to tackle the invaders outside the defence-works of York. Admittedly, the southern walls of the city had long since fallen into disrepair, but the brothers might still have made their stand, with advantage, on the line of the Foss river. Possibly they were under pressure from the influential merchant elements of the city, some with interests on the outskirts, to settle the issue at a safe distance. At worst, an undamaged trading complex, with its traditional Scandinavian alignments, might come to terms with a Norwegian régime. At best, the threat could be dispersed without loss of property and investments.

Indeed, the English earls might plausibly have considered their joint command a match for the enemy, for by any conscious precedent their force was a considerable one. To the hard core of Morcar's household guard, plus at least a strong detachment of Edwin's guardsmen, had been added a resolute levy of northern militiamen, including the same hale and purposeful Northumbrian thegns who had earlier ousted Tostig from the earldom. These would have come on horseback from a wide area, each with his armour (much in the Scandinavian style) and his sword or spear. On top of this, the great fyrd of the immediate district, the general body of peasants, roughly but viciously armed with a variety of lethal implements, would have mustered to the banner of Morcar, prepared to fight for its homes and its own. Doubtless the sum was as powerful and belligerent an array as could be remembered in the ancient military centre of York. But it was still, in a sense, a provincial army set against the military élite of a nation; an earl's following against the host of a king. And that king, in turn, had earls among his allies.

The armies met two miles south of York near a place named Fulford, now a suburb of the city, but then a village. According to Scandinavian tradition, the invaders, drawn up by the Ouse in prepared position, allowed the English to attack first. The Norwegian king, an ageing but flamboyant figure beneath his banner, the so-called Landwaster, allegedly held ground on the left of his formation, a wing arrayed by the river bank.

. . . and one arm of the array was ranked beside the river, while the other stretched inland towards a dyke, where there was also a deep marsh, broad and full of water. The [English] Earls ordered their whole multitude to advance by the river. Now the banner of the King was near the river and there the [Norwegian] ranks were shoulder to shoulder, but near the dyke they were thinner and the men less reliable. The Earls then switched their attack to the dyke and the arm of the Norwegian formation there gave way, whereupon the English pushed forward, expecting the Norwegians to flee. The banner of Morcar advanced. But when King Harald saw that the English had fared alongside the dyke and were advancing, he commanded the charge to be sounded, and eagerly encouraging his men, let the banner Landwaster be carried forward. . . .[1]

---

[1] 'The Saga of Harald Hardrada.'

Unfortunately, Snorri's saga, which might otherwise have been regarded as the one detailed clue to the mechanics of the battle, is demonstrably untrustworthy of its treatment of the Norwegian campaign in England. In truth, this great pitched battle, more terrible in its proportions than anything then heard of, is pretty well a blank page in modern historical knowledge. It is thought that the struggle raged for the best part of a day, and the Northumbrians unquestionably stood with immense tenacity to hold the many thousand invaders. A brief mention of the engagement in the *Anglo-Saxon Chronicle*, where it was overshadowed by the epic events to follow, stated that the defenders 'made great slaughter' of the Norwegians, 'but a great number of the English were either slain or drowned or driven in flight. . . .'

There is little reason to doubt that Harald of Norway, probably stronger numerically than his opponents, and certainly in the overall fighting efficiency of his army, forced the issue at some stage of the day with a grand charge. A favourite Scandinavian battle device for breaking enemy resistance was the *svin-fylking*, or swine-formation— a packed arrowhead pointed by a handful of the most rugged and fanatical warriors, and employed, rather like a giant snow-plough, to sweep through the opposing lines. The array had a special advantage for the commanders of unsophisticated armies whose men were far readier to receive an attack than to press one home against determined resistance, in that the bulk of the weight was at the back. The front ranks, like those of a surging football crowd, had no option but to keep advancing. In such an instance, the type of warrior given to *berserker* behaviour would have been particularly useful for the somewhat suicidal role of 'tipping' the wedge. The trumpeter would sound a war-blast on his horn, the Norsemen would utter a blood-curdling yell to demoralise their enemies, exhortations would be offered to Odin, the god of battle, and to other holy ones both Christian and pagan, and, with the crimson Landwaster fluttering at the centre, the whole formation would sway into motion. Harald can well be pictured swinging his massive sword double-handed in the midst of the ensuing fracas, as can the appalling butchery received and inflicted by both sides.

Among the English dead, it was told later, was a number of priests.

They had died exchanging blow for blow with the Norwegians. Many of the wounded, crawling into the marshes to escape the death-blows of the victors, perished instead by drowning. Before the day was out, the Northumbrian resistance was broken, 'and the Norwegians had possession of the field of slaughter' (*ASC*). Snorri's description of the fate of the English remnants corroborated, if more luridly, the native chronicler. 'Some fled up alongside the river, and some down, but most of them ran straight into the dyke, and there the fallen lay so thick that the Norwegians could walk dry-shod . . .'[1] By evening, the invaders were planning their next step. It was Wednesday, 20 September, the vigil of St Matthew. The road to York lay open.

★

Meanwhile, events had moved quickly in the south. Harold God-winson, having dismissed his standing forces in Hampshire on 8 September, rode to London. Some time within the next few days, intelligence reached the capital of a kind which convinced him that the King of Norway either had made, or intended to make, a full-scale landing in the north of the country. It is possible that this intelligence consisted of news of one or more of Hardrada's pre-liminary landings on the Northumbrian coast, linked with the reputed presence of the former earl of that territory. On the other hand, it might have embraced the more conclusive information that the Norwegian fleet had turned into the Humber. It may even be, though the timing of following events makes it appear unlikely, that the king in London determined his strategy in the knowledge of the ultimate landing at Riccall. Whatever the case, the drama of the situation was stark. To the south, William of Normandy was now waiting for the slenderest nod from the weather to make his bid before winter brought all his preparations to nothing. Harold was faced with a choice between two propositions: (1) that the need to maintain his watch in the south, ready for immediate remobilisation against William, was sufficiently vital to warrant gambling on the ability and resolution of the northern earls to repulse Hardrada;

[1] This picture of the living walking on bridges of corpses is proverbial in early western literature.

(2) that the actuality of the Norwegian invasion, and the need for its immediate suppression, justified the chances of a two-hundred-mile march, a quick and decisive victory against Hardrada and a return in good enough order to rally Wessex, if need be, against a Norman landing. In another sense, Harold was confronted by the classic strategic crisis: a straight choice between the dangers of doing too little or attempting too much. He acted with Napoleonic resolution.

On a day now unknown, probably about the end of the second week of September, the King of England set off northwards from London at the head of his housecarles and such of the Home Counties fyrd as was available for service at short notice. For the bulk of his men it was to be a trek into unfamiliar regions, an adventure that would take them further from home than perhaps many had ever dreamed of travelling in that land still fundamentally parochial. For all, it was to prove a march into history; a place in one of the most vivid military operations in early English times. 'By day and by night' (*ASC*) Harold's column drove north, ponies and wagons clattering noisily through the towns and villages on the way, surrounded by silence in the woods and the great open spaces.

Ermine Street, the most direct route then in use to the north-east, followed the Lea valley away from London between the woods of Middlesex and Essex, passed by Hertford, crossed the eastern Chilterns and thence through the lowlands of Cambridgeshire to Huntingdon. Here the rough and ready line of march jogged past the battered border-fortress, demolished in turn earlier by both English and Danes, and, picking its way round the vast fenlands of the east, across countless ditches, streams and rivers, pushed on through the thinning forests of Kesteven to Lincoln. Harold's audacious bid to check the Norwegians was all the more remarkable, as a personal effort, if his biographer, Ailred of Rielvaux, can be believed. According to the tradition accepted by this writer, the forty-year-old king was not a fit man at the time of the journey. He appears to have suffered from some form of seizure in the leg, perhaps rheumatism or gout. If so, it did little to delay him. Leaving Lincoln through the northern gate, which still sported its fine Roman masonry,[1] the now travel-worn column veered westward to miss

---

[1] The Roman gate was a great arch between two smaller ones, one of which survives.

the Humber, passing by Torksey, across Hatfield Chase to Castleford. On its left rose the bleak, wolf-infested slopes of the Pennines. It would seem reasonable to expect that the less well-fitted of Harold's levies were finding it hard to keep pace with the royal guards; that sections of the force were straggling. But at least the object of the strike was drawing nearer. On Sunday, 24 September, the masts of English ships appeared in view across the meadows of the Wharfe, and the weary soldiers descended gratefully upon Tadcaster, having missed the battle of Fulford by four days.

Edwin and Morcar had escaped from Fulford with their lives, but their army was demolished. With nothing to stop them, Harald of Norway and Tostig had entered York, taking hostages and provisions. The Norwegian king had been discreet enough, however, not to let his men occupy the city. It was important for him to gain not only the recognition of the capital, but also the co-operation of the province in his prospective southwards march to conquer the rest of England, and a horde of loot-conscious warriors turned loose in the streets would not help in the slightest. Instead, Harald Sigurdson had retired to his ships, having arranged a further meeting with local representatives at Stamford Bridge, a convenient road junction some eight miles east of York, where hostages were to be brought to him from all over the shire. Here, trails from many parts of eastern Yorkshire converged on the River Derwent, running on through the nearby village of Gate Helmsley to the capital itself. It was a pleasant, if rather featureless spot. The bridge, of wood, stood at a shallow point in the reedy stream, probably where a broken causeway of stones had once served as a crossing.[1] To the east, the land sloped gently upwards towards the Wolds. To the west, it was mainly flat, with a slight rise for about a mile to Helmsley. The Norwegian army arrived at this tranquil rendezvous, it seems likely, late on Sunday. At about the same time, Harold Godwinson was posting his guards at Tadcaster.

First light on Monday saw the southern army advancing on York, where, if the news had not reached him already, Harold learned that his brother and the King of Norway were camped with the best part of their forces several miles to the east of the city, awaiting the

---

[1] The existing stone bridge is a few hundred feet downstream from the original site.

hostages as promised. The hostages never arrived. Barely pausing in York lest news of his presence went ahead of him, Harold left the city by Walmgate, approached Helmsley in battle order and launched his warriors 'unexpectedly upon the Norwegians' (*ASC*). Two of the Anglo-Saxon chroniclers mentioned the surprise element of the battle at Stamford Bridge, and all implied its ferocity, but it was left to writers working from the traditions of later times to provide most of the now familiar detail, much of which, unfortunately, appears to be more colourful than valid.[1]

In fact, the conflict progressed through three distinct phases, from each of which can be drawn some reconstructive deductions. The first, and least clarified phase, was staged on the west bank of the river. The Norwegian army seems originally to have occupied both sides of the Derwent in a fairly relaxed and casual manner, so that a portion of it was in the hapless position of being not merely in random order on the English downhill approach, but caught with its backs to the water. Clearly, the primary aim of this section was to remove itself to the east bank. To what extent the movement was achieved before action was engaged is uncertain. The stream was perhaps twenty yards wide at that point and, if fordable, certainly a considerable obstacle. Alternatively, the bridge represented a very narrow bottleneck. Henry of Huntingdon portrayed this phase of the operations as a fighting withdrawal on the part of the Scandinavians. On the other hand, a twelfth-century addition to the *Anglo-Saxon Chronicle* suggested that the Norwegians fled across the river, the writer giving special mention to a single warrior who fought a stubborn delaying action with the English vanguard on the bridge. He was despatched, eventually, by one of Harold Godwinson's men who 'went under the bridge' and reportedly stabbed upwards into the Norseman's guts.

[1] The Scandinavian tradition is regarded as unreliable by many modern historians (for an opposite view see Richard Glover's *English Warfare in 1066*). Snorri's description of Harold Godwinson's army seems to have been based on an English army of Snorri's own time, i.e. a Norman-influenced force using cavalry. In parts his version of Stamford Bridge reads more like the Battle of Hastings, with the English taking the Norman role and the Norwegians taking the English one. Two preliminary incidents in Snorri's account of the battle—Harold Godwinson's promise that his adversary would be given 'seven feet of ground or as much as he is taller than other men', and Harald Sigurdson's observation on taking an accidental tumble that 'Falling when faring betokens fortune'—were both applied in substance by earlier writers to William, and probably were dramatic clichés long before that time.

The second phase of the battle was a desperate hand-to-hand tussle to the east of the river. With at least the slope in his favour, Harald of Norway fought to stem the English advance and to organise his forces in some solid defensive formation. Against this, Harold of England's men, sensing victory, pressed forward with a vigour which belied the strenuousness of their recent march. The royal housecarles, in particular, mail-clad and heavily armed with axes, won an awesome reputation that was to linger long in Scandinavian history where each came to be regarded as a match for any two other men. Much was to be made in various accounts of the battle of the tactical unpreparedness of the invaders, but the crux of their misfortune went deeper and was less redeemable. They had fought the battle of their lives only five days earlier, and paid a high price then for victory. Armed belligerence and sabre-rattling might have been mediaeval commonplace, but pitched battles at national, or even regional level, were not. They were entered upon rarely and usually reluctantly, for commanders staked their entire resources upon the result, which was normally conclusive. Losers lost all; victors expected good time to recoup. In fact, when Harold of England hit them, the Norwegians and their allies had scarcely had breathing space since burying their dead from the previous engagement. Physically debilitated by their mauling from the vanquished Northumbrians, they must have suffered as well from the delayed action of battle-shock. Two conflicts on such a scale within five days were to prove one too many, even for the resourceful old Viking general. Harald could not fight the ghosts of Fulford.

Nevertheless, the battle ebbed on through the afternoon. From the far side of the Derwent, those minding the ponies on which the southern warriors had ridden to Helmsley must have watched anxiously as, time and again, the grey figures of the royal guards led the English against the combined defences of Scandinavians, Scots and Flemings. Often it would have been difficult to distinguish side from side in the mêlée. Somewhere near the banner of Wessex, a golden dragon, the King of England was roaring exhortations and orders. Somewhere in that crowd of frantic men clustered round the Norwegian banner, Harald Sigurdson, Tostig Godwinson and many others unknown by name were striking the last violent blows of their lives.

A fleeting image of Hardrada in action at Stamford Bridge was preserved: 'In battle fast the chief's heart never quaked, and the greatest
courage was shown by the strong king amidst the war-cloud's
thunder . . . by his bloody sword the men to death were wounded.'[1]
Some time after noon he received a fatal blow. Tostig, it seems, fell
later. Their carcasses had done bleeding and were cold before dusk.

With victory assured, Harold of England turned his attention to
dissecting the remaining areas of enemy resistance. His own losses
had been heavy and his soldiers were tired. It was necessary to
perform the final act of surgery before the stimulant of battle
delirium subsided. The last phase was the dogged butchery of a
broken and hopeless army:

> *Mishap has fallen on us. . .*
> *In vain has Harald brought us*
> *On this journey from the east*
> *The shrewd chieftain's life-span*
> *Having ended, we now . . .*
> *Fare in peril of our lives.*[2]

Harold Godwinson organised the relentless pursuit of his enemies
until they were wiped out. 'While the English savagely harried their
rear, the remaining Norwegians were put to flight . . . some were
drowned, some were burnt to death . . . diversely they perished,
until there were few survivors . . .' (*ASC*). Presumably the drowned
had tried to recross the Derwent to gain the shelter of their ships on
the Ouse. The burning seems more mysterious. Perhaps parties of
desperate Scandinavians were surrounded in nearby churches or
farm buildings which were then set on fire by the English.

Only the detachment left to guard the fleet under Olaf and the
Orkney earls was spared to return to its homelands. A pathetic
residue. Of the three-hundred-odd ships which had brought Hardrada's army to the Humber, twenty-four were sufficient to remove
the survivors. Stamford Bridge was to mark the failure of the last
Scandinavian invasion in English history. Three days later, at
approximately 9 a.m. Thursday, 28 September, William of Normandy's army splashed ashore unopposed on the Sussex coast.

[1] The earl's *skald* Arnor quoted in the 'Saga of Harald Hardrada'.
[2] The *skald* Thiodolf quoted in the 'Saga of Harald Hardrada'.

14

The Duke Strikes

By the final week of September, William's frustration had been almost complete. Day after day, an overcast sky had brought rain, turning the Somme into a grey and forbidding trough, seeping through the woollen cloth of tents, softening grassland to mud. The horse lines were a quagmire, the duke's men damp and forlorn. Winter drew ominously near, and still the vane on the church tower of St Valéry refused to offer hope. Then, quite suddenly, the outlook brightened. The clouds parted and autumn threw a dazzling finale. On Wednesday, 27 September, the wind veered to blow at last from the south. Caution might have prompted William to let the weather settle, but his army was at the end of its tether. He ordered its immediate embarkation.

The long-awaited command produced a frenzy of action. The old Norman chronicles told how men raced each other to be the first aboard, some even forgetting their goods and chattels in their anxiety not to be left behind. Captains barked instructions; men exhorted each other to hurry; pipes, drums and cymbals took up the theme of martial urgency. Throughout afternoon and evening, preparations continued. Masts were set, sails unfurled, horses loaded, equipment stowed in position. It was dark before the ships began to weigh anchor, slipping away individually or in batches to take up convoy formation at an assembly point near the mouth of the estuary. The plan was for the duke's galley, the *Mora*, to act as 'pathfinder', her nearest sisters following a bright light at her masthead while the rest kept in touch down the line. When all had had time to take stations her master gave the final order for the great fleet to sail.

Through the night the *Mora* plunged and creaked northwards. A queenly vessel, her performance was excellent, and William must have congratulated himself on his progress. But first light brought a nasty surprise. The speed of the flagship had been too much for the heavily-laden transports. Sometime in the hours of darkness, they had lost touch with her guiding lantern. William and his crew were alone in mid-Channel. It was a moment of outstanding peril. The appearance of two or three English ships at this stage could have wrecked not only the whole enterprise but possibly the very future of Normandy. Ordering his apprehensive crew to heave to, William set its members a cool example. There on the chillingly deserted sea, he called for food, and, opening a cask of wine, proceeded to tackle a hearty breakfast. Such a good face did he put on his discomfort that it was as if, wrote William of Poitiers, 'he were in a room of his own home'. Eventually, a look-out at the masthead announced that four ships were in sight, then 'such a host that their masts resembled a forest'. The wallowing galleys of the armada had held a true course. There was to be no further mistake. In bright daylight, the fleet hove in sight of Pevensey's flat and inviting beaches.

There is some evidence that Pevensey had been strongly garrisoned before the dispersal of Harold's reservists, but now the shore was deserted. It was about nine o'clock. According to the traditional Norman version of the landing, the breeze was soft and sweet, the sea conveniently smooth.

The ships ran aground side by side. Sailors, serjeants and squires could be seen jumping to the immediate business of disembarkation; casting the anchors, hauling ropes, bearing out shields and saddles, landing war horses and palfreys. The first to sally forth were the archers, who landed with bows strung, each with a full quiver of arrows at his side. All were shaven and shorn, and all clad in short garments, prepared to attack, to shoot, to wheel and skirmish. Well equipped and in good spirits, they scoured the whole shore without finding any opposition. When the archers had thus established a beach-head, the armed knights landed, their hauberks on, shields slung at their necks and their helmets laced. Having assembled in mounted formation on the shore, these rode forward into the country-side, swords girded on and lances raised. Then the carpenters landed. They had great axes in their hands, and planes and adzes hung at their sides. They took counsel together, seeking a good position to fortify. They had brought with them from Normandy the elements of three wooden forts, ready for putting together, and they now took enough material for one out of the ships. It was all shaped and pierced to take the pins they had brought cut and ready in large barrels. Before evening set in, they had completed a good fort on English soil, and there they placed their stores. Everyone then ate and drank well, right glad that they were ashore.[1]

The fortifications were placed, it seems, within the ruins of the old Roman stronghold of Anderida, providing a guard post and stores depot suitably adjacent to the ships. But, as mounted reconnaissance must soon have informed the duke, Pevensey was by no means an ideal base. Neither the town nor the surrounding countryside was rich enough in provisions to support a large army, even for a short while. Moreover, an expanse of marshy flats to the north and east seriously restricted foraging movements and might have proved tactically dangerous. Boggy land offered a special advantage to those with local knowledge. Accordingly, the invaders lost no time seeking a better headquarters with more freedom to manœuvre.

The next day they marched along the coast to Hastings. Near that place, the duke fortified a camp, setting up the two other wooden strongholds. The foragers, and those on the look-out for booty, seized all the clothing and provisions they could find in case their ship-borne supplies should fail them. And the English could be seen fleeing before them, driving off cattle and quitting their houses. Many took shelter in burying-places, and even there were in great alarm.[2]

Hastings, with a useful harbour and relative prosperity, was more to William's taste than the original encampment. To the north lay a ridge of high land, culminating in Telham Hill, from which his riders could descend into the fertile Rother Valley beyond. At the same time, he was immediately covered to east and west by the estuaries of two small rivers, the Brede and the Bulverhythe, and even provided on his seaward side with a small peninsula which, if the worst came to the worst, could become a handy point of retreat while his force re-embarked. Within a day or two, the whole of the duke's fleet and army had transferred to this new position.

[1] Wace. The Norman tradition includes the familiar story of William falling as he stepped from his boat. To allay the distress of his followers he is supposed to have shouted: 'See my lords! By the splendour of God, I have taken possession of England with both hands. It is mine; and what is mine is yours.' As noted in the previous chapter, the incident is suspiciously unoriginal.

[2] Ibid.

What has been described as one of the most important amphibious operations in the history of war, was now complete. Though there is some suggestion in Norman writings that a small number of ships might have been lost on the voyage, perhaps due to overloading or straying from convoy in the night, the crossing and landing could hardly have been more successful. Potential local opposition had been shocked into impotence by the scale of the invasion, which appears to have proved sufficient in itself to awe even such an important naval station as Hastings into lame submission. Perhaps a fair proportion of Hastings men had sailed to London under Harold's orders from the Isle of Wight. In any case, the town specialised in seamen, not in land soldiers. William was now well enough placed to pause and consider his strategy. At a council of war portrayed in the Bayeux Tapestry, he was shown in conference with his half-brothers, Bishop Odo and Robert of Mortain. Their talk must have turned on a number of imponderables.

To begin, where was Harold and how strong was his army? In the second place, what was Hardrada up to? If William had some inkling of the Norwegian's plans, he was ignorant as yet of their outcome. Supposing the Scandinavians had already defeated Harold? Then he would have a Viking army to contend with. He could have no idea of its strength. Again, supposing nothing decisive had occurred between Hardrada and the English? Then fighting Harold would, at best, be only half the story. Even in victory, he would have to prepare afresh for battle. And where did Tostig fit into the picture? Was he once more a power in this country? If so, the outlook became increasingly complex. Some answers were urgently needed, and until he had them William was loath to push his luck further. His only sensible course was to stay near his ships. This resolved, the need was to draw the enemy before the supply sources of the area ran dry. The method employed was the familiar one of harrying, in which, quite apart from foraging and plundering for gain, the destruction of civilian homes and property was pursued for its own sake. Crude and unoriginal, indeed as old as tribalism itself, this barbarity was invested by William with his own special thoroughness and cruelty. Twenty years later, the territory involved had not recovered fully from his ravages. Such measures were symbolised poignantly in the Bayeux Tapestry by a scene in which a woman and her child, hand in hand, stood by their house while Norman soldiers put it to flames.

The first reliable news William appears to have received about the forces ranged against him came from Robert fitz Wimarc, an English landowner of Breton origin. As a member of Edward the Confessor's circle of French friends—he was a high official in the royal household at Edward's death—yet also a man who had come to respect, and live peacefully under, Harold, Robert seems to have been motivated by a sincere desire to prevent bloodshed between the men of the Continent and of his adopted country. To this end, he sent a messenger to Hastings—possibly the messenger shown speaking to William in the Bayeux Tapestry—with the information that Harold had recently overwhelmed a great Scandinavian invasion, killing Hardrada, Tostig and an immense number of their men, and was now marching south to deal with the Normans. William of Poitiers represented Robert counselling the duke as a friend and kinsman. The picture the Breton painted was gloomy in the extreme for the army at Hastings. The Normans would not stand a chance against the forces which had just defeated the greatest warrior king in the world. Against such men, declared Robert, the defiance of the duke's army would be no more effective than 'the barking of curs'. Let William act prudently and withdraw to his own land. At the very least, let him remain within his fortifications and avoid an open battle, for it could bring nothing but utter destruction to the Frenchmen.

William seems to have been less than dismayed by the warning. For such interest, if not entirely for the gratuitous comparisons, he thanked Robert fitz Wimarc politely, disdaining, however, to modify his tactics. The answers to most of his questions were now before him. The crown of England rested on the result of a straight fight.

*

According to the generally accepted tradition, Harold was still at York when news of William's landing reached him, though it is possible that he had begun to retrace his way south. Wace ascribed to him at that moment the boast that, had he been on the spot, the invaders would have been driven back into the sea, or killed where they landed. 'But,' the poet put into the king's mouth, 'God ordained otherwise. I could not be everywhere at once.' It was not for the want of trying. On 24 September he had rested at Tadcaster on his northerly march against Hardrada. By 6 October, he had completed the journey to Stamford Bridge, engaged and routed the Norwegians, reassembled his weary and depleted army at York, rallied and reorganised the northern government, and amazingly supervised and completed the return march of his forces to London. An astonishing feat in less than a fortnight. Within eight days of the Norman landing, some of which were lost in the conveyance of the tidings, Harold was back in his capital arranging the defence of the south.

He had returned to London, however, with only part of the force he had taken to the north. English losses, especially among the royal housecarles, had been heavy at Stamford Bridge, and the rapidity of his subsequent march south had outstripped the weary, the sick and the ill-mounted among his followers. Though elated by victory, and toughened by campaigning, the residue badly needed reinforcing before another major engagement. So far, Harold had drawn on the reservists quickly available to London, or adjacent to his route through the midlands. Expansion now depended on mustering those from the more distant shires, and here he was up against the delays inevitable in widespread mobilisation. Summonses had to be written and dispatched by horse transport to the appropriate provincial centres, where, through the slow-moving medium of local government, they would be relayed to outlying districts. Individual reservists, having been tracked down in their villages or on their estates, then had to make their various personal arrangements: to brief substitutes to act in their absence, to bring up to date bequests and other provisions against death in action, to organise subsistence for themselves and perhaps for servants on their travels, to shoe horses, sharpen weapons, make family farewells, and so on. And finally, each warrior had to trek, with all the attendant mediaeval hazards of the road before him, to the appointed place of assembly. Whether Harold sent out summonses from York, from London or from points on his march south, he could expect little response at the capital within the first few days of his arrival, and large sections of the reserve might take anything from a week to a fortnight to muster.

Meanwhile, William's calculated destruction and terrorisation in Sussex, was to prove, as intended, a sore provocation. Each day of waiting in London might bring Harold fresh troops, but it also brought new and anguished reports of Norman activity in the family earldom. Honour and anger urged prompt intervention. So, in cooler reason, did the success of his recent strategy. If the swift, long-range strike which he had once tested so effectively against the Welsh, and later studied at first hand in Brittany, had caught the experienced Harald of Norway off balance, why not William of Normandy too? Indeed, in some ways the situation was more favourable to a surprise move than had been the northern campaign. The distance from London to Hastings was less than sixty miles, against two hundred to York. Much of the way he would be covered by the dense woodlands of the Andredesweald. And, as distinct from the prospects of the Northumbrian manoeuvre, the loyalty of the people of Sussex was guaranteed. On the other hand, the arguments for delaying the move from London were powerful ones. Such a delay would make the difference between challenging William with all, as opposed to only part of Harold's available resources; it would mean a better rest for the men who had been at Stamford Bridge, and, given time enough, it would force the Normans to extend their communications, perhaps even allowing the English to cut them off from their ships.

Harold's dilemma was a harsh one. According to a Waltham tradition, the king sought spiritual aid there, at his church of the holy rood, before taking action. The local writer described a solemn ritual in which the rugged patron of the shrine, exhausted by one ordeal and facing another, placed a special gift of saintly relics on the altar and proposed a touching bargain with his god. If victory was granted him over the Normans, he would devote his life in slavish service to the king of heaven. He also promised that the foundation at Waltham would receive further lands and donations, and that he would undertake to increase its congregation. Surrounded by the canons and other members of the church, he then prostrated himself beneath the holy cross. A single witness, one

Thurkill, the keeper of the sacred vessels, later claimed that at that moment he saw the head of the holy image droop sadly forward. Legend apart, there can be little doubt that, with fate timing its blows so chasteningly against him, Harold was not unmindful of his spiritual status, especially the pressing aspect of his oath to the Duke of Normandy. William of Malmesbury, along with several Norman authorities, had it that Harold's brother Gyrth, the Earl of East Anglia, offered to lead the English army against the invaders while the king remained in London, suggesting not only that his brother needed a rest after the Northumbrian campaign but that for Harold to ignore the implications of the controversial oath to the extent of actually meeting William in battle would be tempting providence too far.

If this were true, Harold rejected the offer. It would, in any case, have smacked of compromise, and could hardly have helped the morale of his followers. He appears also to have rejected a number of ostentatious demands and challenges from William. It is a pity that the English chroniclers had nothing to say on this matter, for the Norman writers were so full of conflicting and inflated statements concerning messages, counter-messages, bribes, threats and summonses, that the tradition which later hardened from their literature can be offered only as a pertinent myth.

As a later historian resolved it:

A monk named Hugues Maigrot [Hugh Margot or Maigret] came in William's name to call upon the Saxon king to do one of three things, either to resign his royalty in favour of William, or to refer it to the arbitration of the Pope to decide which of the two ought to be king, or to let it be determined by the issue of a single combat. Harold abruptly replied, 'I will not resign my title, I will not refer it to the Pope, nor will I accept the single combat.' He was far from being deficient in bravery; but he was no more at liberty to stake the crown which he had received from a whole people on the chance of a duel, than to deposit it in the hands of an Italian priest. William was not at all ruffled by the Saxon's refusal, but steadily pursuing the course of his calculated measures, sent the Norman monk again, after giving him these instructions: 'Go and tell Harold that if he will keep his former compact with me, I will leave him all the country which is beyond the Humber, and will give his brother Gyrth all the lands which Godwin held. If he still persist in refusing my offers, then thou shalt tell him, before all his people, that he is a perjurer and a liar;

that he and all who support him are excommunicated by the mouth of the Pope; and that the bull to that effect is in my hands.'

The English chiefs were represented in the story as sceptical:

'The Norman has given our lands to his captains, to his knights, to all his people, the greater part of whom have already done homage to him for them; they will all look for their gift if their Duke become our king; and he himself is bound to deliver up to them our goods, our wives and our daughters: all is promised to them beforehand. They come not only to ruin us, but to ruin our descendants also, and to take from us the land of our ancestors. And what shall we do—whither shall we go—when we have no longer a country?' The English promised, by a unanimous oath, to make neither peace, nor truce nor treaty, with the invader, but to die or drive away the Normans.[1]

In fact, Harold waited just long enough for some of the least distant reservists to join him, and, on 11 October, the fifth day after his return from the north, led his force out of London and struck the road for the south coast. Rightly or wrongly, he had decided on an early attack. Many historians have questioned Harold's generalship at this stage, but none has doubted his courage. It was a loyal army that followed him, though much of it still sore and scarred from recent combat. At its core were the royal housecarles, veterans of the wars with Gruffyd and Hardrada, strengthened by the guards of Harold's brothers, Gyrth and Leofwine. Beside this clique of professionals, rode the thegns and mounted ceorls of the select fyrd who had joined the king on his march to or from York, plus a fresh territorial element comprising the early body of response to his latest summons. Among the various ranks, now moving in a noisy haphazard column over the North Downs and into the Vale of Kent, could be heard the accents of London, Kent, Essex, Surrey, Sussex, Suffolk, Norfolk, Dorset, Somerset, Hampshire and Berkshire, together with such other places as Bedford, Huntingdon, Northampton, Buckingham and Nottingham (Wace). The northern earls, having spent their resources in the bloody stand at Fulford, were not represented in any strength, though a number of mounted warriors from York, Lindsey and Lincoln appear to have attached themselves to Harold. Purposefully, the army pressed on through the

[1] Thierry—there have been many different versions.

forest belt. Hatred of the Norman invader drew the peasants in arms from their villages to swell the hosts. Those who could not lay their hands on better weapons, came with slings and stones, and with cudgels and pitchforks.

Reinforced by this motley but numerous following of the great fyrd, the king's army probably totalled something between 6,000 and 7,000 men. Unfortunately few records have survived to identify the individuals who made that fateful journey with Harold. At his side were his younger brothers. Among other members of his personal retinue, was a deacon named Eadric who had first taken service with his lord when Harold had been Earl of East Anglia. Two prelates, the king's uncle Aelfwig, abbot of the New Minster, Winchester, and Abbot Leofric of Peterborough, rode doggedly behind, surrounded by armed monks. The monastic costume beneath their hauberks distinguished them quaintly from the leather-and-iron-clad housecarles. Then, with the men of Kent, came a sheriff named Esegar, and from Berkshire another sheriff, Godric, and a man named Thurkill. From all the rough and colourful warriors straggling in the wake of Harold's banner on that Hastings road, only two others were to linger by name in history, a certain Aelfric of Gelling, a thegn from Huntingdonshire, and 'a freeman' of unknown origin, Breme.

The English army reached the slopes north of Hastings on the night of 13-14 October, much of it in a state of considerable exhaustion. Whether or not it would have been in a condition to mount a surprise attack on William the next day, assuming this was Harold's intention,[1] is doubtful. As it happened, the opportunity never arose for by sunset on Friday, the 13th, the king's movements had been spotted by Norman scouts. Suddenly, the initiative landed squarely in the duke's lap. Seven miles away, that night, a travel-worn enemy was camped rough in the chill and darkened countryside. The information was almost too good to be true, and William seized his chance avidly. First thing next morning, the invaders left Hastings, advancing rapidly towards the ill-prepared English lines.

[1] Freeman, among other authorities, maintained that Harold never intended to attack the Norman army, simply to adopt a defensive position in the Hastings area and wait to be attacked. The theory, hard to reconcile with his haste and with some of the best evidence, is not generally accepted by present-day experts.

15

The Battle at Senlac

Saturday, 14 October, dawned on a Sussex in the full flush of her seasonal brilliance. There are still wooded views in that part of England whose colourings catch at the breath in autumn. Then, the forests spread wider and denser. Ahead of William's knights stretched a golden island, and their path, the customary route from Hastings to London, led north-west along a neck of high land, offering an admirable vista of the promised country. For some five or six miles, the scouts reported no sign of hostile activity. Then, rather less than seven miles from Hastings, the ridge came to an end in Telham, or Heathland, and across an intervening valley the invaders caught their first glimpse of Harold's army. It was positioned on a grassy, peninsula-shaped hill known as Senlac, a barren and normally deserted place standing more or less at right-angles to the Hastings road. Behind it, a rough causeway of high ground linked the hill with the thickly-wooded downs through which Harold had approached from London. According to tradition, the English king had placed his two standards—the victorious Dragon of Wessex, and his personal ensign, a bejewelled and gold-embroidered gonfanon representing a fighting warrior—near the crown of the hill, on the spot later occupied by the high altar of Battle Abbey. About two hundred yards to the east of this, and four hundred to the west, the hill fell away sufficiently to provide readily defensible gradients on either of Harold's flanks. To his front, the slope was less pronounced, the easiest ascent from the valley bottom rising little more than fifty feet in the four hundred yards to his personal station on Senlac. Around him, the hill was swarming with Englishmen.

For William, everything now depended on the temper of his warriors. His army, though somewhat less numerous than Harold's, contained a higher proportion of select men. Furthermore, it was fresh, and eager for conquest. But it had still to be tested in action as a cohesive unit. Moreover, it had yet to face English tactics. The task ahead was more onerous than that of sitting in siege outside some French castle. Senlac bristled with swords and axes, and if the grim task of engaging it proved too much for French and Norman hearts, at least England, if not all, was now lost to William. The danger that his force of adventurers might prove less than venturesome when it came to real business can have been no less worrying to the duke than to any other commander of the time whose fortunes depended on attacking in the face of strong and determined resistance. In an address to his men on the morning of the battle, it seems he was at pains to stress their lack of alternative.

For God's sake spare not [he was quoted as pleading], strike hard at the beginning; don't stop to take spoil; all the booty shall be in common, and there will be plenty for everyone. There will be no safety in asking quarter or in flight; the English will never love or spare a Norman. Felons they were and felons they are; false they were and false they will be. Show no weakness towards them, for they will have no pity on you. Neither the coward for running well, nor the bold men for smiting well, will be the better liked by the English, nor will any be the more spared on either account. You may fly to the sea, but no further ... the English will over-take you and slay you in your shame. More of you will die in flight than in battle. Therefore, since flight will not save you, fight and you will conquer. I have no doubt of the victory: we are come for glory, the victory is in our hands and we may be sure of obtaining it if we so please.[1]

Harold was not without his own troubles. Certain sections of his army, it seems, had reservations about becoming the subjects of violence. A contemporary English chronicler had no doubt that William's prompt advance had taken the king by surprise, 'before his army was set in order' (*ASC*), and the resulting confusion perhaps inspired part of the great fyrd to make good its retirement. The theory is partially backed by Florence of Worcester, who claimed that many of the Englishmen deserted because they found the position on the hill too cramped. Such an objection would hardly have

---

[1] Wace—the quote, of course, is not verbatim but reported tradition, nevertheless it is interesting as an insight into a psychological problem appreciable a century after the event, also as a description of an old technique for persuading men to fight.

occurred to the regulars and territorials, for whom a tight formation was the accepted defensive procedure, but might well have been a contributing factor to the discomfort of the peasant levies, who liked to spread out and pick their own ground. On receiving news of the Norman approach, Harold had hastily marshalled his best troops, including the housecarles, shoulder-to-shoulder in readiness to receive an attack. Aptly known as the wall of shields, this type of array was a favourite Anglo-Saxon and Danish war formation.[1] Behind the phalanx of shields, each normally held on the left arm, the mail-shirted and helmeted warriors would keep a supply of javelins ready to hurl at the oncoming enemy. Normally, these either halted or broke the shock of the attack, which was thereafter contested with sword, spear and axe. With steady men in the line, the whole wall could move slowly and crushingly forward should the enemy show signs of wavering. Behind this barrier, and on the relatively safe ground to his flanks, Harold now deployed the less effective elements of his army, including the men of the great fyrd.

From its station on the crown of Senlac, the English headquarters group could watch the final Norman preparations on the high ground across the valley. In armour, the Frenchmen looked much like the housecarles and thegns of the home force. The main difference, at face value, between the two armies was the high proportion of mounted men under William, whereas the English stood to fight entirely as infantry. There seems also to have been a significantly larger contingent of archers with William than with Harold, who, if he had used bows and arrows in any numbers at Stamford Bridge, had probably outstripped his dismounted bowmen on the ride south. According to Wace, the Norman foot-soldiers

were well equipped, each bearing bow and sword; on their heads were caps, and to their feet were bound buskins. Some had bound strong hides round their bodies; and many were clad in frocks, and had quivers and bows hung to their girdles. The knights had hauberks and swords, boots of steel and shining helmets; shields at their necks, and in their hands lances. And all had distinctive insignia or emblems, so that each might know his fellow, and Norman might not strike Norman, nor Frenchmen

---

[1] It was probably a misunderstanding of the shield-wall principle that led later writers into the belief that the English actually constructed a true wall or barricade of wood at Hastings.

kill his countryman by mistake. Those on foot led the way, with serried ranks, bearing their bows. Then rode the knights, supporting the archers from behind. Thus both horse and foot kept their course and orders of march as they began; in close ranks at a gentle pace, that the one might not pass or separate from the other.[1]

Heavily-armed infantry of the housecarle type were relatively scarce in William's force. They appear to have occupied a position between the bowmen and the mounted knights during the advance, which was made in three divisions abreast. In the central division, with William himself, were the true Norman contingents under such familiar campaigners as Walter Giffard, William of Warenne, Hugh of Montfort, Ralph of Tosny, William Malet and others. On the right were a mixed bag of French mercenaries, led, if the tradition can be believed, by two more Normans, Roger of Montgomery and the ever-loyal William fitz Osbern. On the left were the men of Brittany. Now, as the invaders descended into the valley, the English could observe in more detail the trappings of the Norman horsemen. They rode with long stirrups, their legs mail-clad at least to the knee, and wore spurs with pyramidal or ball-and-point goads. The saddles on their mounts, attached by girths and breast-bands, had tall, upright bows and cantles, rather like the saddle of the American cowboy, except that the flaps were angular instead of rounded. Though the horses were unprotected by armour, the knights carried long, kite-shaped shields on which were daubed brightly-coloured birds, dragons and other wild beasts, real or imaginary, or simply stripes, wavy lines, crosses, saltires and so on. Grasped in the left hand, together with the reins, each shield was also attached by a loose strap round the neck of its owner so that it could hang conveniently at his side when not wanted in action. To William's neck was additionally attached a casket or charm containing holy relics. Reputedly mounted on a charger donated by a royal admirer in Spain, the substantial figure of the Norman duke could be seen, perhaps alongside his second-in-command, the warrior-prelate Odo of Bayeux, beneath the consecrated banner of Rome and Hildebrand.

[1] Much of this description tallies with the Bayeux Tapestry, from which, however, it would seem that the knights wore boots of leather rather than steel, though in some cases chain-mail reached down to their ankles. The word 'lance' is perhaps misleading. The Norman lance was a light weapon more akin to a javelin than the heavy lance of the later Middle Ages.

According to William of Malmesbury, the duke's army advanced chanting a song about the French epic hero Roland, possibly an early version of the *Chanson de Roland* which was to be written in its surviving form at the end of the twelfth century. William of Malmesbury's older contemporary, Henry of Huntingdon, among other authorities, claimed that the force was preceded by a lone rider, the minstrel Taillefer, who not only sang but flourished and tossed his sword like a bandmaster's baton. From the English ranks broke a responding volley of taunts, oaths, challenges and the braying of horns, until the whole valley resounded with the clamour of vocal aggression. It was about 9.30 a.m. when a sally from the Norman archers, followed by the swish of flying arrows, announced the start of the battle proper. The bows of the period, some four feet long and drawn to the chest (rather than to the ear, as with the long-bows of a later date), could penetrate chain-mail at up to fifty yards, but the opening barrage, fired from the disadvantage of lower ground, merely stuck harmlessly in the wall of English shields, the projectiles stopped dead by reinforced wood. When the archers, supported by William's infantry, moved in closer, they were met with a withering shower of javelins, hatchets, sling-stones and other missiles from Harold's ranks. Those who tried to press home the attack, found themselves hand-to-hand against the finest infantrymen in Europe. The attacking line reeled and drew back.

It was in this action, seemingly, that Taillefer, moved to inspire the duke's men by his own example, spurred his horse at the English and met a punctilious death. The day had started badly for William. With his bowmen unsuccessful and his infantry wavering, the cavalry had to be thrown in sooner than intended. He ordered his knights to attack. Setting their horses at the slope, they raced, cheering, towards the English line. But the Norman horsemen were not accustomed, as were latter-day cavalrymen, to carrying a charge through to the bitter end. Instead of riding as an organised body, sweeping all before them and regrouping in the rear of the enemy, they operated rather on an individual basis, each choosing his own course of action. They had not learnt to exploit the momentum of the charge. For instance, few of them couched their lances under their arms. Most of them carried these weapons like spears or javelins, ready for stabbing or throwing (Bayeux Tapestry). Instead of riding straight into the English ranks, they either halted on the fringe and hurled their lances over their horses' necks, or they attempted to stab and cut at the closest of the opposing footmen without becoming enmeshed in the enemy formation. All the same they would have stood a better chance had their charge been less premature. Given a breach or two in the English line, the knights could have poured in and used the weight of their mounts to greater advantage. As it was, they came up against a steadfast and unbroken formation, a veritable wall of wood and steel, manned by axemen quite capable of felling a horse with a single blow.

For all that, William's riders, the pride of his army, tried desperately to succeed where his footmen had failed. Those who had launched their lances at Harold's thegns, or had had them splintered by the hatchets of the housecarles, drew their swords and attempted to hack a path through the shield wall. Single incidents, probably typical of many in the fierce hand-to-hand fighting that followed, were graphically depicted in the Bayeux Tapestry: a mounted knight slashing at an Englishman's face with his sword; a housecarle severing the neck of a horse with his axe; an armoured Englishman falling, contorted, with an arrow in his jaw; horses and riders crashing to the ground; a man cleanly beheaded despite the mailed collar of his protective hauberk; dead and dying warriors being divested of their armour, even in the heat of battle, by peasants anxious to acquire such protection for themselves. Yet, for all its ferocity, the attack failed in its objective of breaking Harold's front. Where men fell, and gaps appeared in the shield wall, other men came forward to take their place, or else the line simply closed up. Finally, the French knights, losing heart like their footmen before them, began to withdraw down the hill in confusion (William of Poitiers). Among the bleeding and wild-eyed horses, William's footmen lurched and scrambled for safety. To add to their despondency, a rumour seems now to have spread that the duke had been killed in the mêlée.

At this moment of crisis for the invaders, Bishop Odo, wearing some form of clerical garb with his hauberk, and wielding a cudgel, was prominent in his endeavours to rally the Normans (Bayeux Tapestry). At the same time, Eustace of Boulogne, the man once put to flight by the townsmen of Dover, rode forward waving the papal banner, accompanied by a livid William, who had now removed his helmet to let everyone see his face. According to William of Poitiers, the duke grabbed a spear and, in his fury, forced some of his despondent followers back to their duty at its point. Had the invaders lacked horses, Harold well might have used this critical phase of the battle to clinch total success, for, under such circumstances, a controlled advance behind his shield wall would have been very hard for William to counter. However, the English king could not pursue riders with footmen, and it was thus, as an efficient vehicle of retirement (rather than as an irresistible force in attack, as has sometimes been suggested), that William's 'cavalry arm' perhaps saved the contest for the Normans. Well aware of the superior mobility of his enemy, Harold decided to stay where he was.

Not all of his army was as wise. Exhilarated by their success, especially against the Breton flank of William's force, which had been most severely repulsed, many of Harold's untrained levies took it upon themselves to mount an unauthorised offensive. Breaking from their allotted stations, they streamed down the hill after the retiring Frenchmen. William's lieutenants could not have hoped for anything better. Wheeling their chargers, and calling upon their knights to follow, they were among the loose mob of English peasants almost before its members had time to realise their mistake. Some made a grim stand on an isolated hillock, plainly marked in the Bayeux Tapestry, and which can still be identified on the ground today. But the majority were annihilated or routed by the horsemen. So gratifying was this development to the Normans that, on the evidence of William of Poitiers, among others, similar episodes were contrived by the invaders later in the battle, the French troops luring the English into the open by simulated retirement. Modern historians have tended to part company over the authenticity, or otherwise, of these so-called feigned-flight incidents, some holding that such a dangerous and sophisticated manœuvre was beyond the capabilities of the rough warriors of Hastings. Nevertheless, the tactic reputedly had assisted Norman knights in at least one earlier engagement (Messina, 1060), and was claimed by Scandinavian chroniclers as a favourite Viking war-ruse.

At all events, the first disastrous sally of the English great fyrd, with its tragic outcome, levelled the scoring, and gave William time to reorganise his main offensive. The morning had gone and both sides were tiring under the strain of their efforts. Since the best of the English soldiers had started the day with little enough in reserve, time was playing in William's favour. Yet the wall of shields on Senlac held firm. Bowmen, infantry and knights had tried, and failed, in turn to demolish it. William now resolved to use his three main arms in an all-out combined offensive. This time the archers were employed at longer range, firing with a high trajectory. The technique, though reducing the impact of their arrows, enabled them to produce a covering barrage for their advancing compatriots. It also induced the English defenders to raise their shields against the shower of descending missiles. And, with this much to hearten them, the duke's knights and footmen hauled once more up the slope and fell fiercely to their unenviable task. At last, the sheer weight of the attack forced Harold's line to give ground in places. It was the beginning of the end. Here and there, the 'wall' was breached. The Norman knights hacked their way in. Several English leaders must have fallen about this time, attempting to rally the defenders. It was now, as William of Poitiers saw it, that Harold's brother Gyrth was killed, while, according to the Tapestry, Leofwine died by his side, one jack-knifing in mortal agony, the other knocked flying by charging horsemen.[1] By mid-afternoon, the scene on the hill was a confusion of isolated sallies and counter-sallies, some spontaneous, some relatively organised, amidst an even greater bedlam of hand-to-hand encounters. Wace's description, if not the most reliable in detail, perhaps came the nearest to capturing the character and atmosphere of the contest:

The English fell back towards the standard, on rising ground, and the Normans followed . . . attacking them on foot and on horseback. Hugh of Mortemer charged with the knights of Auviler, Onebac and St Cler, overthrowing many. Robert fitz Erneis, grasping his shield and galloping towards the standard, struck and killed an interposing Englishman with

[1] Among other versions of the battle, however, the Tapestry appears to place the deaths of the brothers at an earlier stage. It does not lend authority to a later tradition that Gyrth was killed by the duke's own hand.

his sword, withdrew the blade and, defying many others, pushed straight for the emblem, trying to beat it down. The English surrounding it killed him with their axes. He was found on the spot when they sought him afterwards, lying dead at the standard's foot. Duke William pressed the English hard . . . now striving to reach the banner with a large troop of followers, and searching keenly for Harold. . . . Hacking at the enemy, the Normans followed, ganging round their leader as the Englishmen returned blow for blow, fighting a stubborn defensive action. One of them, a wrestler of great strength, caused serious harm to the Normans with his axe. So many had suffered at his hand that everyone feared him. The Duke, spurring his horse, aimed a blow at the man, but he ducked, jumped to one side and raised his weapon aloft. As the Duke bent to avoid the stroke, the Englishman struck at his head, denting his helmet but not causing much injury. . . . The ceorl then sought cover among his comrades, but he was not to escape long, for the Duke's followers went after him, caught him and pierced him through and through with their lances. . . .

At the fiercest point of the battle, the men of Kent and Essex fought magnificently, turning the Normans again and again. . . . Then about a thousand armoured men, led by the Duke, rushed with closed ranks upon the English. The weight of the horses and the blows of the knights now broke the enemy pack, scattering a crowd before them. Many pursued while many fled; many were the Englishmen who fell around and were trampled under the horses, crawling on the earth, unable to rise. Many of the richest and noblest men fell in that rout, but the English still rallied . . . smiting those who came within reach, continuing to fight as best they could, beating down men and killing horses. One Englishman kept his eyes on the Duke, intending to kill him. He would have struck with his spear, but he was too late, for the Duke struck first, and felled him. . . . Loud now was the clamour and great the slaughter; many a soul then quitted the body. The living marched over the heaps of dead, and each side was weary from striking. He who could still charge, did so; he who could raise an arm no longer, still pushed forward. The strong struggled with the strong, some failing, others triumphing; cowards fell back, the brave pressed on; and sad was his fate who fell in the midst, for he had little chance of rising again. In truth, many fell and were crushed beneath the throng.

By the approach of evening, all hope for Harold had gone. He had resisted, wrote Florence, from the third hour of the day until nightfall, displaying such courage and tenacity that, almost to the end, the invaders despaired of taking his life. Around him stood the last of his thegns and housecarles, bloody and exhausted, still fighting shoulder to shoulder. So impressed were the Normans by the strength of the English infantry formation that for the best part of a century to come, in almost every great battle of the Anglo-Norman age, a preponderance of knights fought after the Anglo-Saxon fashion. But now, not even the loyalty of the English housecarles could save their king from the final blow in a reign of incomparable military challenge and misfortune. In the waning light of 14 October 1066, Harold Godwinson, the last Anglo-Saxon ruler of England, was smashed down by an unknown assailant, or assailants, and his body trampled to anonymity in the soft turf of the Sussex downs—the same downs that had once helped to mould his identity. Posterity was to dramatise the moment of his death in the familiar story that a random arrow struck him in the eye, a form of injury with a strong anecdotal appeal to the morbidity of the period.[1] In fact, the earliest surviving record of Harold's alleged death in this manner can be attributed to a poet named Baudri, Abbot of Bourgueil, who wrote in the early twelfth century of a contemporary embroidery. If this reference indeed applied to the Bayeux Tapestry, the origin of the legend could well lie in a misinterpretation of the picture dealing with the incident, for though the artist depicted Harold falling to the sword of a mounted knight, a figure nearby, and similar to that of the king, was shown with an arrow lodged close to the helmet.

Even with the king dead, the royal housecarles fought on around his body, and many thegns and ceorls of the select fyrd with them. It was said that not a man of his personal retinue fled, nor was taken captive. There can be no doubt that, like the followers of Byrhtnoth, they sold their lives dearly, in the classic heroic tradition. Beside the nameless many fell Thurkill, Godric and Harold's friend Eadric, the deacon. Of the prelates, Aelfwig died on the field with his royal nephew; Abbot Leofric managed to return to Peterborough, but the campaign had left him a sick man and he died soon afterwards.

---

[1] According to legend, Harald Hardrada was killed in precisely the same manner, a remarkable coincidence if the traditions are taken literally. The convenience of the story, as applied to warrior heroes, is apparent: from one point of view it spared the humility of defeat in hand-to-hand combat, while, from another, it served as a token of heaven-sent justice.

'Then "Golden Borough" became "Wretched Borough",' it was written in the *Anglo-Saxon Chronicle*. Others took advantage of the closing darkness to escape into the woods behind them, and it was while pursuing these remnants of the English army that, as William of Poitiers recalled it, the Normans ran into their final set-back. Intoxicated by success, and blinded by the poor light, a party of mounted knights careered down the north slope of the hill on the tail of some fleeing Englishmen. The steep incline and the rough ground were more than the horses could manage, and their riders were hurled from their saddles. For the fugitives it was a moment of bloody revenge. Leaping on the unseated horsemen, they slaughtered them savagely, before melting into the shadowy forest. The site of the incident was known afterwards to the Normans as Malfosse.

At this stage, the duke wisely abandoned further pursuit, recalling his troops to the hill itself. Here, amid the carnage, he made camp for the night, and, having received the cheers of his warriors and offered prayers to heaven, sat down to a feast of victory. Next morning, the women of the surrounding district appeared cautiously on the battle-field, seeking the bodies of husbands, sons and brothers. According to one tradition, Harold's Danish mother, the widowed Gytha, offered William the dead king's weight in gold for possession of his corpse. It is hard to conceive a figure more tragic than this ageing princess, already deprived of a husband and two sons through either violent or premature death, and now bereaved of three more in a single battle. But her request was not granted. Indeed, it would seem that for some time Harold's body, mutilated and stripped of armour and ornament, defied identification. His wife, Ealdgyth, was not available to help in the matter, perhaps already on her way north to the lands of her brothers, while his sister Edith in Winchester could hardly have been looked to for sympathy. A touching, though questionable story, which was to gather popularity as time passed, told how two priests from Harold's minster at Waltham, Osgod and Aethelric, eventually arrived on the scene with the king's early and devoted mistress, Edith of the Swan Neck. Edith allegedly recognised the remains of her lover by the means of certain body markings familiar to her alone, and William ordered its burial at Hastings. In a later and less turbulent period, Harold's bones were supposedly removed to Waltham.

*

The winner of Hastings was the winner of England. In nine hundred years, no other invader has repeated the achievement, though huge forces and vast resources have been marshalled in the effort. The feat, imposing enough in its own definition, was the more remarkable for the manner of the operation. In a single day of fighting, a polyglot band of some 5,000 adventurers, led by a brilliant and daring general, had decided the fate of a nation. Yet, to William on the morrow of the battle at Senlac the situation must still have seemed far from conclusive. Not only had he an unknown factor to contend with in the northern earldoms: so far he had not even tested his strength against any of the southern cities. London in particular was strongly manned. Large numbers of reservists, arriving too late to march south with Harold, had stayed on there, awaiting fresh instructions. There were still ships in the Thames which could menace the duke's communications. There was even the possibility that an alternative king might be named in the person of Edgar the Atheling, a course indeed recommended in the crisis by Archbishop Stigand and backed by Edwin, Morcar and the Archbishop of York. As the last male of Cerdic's line, Edgar might have proved a figurehead to whom Englishmen could rally, though, as it happened, the proposition came too late and was soon abandoned by the northern earls.

William was too prudent to attempt a direct assault on London with his weakened army. Instead, he rested a few days at Hastings before embarking on a campaign of psychological warfare calculated to break the morale of the capital. His first move was against Romney, which he savaged ruthlessly as a retaliation for some early opposition from the townsfolk. He then proceeded to Dover where the people were sufficiently intimidated to submit without resistance. Canterbury likewise yielded. By November the strain of prolonged operations in a hostile country was telling on the Normans. Dysentery was rife among the troops, and William himself was ill. For several weeks he was in the dangerous position of having to remain immobile while his men recuperated. But the English force in London still lacked a leader who could grasp the initiative, and, by December, the duke was continuing his circuitous advance on the capital. His next success was one of greater significance. Soon after leaving Canterbury, he received an offer of submission from the late king's sister, Edith, who, as Edward the Confessor's widow, held the city of Winchester in dower. The collapse of the ancient seat of the West Saxon kings must have signalled an end to potential resistance in many parts of the south. William followed it by a bold march to the south bank of London, where an abortive attack by supporters of the Atheling decided him against trying to force the bridge. Once again, he resorted to terror, burning the suburb of Southwark before making a wide, clockwise orbit of the city. Ravaging and despoiling as they went, the raiders moved in a ruinous arc across Surrey, northern Hampshire and Berkshire, eventually crossing the Thames at Wallingford. There the duke encamped on the Oxfordshire bank.

The war of nerves was telling on the city. At Wallingford, Stigand came over to William's side, a fair sign that the vessel, as it were, was sinking. By the time the duke had skirted the Chilterns and arrived at Berkhampstead, the Atheling's party was no longer a power for resistance. 'There he was met by Archbishop Ealdred, Prince Edgar, Earl Edwin, Earl Morcar, and all the best men of London, who, of necessity submitted, though not before the damage was done. . . . They gave hostages and swore fealty to him, and he promised to be a gracious lord to them' (*ASC*). The writer added that only folly had prevented an earlier submission, but, though the bulk of city opinion was clearly against provoking any further destruction, it seems that not everyone was of the same mind, for Norman chroniclers spoke of pockets of resistance on the outskirts. These, however, were soon overcome. A few days before Christmas, William the Conqueror triumphantly entered his new capital.

He was crowned on Christmas morning itself. As the bells rang out from London's churches, the duke's mercenaries formed guard outside the West Minster. The approaches were thick with Norman horsemen. Others patrolled the streets of the city. Inside, where the grave of the founder was not yet a year old, the surviving lords of England and Normandy, whose blood was to mingle henceforth in the history of the country, kept uneasily in their own divisions. Preceded by cross-bearers and bishops, and surrounded by the chief men of the duchy and his new kingdom, the Conqueror made his way to a throne set before the high altar. The service was conducted by the Archbishops Ealdred and Stigand, assisted by the Bishop Geoffrey of Coutances. When the time came for the assembled crowd to mark their consent by acclamation, Ealdred presented the new king in English, Geoffrey in French, and the people roared assent in their appropriate tongues. So strange was this mingling of two languages to the troops on duty within earshot of the minster, that, believing a riot had broken out, they hastened to take what was probably the decreed line of action. They promptly set fire to the neighbouring buildings. Confusion now became real. Many people rushed from the minster to help fight the blaze. Orderic described the scene as one of terror, and claimed that even William trembled. But the coronation went on. With flames devouring the houses outside, Ealdred shakily placed the royal crown of England on the head of the Norman who had finally won its possession.

16

Reckonings

Three months after his coronation in England, William returned triumphantly to Normandy to receive the acclaim of its people and to parade the spoils of victory. Wherever he went the Conqueror was applauded and feasted as he dispensed grants of his newly-won land and wealth. With him, as some guarantee of England's good behaviour in his absence, travelled Stigand, Edgar, Edwin, Morcar and other English nobles. According to the Norman chroniclers, these were greatly admired in the duchy for their appearance and dignity, while people everywhere wondered at the splendours in gold, silver and embroidered cloths wrought by the island craftsmen. Norman prestige had never flown higher, nor had any of her dukes commanded more authority. William had touched the zenith of his personal glory.

In England, however, the scene was less rosy. Martial law, symbolised by newly-built Norman castles at London, Dover and elsewhere, had aroused considerable resentment among the population of the south-east. Heavy taxes imposed on the country as a whole had spread the mood to territories yet unoccupied by the governing forces. While Normandy rejoiced, England rumbled on the verge of rebellion. William had left the government of his new kingdom under the joint command of Bishop Odo and William fitz Osbern. The latter, appointed Earl of Hereford, with his headquarters at Norwich, bore the responsibility of guarding the eastern approaches. Many Englishmen had taken refuge in Denmark, and the chance of attack from this quarter could not be neglected. Odo, based at Dover, had the job, among other duties, of watching the Kentish ports, and it was from this part of the country that the first serious trouble arose. Backed, oddly enough, by Eustace of Boulogne, who had fallen out with William after Hastings, the men of Kent took arms against the new authority. Eustace himself gained possession of Dover, but he was unable to capture the castle and its garrison was largely responsible for his ultimate defeat and flight across the Channel. Challenged by the full army of the Norman regent, the insurgents now dispersed, but the episode had done nothing to reduce tension in the island, and the presence of William was to become an urgent necessity if the régime was to last.

He returned from Normandy in December to find Exeter and other parts of the south-west in open defiance, and was forced to mount a full-scale campaign against Devon (his force, comprised partly of English mercenaries, was the first Anglo-Norman army) before the rebels submitted. Even then, Exeter itself repulsed all attempts at capture for eighteen days, surrendering only on terms. The real trouble, however, was yet to come, and from a part of the country a good deal less amenable at the best of times to crown authority than the south. Northern England, still uncowed by the clatter of Norman knights, was busy threshing out its own political salvation in which William was scarcely regarded as a guiding light. Shortly after his accession, the Conqueror had dispatched Tostig's friend Copsi to Northumbria as his representative. He need hardly have troubled. Within a few weeks, Copsi had been ambushed and killed at Newburn on Tyne by one Oswulf Eadwulfson, the scion of an aristocratic house with pretensions to the earldom—who, in turn, was killed by his cousin Gospatric. Gospatric then made a bid to rally northern allegiance. By now, Morcar, Edwin and Edgar the Atheling had deserted William's court for the north, and a strong anti-Norman movement had centred on York. To make matters worse for the new king, both Malcolm of Scotland and Sweyn Estrithson of Denmark were in sympathetic contact with the northern resistance. The growing danger of a three-cornered alliance between these elements, perhaps with the pretender Edgar as a figurehead, finally forced William to act.

In a whirlwind display of strength, he marched his army into Yorkshire, via Warwick and Nottingham, and entered the northern capital as its citizens stood and gaped. They were still gaping when he left, having built the customary castle and installed his garrison. It was an impressive act, but this time William had underestimated the audience. If the Northumbrians were slow to react, they were not quickly intimidated. Moreover, the Conqueror had stopped short of the far north. From York, he turned south to repeat the show at Lincoln, Huntingdon and Cambridge, leaving unvisited in his rear the ruggedly independent northern centre of Durham. Here, late in January 1069, the natives showed their contempt of the new king by setting on the troops of a Norman commander, Robert de Commines, who was visiting the bishop of the city. The soldiers were massacred in the streets while Robert, trapped in the bishop's house, perhaps wisely chose to perish in the flames designed to burn him out rather than face the waiting crowd. In York, news of the Durham episode came as a spur to those with rebel sympathies, provoking a fierce attack on the garrison. The commander of the force was killed and the city declared itself for Edgar, but the castle itself held out against the insurgents and its defenders managed to get a message to William. Furiously, the Conqueror retraced his steps north, this time with the briefest of stops on the way, arriving in York earlier than his enemies anticipated. As an echo of Harold's famous march against Hardrada, it was suitably successful. William raised the siege of the castle, occupied the city with his troops and exacted a bloody revenge on the rebels. But he could not afford to remain in the north for long, and, having reinforced his interests in York with a second castle, he returned to the south for the summer.

So far, the threats to William's régime in England, though widespread and frequent, had lacked cohesion and any sense of real leadership. Able to tackle them piecemeal, the king had snuffed each in turn without too much trouble. With the coming of autumn, however, the situation took on a very different complexion. William now received news that a large Scandinavian fleet was off the east coast, and that invasion in that quarter was imminent. Sweyn Estrithson had launched his challenge. In fact, Sweyn had not committed himself to the venture as wholeheartedly as had Hardrada before him, leaving the enterprise in the hands of his sons Harold and Canute, and his brother Osbern. Nevertheless, the force at their command was a strong one. Some 240 Danish and Norwegian ships were involved, fully manned by well-armed warriors. These, having anchored eventually in the Humber, were soon reinforced by an English host gathered under the Atheling and various northern leaders, whereupon the combined army marched towards York. Nothing could save the hopelessly outnumbered garrison. In a vain effort to deter the advance, William's men set fire to the city, but the invaders were already on top of them and the castles were taken. Most of the defenders perished, seemingly in a desperate attempt to fight their way to safety through the blazing streets. By 20 September York was in Anglo-Danish hands. Before long, villages in many parts of the north were welcoming the Danish warriors and preparing to celebrate William's defeat. At last, the whole movement of resistance in England had a focus. The Norman position in the land was critical.

Had the captors of York now swept south to join with the rebel factions in Mercia and East Anglia, they might well have carried the country in an avalanche that not even William could have stood against. But it appears not to have been any part of the Danish plan to bear the brunt of a liberation campaign for the benefit of the English. Having brought the pot, as it were, to the boil, they were content to sit back and await developments. Accordingly, they now retired to the vicinity of their ships, the richer by prisoners and loot, and left the next move to the freshly-roused English insurgents. The strategy gave the Conqueror vital breathing space. Characteristically, he used it to the utmost effect. In Devon and Cornwall, the furthermost reaction to Danish intervention took the form of a rising centred largely round Exeter. Luckily for William, the city itself did not join the rebellion, and the forces there were able to hold their own against the rebels. In Dorset and Somerset, a more formidable rising, directed against a Norman castle at Montacute, necessitated the deployment of loyal troops from Salisbury, Winchester and London. These William left in the hands of Geoffrey, Bishop of Coutances, who eventually suppressed the insurgents. Marching his main army north, the king now placed part of it to check any possible southward movement by the Danes while he struck westward with the rest at a rising based on Stafford. Here a Herefordshire resistance leader known as Edric the Wild had concentrated a numerous following, including contingents provided by Welsh princes. According to the Norman evidence, William dispersed them with relative ease and was soon heading back towards Lincolnshire. He had travelled as far as Nottingham when news reached him that the Scandinavians were preparing to reoccupy York.

From now on, his seemingly tireless cross-country shunting was to mount to a remorseless climax as William pursued perhaps the most notorious *tour de force* of his whole career. Altering course once more, he struck north in hopes of foiling the Danish intent, only to find his bridge broken at the intervening Aire river and the far bank held by insurgents. By the time he had cleared this obstacle, the Scandinavians had achieved their destination and were firmly entrenched in the city. Undismayed, William embarked on the tactics that had successfully terrorised London. In a looping march to the west and then to the north of the city, he proceeded to devastate every acre of cultivated land and habitation in his path. Every male Northumbrian his men could ride down was murdered; every dwelling burnt; every crop destroyed; all cattle either slaughtered or driven off. Surrounded by a wasted countryside, it was not long before the Danes withdrew to the Humber and later agreed to be bought off. William entered a charred and battered York in time for Christmas. There, he celebrated, solemnly, the day of Christ's birth.

Now, in the heart of winter, he might have been expected to rest. But William's deliberate ruination of the area had so far extended only a limited distance from the city: his intention was to subjugate Yorkshire for good. The method was simple. He gave orders for the immediate and systematic destruction of human livelihood throughout the entire county. So appalling was the havoc wrought by the king's marauders that the results were still clearly evident two decades later. Northern writers recalled the mouldering corpses scattered everywhere, and the disease and starvation which followed. Not even William's most consistent admirers, men hardened to the customary brutalities of eleventh-century warfare, could condone such measures. Wrote Orderic: 'Often I have seen fit to praise William according to his merits, but I cannot applaud him for an act which reduced both the bad and the good to common ruin through overwhelming famine . . . such barbarous homicide ought not to go unpunished.'

Leaving the grim task to his lieutenants, the Conqueror next pushed up to the Tees, where he received the submission of Gospatric and other northern leaders before crossing the Pennines to complete the chastisement of the last of the Mercian rebels at Chester. Consumed by his ferocious endeavours, William had ignored alike bad weather and the increasing weariness of his troops. At one stage, the latter came close to mutiny. The king pressed on to a triumphant, if bitter end. By Easter, the backbone of resistance pulverised, he felt safe enough to pay off the mercenaries in his army.

It remained to secure the departure of the Danish fleet which still lingered in English waters. Indeed, in spring 1070, it was joined by Sweyn himself who, leading his ships south from the Humber to the Wash, entered East Anglia to squeeze a final profit from the venture. Here, in the marshy fastnesses of the Isle of Ely, the Scandinavians were joined by a band of local rebels led by a Lincolnshire thegn named Hereward. William showed no signs of being unduly worried. The threat was a tame sequel to the earlier crisis, and, having bribed or cajoled Sweyn into withdrawing his plunder-laden force from the country, the king took his time in dealing with Hereward. As it happened, this delay lured a number of other fugitives to the fens, enabling the Normans, when they moved seriously against Ely, to make a useful killing. Among the bag of prisoners was Earl Morcar, who died shortly afterwards, while, at about the same time, his brother Edwin perished trying to reach the safety of Scotland. For a time, Edgar the Atheling found sanctuary with Malcolm, later fleeing abroad. Hereward's fate, though the subject of much romance, is unknown. Thus, with a final scuffle in the marshes, it could be said that the conquest had ended. All England was William's. There remained the reckoning. . . .

*

To the English thegnhood or aristocracy of the period, the Norman conquest was a disaster of the utmost magnitude. Many left the country to take their chances abroad as soldiers of fortune rather than stay where, as the northern poet Thorkil Skallason put it, 'Cold

heart and bloody hand now rule the English land'. Indeed, by the
end of William's reign almost every magnate with any power in
England was a foreigner. Among the majority of people, however,
conditions can hardly have worsened to the same extent. For the
peasants, servitude was servitude under any régime, and, if they
gained little from the wars of their masters, on the whole they had
little to lose. New tricks to learn, old tricks to impart. William of
Malmesbury made it sound simple. If his comparison of Norman
and English attributes can be accepted, the Normans set the English
an example of frugality, perfidy, piety and, among many other
things, avarice, while the English taught their conquerors 'to eat till
they became surfeited and to drink till they were sick'.

The broader significance of the Conquest on English life has been,
and perhaps always will be, a subject fraught with controversy.
For some historians the episode has represented the destruction of a
relatively benevolent and cultured society by a harsh, aggressive
people who had little to contribute of intellectual and aesthetic
importance. For others, it was the replacement of an obsolescent and
insular system by a virile, cosmopolitan order, an infusion of new
blood. As some have seen it, William introduced the feudal system
to England; for others, it had already emerged in that country, or at
least was emerging, by the time he arrived. For some, the Conquest
brought an architectural revolution to the island, replacing humble
English styles with Norman majesty; for others, England was evolv-
ing a Romanesque style of her own, sufficiently aware of foreign
developments to proceed without Norman help. For some, William
was uniquely qualified to reorganise and revitalise the affairs of
Church and State in his new kingdom; for others, his merits as a
ruler were vitiated by arrogance, greed and destructiveness, while
the loss of Harold robbed England of a potentially great king, a king
who might well have possessed the strength and inspiration to lead
his country peacefully into a new era.

William, for his part, appears to have had no doubts about the
merits of his case. In 1070, Stigand, having served his purpose, was
deposed and replaced as primate of England by Lanfranc. But not
even the shrewd Italian could moderate the poor image the king
created for himself in the country. 'The rich complained and the

poor lamented,' wrote a contemporary Englishman, 'but he was too hard to care had everyone hated him, and those who wished to retain the king's favour, their lives, lands and goods, were compelled to submit utterly to his will' (*ASC*). As time passed, the crown brought him neither security nor abiding satisfaction. The closing years of his life saw his son Robert in revolt against him, backed by King Philip of France; his half-brother Odo fostering treason; the Count of Flanders his open enemy; a hostile Malcolm on the Scottish border of the Anglo-Norman kingdom; a new threat in Anjou, and yet another challenge from Denmark. In 1083 his wife Matilda died, depriving him of one of his few enduring sources of loyalty and sustenance, while his own health was suffering from his excessive corpulence.

William's last act of aggression was the sack of Mantes in 1087. The French garrison of the town had been raiding into Normandy, and he was hungry for vengeance. In a final spasm of barbarity, the Conqueror wiped out the city. He was still absorbed with his work of ruin when he was seized by violent intestinal pain and forced to retire in agony to Rouen, where, it seems, he developed a sudden and remarkable concern for the victims of his ambition. For six weeks he lay ill at the priory of St Gervais, confessing and repenting. Then, on the morning of 9 September, he was awakened by the sound of a bell tolling in the city. 'On asking why it rang,' wrote Orderic, 'his attendants replied: "Lord, it strikes for the hour of Prime in the church of St Mary." Whereupon the king raised his eyes and lifted his hands and said: "I commend myself to the holy Mary, Mother of God, that through her I may be reconciled with her Son, our Lord Jesus Christ." And having said this, he died.'

It was now the turn of those around him to look to their own salvation. 'The wealthiest took to their horses, leaving rapidly to guard their property, while those of subordinate rank, seeing that their masters had gone, grabbed the arms, the plate, the linen and the royal furniture before hurrying after them, leaving the corpse almost naked on the floor. . . .' After some trouble with the funeral arrangements, seemingly due to a general reluctance to take responsibility for the expense, the body was conveyed to Caen where a stone coffin was prepared in William's own foundation, the abbey of

St Stephen. The burial service was actually under way when a man named Ascelin interrupted the officiating bishop, Gilbert of Lisieux, with the observation that the ground in which the body was to be interred had belonged to his father, that William had taken it unlawfully to build the church, and that he, Ascelin, now claimed rightful compensation. At this, the ceremony came to an abrupt halt while a deal was hastily concluded for the site of the tomb. Ascelin settled for sixty shillings, but it was now found that the coffin was too small for the body. Impatient to be finished with the whole unnerving affair, the attendants broke the corpse. The church was filled with a noxious stench. Piling incense on the burners, the priests completed the service and thankfully left St Stephen's to its founder.

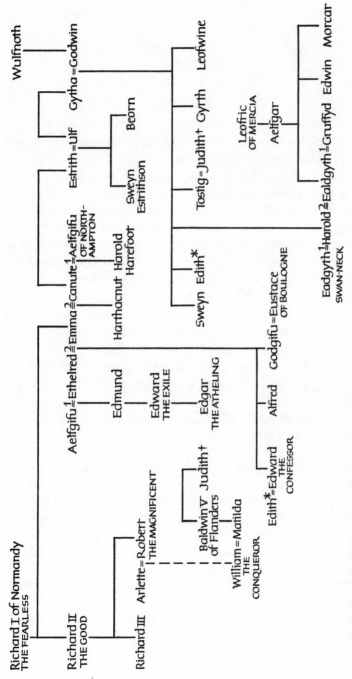

* indicates the same person   + indicates the same person

Sources

The earliest references to Britain are found in the literature of other countries, notably in the works of the Greek geographers Strabo and Ptolemy, and of the Latin encyclopaedist Pliny. Caesar and Tacitus are the chief literary authorities for the Roman conquest of the island, while, in the sixth century, a native author, Gildas, provided a brief glimpse of the post-Roman period. Gildas, like most of the British authorities who followed him for many centuries, including the eighth-century English historian Bede, was an ecclesiastic. Indeed, it was a series of monks, writing between the period of Alfred the Great and the second half of the twelfth century, who provided the remarkable annals which are the basic authority for the foregoing story, at least as far as it takes place on British soil. These annals, scripted in a number of English monasteries, are known collectively as the *Anglo-Saxon Chronicle* (ed. B. Thorpe, Rolls Series, Longmans, 1861). An excellent modern translation is also available at a modest price in Everyman's Library (tr. G. N. Garmonsway, Dent, 1953).

Among other original authorities to whom reference is made in the preceding pages are:

FLORENCE OF WORCESTER. A monk of the immediate post-Hastings generation. Primarily a compiler of existing works, but some of his observations usefully supplement the *Anglo-Saxon Chronicle*. *Chronica ex Chronicis* (ed. B. Thorpe, English Historical Society, 1848-49).

HENRY OF HUNTINGDON. Born about two decades after the Norman conquest and became archdeacon of the diocese of Lincoln. Henry wrote a colourful but often questionable history of England at the bidding of his bishop. *Historia Anglorum* (ed. T. Arnold, Rolls Series, Longmans, 1879).

WILLIAM OF MALMESBURY. A younger contemporary of Henry of Huntingdon, and a better historian. His work, reflecting the new continental influence of the Normans, was quickly accepted among a wide following. *Gesta Regum* (ed. W. Stubbs, Rolls Series, Eyre & Spottiswoode, 1887-89).

GEOFFREY GAIMAR. A twelfth-century poet-historian of uncertain origin. If he was a Norman, he took the trouble to learn Old English for much of his own rhyming chronicle is based on the *Anglo-Saxon Chronicle*. *L'Estorie des Engles* (ed. T. D. Hardy and tr. C. T. Martin, Rolls Series, Eyre and Spottiswoode, 1888-89).

WILLIAM OF POITIERS. Norman chaplain to Duke William, he is best known for his valuable but eulogistic life of the Conqueror. He was also Archdeacon of Lisieux. *Gesta Guillelmi ducis Normannorum et regis Anglorum* (*Scriptores rerum gestarum Willelmi Conquestoris*, ed. V. A. Giles, Nutt, 1845).

WILLIAM OF JUMIÈGES. Also a contemporary of William the Conqueror. *Gesta Normannorum Ducum* (ed. J. Marx, Société de l'Histoire de Normandie, 1914).

ORDERIC VITALIS. Born in England on the morrow of the conquest and sent, at the age of eleven, to a Norman monastery. Orderic met many war veterans of the conquest period and wrote shrewdly of their lives and times. *Historia Ecclesiastica* (ed. A. le Prevost, Société de l'Histoire de France, 1838-55).

ROBERT WACE (otherwise known as William Wace). Twelfth-century poet-historian, born Jersey, Channel Islands, who wrote most vividly, though not always factually, of the conquest in his rhyming chronicle of the Norman dukes: *Roman de Rou* (tr. Sir A. Malet, Bell & Daldy, 1860).

THE BAYEUX TAPESTRY. A vitally important picture-story worked by unknown craftsmen, possibly under the orders of Bishop Odo of Bayeux. For a complete reproduction, partially in colour plates, and many interesting notes, see *The Bayeux Tapestry*, by Sir F. Stenton and others (Phaidon Press, 1957).

SNORRI STURLASON. The greatest of early Scandinavian historians, born a little more than a century after the conquest in Iceland where he became chief magistrate. Snorri wrote with grandeur and feeling of the Northern kings, though with some confusion regarding events in England, 1066. *The Heimskringla* (tr. S. Laing, Longmans, 1844).

ADAM OF BREMEN. An eleventh-century German writer with a keen interest in distant places, including Scandinavia. There is no evidence that he travelled north of Denmark, but he derived information from Sweyn Estrithson and others who had. *Gesta Hammenburgensis ecclesiae pontificum* (ed. V. C. I. M. Lappenberg, Hanover, 1846).

Contemporary or near-contemporary biographies have survived of Edward the Confessor and the Lady Emma, both by unknown but strictly partial authors.

Vita Edwardi Regis (*Lives of Edward the Confessor*, ed. H. R. Luard, Rolls Series, Longmans, 1858); *Encomium Emmae reginae* (ed. Alistair Campbell, London, 1949).

Some collections of early charters, laws, poems, sagas and other documents relevant to the period:

ATTENBOROUGH, F. L. (ed.) *The Laws of the Earliest English Kings.* Cambridge U.P., 1922.

GORDON, R. K. *Anglo-Saxon Poetry.* Revised edn. Dent (Everyman's Library), 1954.

HADDAN, A. W. and STUBBS, W. *Councils of Ecclesiastical Documents Relating to Great Britain and Ireland.* Macmillan, 1871. Vol. III.

HARMER, F. E. (ed.) *Select English Historical Documents.* Cambridge U.P., 1914.

NAPIER, A. S. and STEVENSON, W. H. *The Crawford Collection of Early Charters and Documents.* Oxford, Clarendon Press, 1895.

ROBERTSON, A. J. (ed.) Anglo-Saxon Charters. Cambridge U.P., 1939.

VIGJUSSON, G. and POWELL, F. YORK (tr.) *Corpus Poeticum Boreale.* Oxford, Clarendon Press, 1883.

— *Origines Islandicae.* Oxford, Clarendon Press, 1905.

GENERAL

ANDERSON, I. *A History of Sweden.* Weidenfeld & Nicholson, 1956.

ANDRIEU-GUITRANCOURT, P. *Histoire de l'Empire Normand et de la Civilisation.* Paris, 1952.

ARBMAN, E. H. *The Vikings.* Tr. and ed. A. Binns. Thames & Hudson, 1961.

BESANT, WALTER. *London.* Chatto & Windus, 1892.

BARLOW, F. *The Feudal Kingdom of England.* Longmans, 1962.

BLAIR, P. H. *An Introduction to Anglo-Saxon England.* Cambridge U.P., 1956.

BROOKE, C. N. L. *From Alfred to Henry III.* Nelson, 1961.

— *The Saxon and Norman Kings.* Batsford, 1963.

BROOKS, F. W. *The Battle of Stamford Bridge.* East Yorks Local History Society, 1963.

BROWN, G. BALDWIN. *The Arts in Early England.* Murray, 1937. Vol. VI, part 2.

BURBIDGE, F. BLISS. *Old Coventry and Lady Godiva.* Cornish, Birmingham, 1952.

CHAMBERS, R. W. *Beowulf, an Introduction to the Study of the Poem.* Cambridge U.P., 1932.

CLAPHAM, A. W. *Romanesque Architecture in Western Europe.* Oxford, Clarendon Press, 1936.

CLARK, J. W. *Cambridge.* Seeley, 1890.

CLOWES, G. S. L. 'Ships of the Early Explorers', *Geographical Journal*, LXIX, 1927.

COMPTON, H. *Harold the King.* Hale, 1961.

CORBETT, W. J. *The Development of the Duchy of Normandy and the Norman Conquest of England.* Cambridge U.P., 1926 (*Cambridge Mediaeval History*, vol. V).

COTMAN, J. S., and TURNER, D. *Architectural Antiquities of Normandy.* Arch, 1822.

COX, J. C. *Canterbury.* Methuen, 1905.

DARBY, H. C. *An Historical Geography of England before A.D. 1800.* Cambridge U.P., 1936.

DARLINGTON, R. R. *The Norman Conquest.* Creighton Lectures in History. 1962. Athlone Press, 1963.

DELISLE, L. V. *Études sur la condition de la classe agricole et l'état de l'agriculture en Normandie au moyen âge.* Paris, 1899.

DU CHAILLU, P. B. *The Viking Age.* Murray, 1889.

FISHER, E. A. *An Introduction to Anglo-Saxon Architecture.* Faber, 1959.

FOWKE, F. R. (ed.) *The Bayeux Tapestry.* Arundel Society, 1875.

FREEMAN, E. A. *The Norman Conquest of England.* Oxford, Clarendon Press, 1869.

FULLER, J. F. C. *Decisive Battles of the Western World.* Eyre & Spottiswoode, 1954.

GARDINER, D. *Historic Haven: the Story of Sandwich.* Pilgrim Press, 1954.

GLOVER, R. 'English Warfare in 1066', *English Historical Review*, LXVII, 1952.

GUIGNEBERT, C. *A Short History of the French People.* Tr. F. G. Richmond. Allen & Unwin, 1930.

HANNAH, I. C. *The Sussex Coast.* Fisher Unwin, 1912.

HASKINS, C. H. *Norman Institutions.* Harvard U.P., 1918.

— *The Normans in European History.* Constable, 1916.

HASSALL, W. O. *They Saw It Happen: 55 B.C.–1485.* Basil Blackwell, 1957.

— *How They Lived: 55 B.C.–1485.* Basil Blackwell, 1962.

HELLENDORFF, C., and SCHUCK, A. *A History of Sweden.* Cassell, 1929.

HODGKIN, T. *Political History of England to 1066.* Longmans, 1920.

HOLLISTER, C. W. *Anglo-Saxon Military Institutions.* Oxford, 1962.

HOME, GORDON. *Roman London.* Benn, 1926.

HYETT, F. A. *Gloucester in National History.* Bellows, Gloucester; Kegan Paul, London, 1906.

KENDRICK, T. D. *A History of the Vikings.* Methuen, 1930.

— *Anglo-Saxon Art.* Methuen, 1938.

KITCHEN, G. W. *Winchester.* Longmans, 1890 (*Historic Towns Series*).

KNIGHT, C. B. *A History of the City of York.* Herald, York and London, 1944.

KNOWLES, D. *The Evolution of Medieval Thought.* Longmans, 1962.

LACROIX, P. *France in the Middle Ages.* New York, Ungar, 1963.

LARSEN, K. *A History of Norway.* Princeton U.P., 1948.

LEMMON, C. H. *The Field of Hastings.* Budd & Gilliatt, 1956.

LOYN, H. R. *Anglo-Saxon England and the Norman Conquest.* Longmans, 1962.

MACDONALD, A. J. *Lanfranc: a Study of his Life and Writing.* 2nd edn. S.P.C.K., 1944.

MACLAGAN, E. *The Bayeux Tapestry.* Penguin, 1943.

MARRIOTT, SIR J. *Oxford: its place in national history.* Oxford, Clarendon Press, 1933.

MEAD, W. E. *The English Medieval Feast.* Allen & Unwin, 1931.

MOORE, SIR A. 'Rig in Northern Europe', *Mariners' Mirror*, XLII.

MORGAN, J. F. *England under the Norman Occupation.* Williams, 1858.

OLRIK, A. *Viking Civilization.* Revised by H. Ellekilde. Allen & Unwin, 1930.

OMAN, SIR C. *England Before the Norman Conquest.* Methuen, 1949.

RAINE, A. *Medieval York.* Murray, 1955.

RIASANOVSKY, N. *A History of Russia.* Oxford, 1963.

ROUND, J. H. *Feudal England.* Swan Sonnenschein, 1895.

SAWYER, P. H. *The Age of the Vikings.* Arnold, 1948.

SCHRAMM, P. E. *History of the English Coronation.* Tr. L. Legg. Oxford, Clarendon Press, 1937.

SHETELIG, H., and FALK, H. *Scandinavian Archeology.* Oxford, 1937.

SLOCOMBE, G. E. *William the Conqueror.* Hutchinson, 1959.

SMITH, C. M. *Northmen of Adventure.* Longmans, 1932.

STENTON, D. M. *English Society in the Early Middle Ages 1066-1307.* Penguin, 1951.

STENTON, F. M. *Anglo-Saxon England.* Oxford, Clarendon Press, 1962.

THIERRY, A. *The Norman Conquest.* Dent (Everyman's Library), 1957.

TILLEY, A. (ed.) *Medieval France.* Cambridge U.P., 1922.

TOUT, T. F. *France and England . . . in the Middle Ages and Now.* Manchester U.P., 1922.

TOWNSEND, G. F. *The Town and Borough of Leominster.* Partridge, Leominster; Hall, London, 1863.

TOYNE, S. M. *The Scandinavians in History.* Arnold, 1948.

VINOGRADOFF, SIR P. *English Society in the Eleventh Century.* Oxford, Clarendon Press, 1908.

WEYMOUTH, ANTHONY. *London and Londoners.* Williams & Norgate, 1951.

WHEELER, R. E. M. *London and the Saxons.* London Museum, 1935.

WHITELOCK, D. *The Beginnings of English Society.* Penguin, 1952 (*Pelican History of England,* vol. II).

WILLIAMS, M. W. *Social Scandinavia in the Viking Age.* New York, Macmillan, 1920.

WILLIAMSON, G. C. *Guildford in Olden Times.* Woodbridge Press, Guildford; Bell, London, 1904.

Index